Business Ethics as Practice

Business Ethics as Practice

Representation, Reflexivity and Performance

Edited by

Chris Carter
University of St Andrews, UK

Stewart Clegg
*University of Technology, Sydney, Australia, and Aston
Business School, UK*

Martin Kornberger
*University of Technology, Sydney, Australia,University of
St Andrews, UK, and University of Innsbruck, Austria*

Stephan Laske
University of Innsbruck, Austria

Martin Messner
HEC Paris, France and University of Innsbruck, Austria

Edward Elgar
Cheltenham, UK • Northampton, MA, USA

Published by
Edward Elgar Publishing Limited
Glensanda House
Montpellier Parade
Cheltenham
Glos GL50 1UA
UK

Edward Elgar Publishing, Inc.
William Pratt House
9 Dewey Court
Northampton
Massachusetts 01060
USA

A catalogue record for this book is available from the British Library

Library of Congress Cataloguing in Publication Data

Business ethics as practice : representation, reflexivity and performance / edited by Chris Carter ... [et al.].
    p. cm.
  Includes bibliographical references and index.
1. Business ethics. I. Carter, Chris, 1970-
  HF5387.B8683 2007
  174'.4–dc22

                                                              2007011661

ISBN 978 1 84542 975 1

Printed and bound in Great Britain by MPG Books Ltd, Bodmin, Cornwall

Contents

PART THREE: PERFORMING ETHICS

Contributors

Olivier Babeau is Assistant Professor at Paris Dauphine University (DMSP laboratory). He has diplomas in management, economy and philosophy. He teaches strategy and business ethics in university and various business schools. His researches are mainly grounded on the idea that ambiguity and contradiction play a positive but neglected role in organization. His doctorate thesis (completed in 2005) is an analysis of the role of ordinary rules transgression practices in management consulting firms.

Thomas Beschorner is Head of the Research Group 'Social Learning and Sustainability' in the Faculty of Business, Economics and Law, University of Oldenburg, Germany. He is currently Visiting Professor in the Department of Sociology, McGill University, Montreal, Canada.

Dirk Bunzel is Lecturer in Organization Studies in the School of Economic and Management Studies at Keele University, UK. He holds a first degree from Humboldt University, Berlin, in Germany and a PhD from the University of Western Sydney in Australia. He has published in books, journals, and encyclopedias on matters of organizational power, rhythms in organizations, and on the historical development of strategies for socially integrating people with disabilities. His research interests include ethics at work in service industries and the management of diversity.

Chris Carter is Professor of Accounting and Organizations at the University of St Andrews, Scotland and is a regular visitor at the University of Technology, Sydney. He is particularly interested in the study of professional labour and ethics. Chris received his PhD from Aston Business School.

Stewart Clegg completed a first degree at the University of Aston (1971) and a Doctorate at Bradford University (1974). Stewart is currently a Professor at the University of Technology, Sydney, and Director of ICAN Research – Innovative Collaborations, Alliances and Networks, a Key University Research Centre. He also holds Chairs at Aston University, and Visiting

Appointments at the University of Maastricht and Vrije Universiteit, Amsterdam in the Netherlands, as well as at EM-Lyon, France. He has published extensively in many journals and has contributed a large number of books to the literature, including the award-winning *Handbook of Organization Studies* (London: Sage, second edition 2006, co-edited with Cynthia Hardy, Walter Nord and Tom Lawrence). His most recent books are *Managing and Organizations: An Introduction to Theory and Practice* (London: Sage 2005, with Martin Kornberger and Tyrone Pitsis) and *Power and Organizations* (London: Sage, with David Courpasson and Nelson Phillips), and has a number of other projects in press or preparation.

Paul du Gay is Professor of Sociology and Organization Studies and Co-Director of the Centre for Citizenship, Identities and Governance at the Open University, UK. He is also an Adjunct Professor at the Copenhagen Business School. He is currently working for the ESRC's Centre for Research on Socio-Cultural Change (CReSC) on the theme of 'Re-working Expertise'. His book arising from this project – *Organizing Identity: culture, person and organization after 'the moment of theory'* – will be published by Sage in 2007.

Daniel E. Esser is working for the United Nations Economic and Social Commission for Asia and the Pacific in Bangkok, Thailand. He has published on a range of issues, including urban governance and management, internal displacement, organizational restructuring, discourse ethics, and achieving socio-economic development in zones of armed conflict. He will soon defend his PhD, from the London School of Economic and Political Science, focusing on urban reconstruction in Sierra Leone and Afghanistan.

Martin Kornberger received his PhD in 2002 from the University of Vienna, Austria. Currently he works and plays at the University of Technology, Sydney as a senior lecturer in the School of Management and the School of Design. He is also a lecturer at the University of St Andrews, Scotland. His research interests include ethics as practice as well as other organizational practices such as strategy making and branding.

Stephan Laske is Professor of Business Management and Business Education, and Dean of School of Management at the University of Innsbruck. He has taught at different universities in Germany and Austria, and has been a visiting scholar at Griffith University (Brisbane, Australia) and the School of Economics and Commercial Law, Gothenburg University (Sweden). As Chair of the University's Academic Senate, he was responsible for a two-year organization development programme. Currently, he is member of the Board of Governors of Innsbruck Medical University, and of the Scientific Commission in Lower Saxony (Germany), an advisory body to the Minister of Science. He has published widely on university management and personnel policy.

Sue Llewellyn holds a Chair in the University of Leicester Management Centre. She has published widely in the areas of management and governance in the public sector, with a particular focus on accountability frameworks, and professional/managerial roles and responsibilities. In health care management research she has collaborated with colleagues in Sweden, Italy, Australia, New Zealand, Japan and the US. She has a particular interest in how people work with others to achieve things in organizations.

Martin Messner is currently Assistant Professor at the Department of Accounting and Management Control at HEC Paris. Before coming to Paris, he was lecturer in management accounting at the University of Innsbruck, School of Management, Austria, from where he also obtained his doctoral degree. His research is focused on management accounting practice and the work of management accountants, on issues of accountability and responsibility in organizations, and on the limits of organizing. He is the editor of the quarterly newsletter of the European Accounting Association.

Martin Müller received his PhD in 2000 from the University of Halle-Wittenberg. Currently he is Associate Professor for Production and Environment at the Faculty of Business, Economics and Law, University of Oldenburg. His research interest includes organizational theory, environmental management, supply chain management and corporate social responsibility.

Karin Oppegaard is a doctoral student at the University of Lausanne, Switzerland. Her thesis focuses on the role of mindfulness in leadership. She is also a Research Associate at IMD, Switzerland, focussing on leadership, sustainability, and Corporate Social Responsibility. Karin's previous roles include a research assistantship at INSEAD, France, working on RESPONSE, a study of Corporate Social Responsibility funded by the European Union. Prior to this, she worked as a dissertation fellow at the Imagination Lab Foundation in Lausanne, researching with Matt Statler the notion of Aristotelian Practical Wisdom as applied to business ethics.

Andreas Rasche is currently working at the Helmut Schmidt University, Hamburg, Germany and is finishing his PhD in strategic management at the European Business School, Germany, where he also teaches business ethics. His research interests include the institutionalization of ethics initiatives in multinational corporations and strategic management in organizations.

Carl Rhodes is Professor in the School of Management at the University of Technoloy, Sydney. He has researched and written widely on issues related to ethics, culture and learning on organizations. His current work is focussing on identity at work management ethics, and organizations in popular culture. Carl is author of *Writing Organization: (Re)presentation and Control in Narratives at Work* (2001), Benjamins; co-author of *Reconstructing the Lifelong Learner* (2003), Routledge; and co-editor of *Research and Knowledge at Work* (2000), Routledge; *Management Ethics* (2006), Routledge; and *Humour, Work and Organization* (2006), Routledge. He has published in journals such as *Organization, Organization Studies, The Leadership Quarterly, The Journal of Business Ethics and Qualitative Inquiry.*

Silke Seemann studied General Management with specialization in HR and Organizational Development at the Management Center Innsbruck, while working as a Consultant for Organizational Development in Germany. She joined the Institute for Organization and Learning at the University of Innsbruck in 2004. Currently she is Research Assistant for the FWF 'Ethics as Practice' project.

Matt Statler is Associate Director of the International Center for Enterprise Preparedness (InterCEP) at New York University, where he conducts research and coordinates special projects. Formerly the Director of Research at the Imagination Lab Foundation in Switzerland, he has also taught at the University of Saint-Gallen, the University of Innsbruck and the City University of New York. Matt has extensive experience facilitating innovative strategy processes for multinational corporations, non-governmental organizations, and SMEs. He studied at the University of Heidelberg as a Fulbright Scholar and wrote his PhD in Philosophy at Vanderbilt University about the philosopher's allegorical return to the cave.

Wim Vandekerckhove holds a PhD in Ethics and is currently a post-doctoral researcher at the Center for Ethics & Value Inquiry (CEVI), Ghent University, Belgium. His research interests include whistleblowing, dissent, shareholder-engagement SRI, global ethics, and general semantics. He recently published *Whistleblowing and Organizational Social Responsibility: A Global Assessment* with Ashgate.

Robert Westwood is Reader in Organization Studies at the University of Queensland Business School. In his writing and research Bob pursues a critical perspective in relation to international and comparative management and areas within organization studies. He is currently working on research and book projects related to humour and organization, the representation of work and organization in popular culture, and postcolonial analysis of comparative management. Additional research interests include the meaning and experience of work, gender, and language-power relations in organizations. His latest book was *Debating Organisation Point/Counterpoint in Organisation Studies* edited with Stewart Clegg and published by Blackwell in 2003. He is Co-Editor of the journal *Culture and Organisation*, and on the boards of three other journals.

Acknowledgments

We would like to thank all participants in the Stream 'Performing Ethics' at the APROS 2005 conference in Melbourne and all contributors to the stream 'Ethics at work: exploring the dynamic relationships between ethics and organizational processes and practices', at the EURAM conference in Munich in 2005. Without their valuable input, critical feedback and openness this volume would have not been possible. We would also like to thank the team at our publisher Edward Elgar and especially Francine O'Sullivan for their support and enthusiasm about this project. Intellectually, the editors' discussions around ethics as practice were largely made possible by a grant from the Austrian Science Fund (FWF) as 'Rethinking Business Ethics', Project Number P16531 and funding from the Australian Research Council Discovery Award, for the research program 'Ethics as Practice – A Study of Organisational Learning and Management Power in Australian Society', Project ID DP0453018. Last but not least we would like to thank Cleo Lester for her never-ending patience with us and support in editing this book.

1. Introduction

Chris Carter, Stewart Clegg,
Martin Kornberger, Stephan Laske and
Martin Messner

When a fairly economically liberal magazine such as *The Economist* features a survey on Corporate Social Responsibility and proclaims that '[m]anagers should think much harder about business ethics than they appear to at present' (20 January of 2005), then something critical must have happened in the world of business. Indeed, discussions about corporate social responsibility and business ethics seem to have gained particular momentum in recent years, since some prominent corporations, and the managers responsible for them, have made it to the news in an all too inglorious manner. Recent corporate scandals such as those of Enron, Worldcom, or Parmalat have brought to the fore, a problem which mainstream economics and management studies have ignored for a long time: the fact that the laws of the market cannot ensure ethical behaviour of its participants. Still worse, some have even argued that the way in which managers are being educated at business schools and universities is part of the problem. Sumantra Ghoshal (2005, p. 77), for example, has argued that a 'precondition for making business studies a science has been the denial of any moral or ethical considerations in our theories'. As a consequence of teaching 'ideologically inspired amoral theories, business schools have actively freed their students from any sense of moral responsibility' (ibid., p. 76). More often than not, theories on how corporations ought to work deal with the optimization of structures, processes, and human behaviour – and not with situations in which managers face moral dilemmas or ambiguous choices, such that any effort to optimize will come at the expense of considerable (social, environmental and/or personal) costs.

If academics are part of the problem, then they can also be part of its solution. If there is indeed 'confusion over what managers' responsibilities are, and over where the limits of those responsibilities lie' (*The Economist,*

20 January 2005), then business ethics as an academic discipline may offer some discussion and clarification. This volume aims to be one contribution in this respect.

The book assembles chapters which can be said to have one thing in common: they agree that moral questions arise *in practice* and have to be dealt with *in practice*. They take the tension between morals or money and profits or principles as the starting point of their investigations into the space in which ethical problems emerge and are managed. If there were a clear set of moral rules that could be applied and that could ensure ethical behaviour, ethics would be a matter of following these rules and policing conformity to them. Rather than taking this perspective, in this volume we argue that ethics are at stake in ambiguous situations in which different, often contradicting sets of moral values and rules clash. The contributions to this volume give testimony to the gap that can often be observed between the ethical statements made on behalf of companies and the practices that these companies are actually engaged in. While sharing this 'practice perspective' on ethics, the contributions differ with respect to the ethically relevant issues they address as well as in regard of the theoretical concepts they draw upon. While some contributions look at ethics in organizations more broadly, others focus on specific practices such as cross-cultural management or accounting. Theorists and philosophers typically referred to include Weber, Habermas, Foucault, Levinas, Derrida, and Giddens. The volume features both conceptual contributions and empirical case studies that explore theoretical concepts as they are situated in different organizational practice contexts and enacted in organizational discourses.

The book is structured in three parts. The first part 'Order and Representation' focuses on the ethical issues surrounding different forms of order, organizing and representation. Ethics are represented in codes of practices, established routines, credos, bureaucracy and such like.

Paul du Gay opens the first part of the book with his chapter 'Office as a Vocation? The Ethos of Bureaucratic Office and Public Service'. As he argues there has recently occurred a considerable upsurge of interest in the concept of 'office' within the social sciences, humanities and among scholars of public law and public management. Traditionally, in the theory of bureaucracy office was defined by practices such as rules and job descriptions, constructing a ladder of job opportunities that were arranged in a career. Although there are a number of important factors contributing to this renewed focus, du Gay highlights two important issues. First, there is a rekindled interest in the moral attributes of public agency inspired not only by a number of well publicized political controversies – from the sexual scandals of the Clinton administration in the USA, to the UK Hutton and Butler enquiries into events surrounding the decision to go to war in Iraq –

but also by growing ethical uncertainties deriving from a rapid and equally controversial series of managerial reforms of a wide range of public institutions. Second, and not entirely unrelated, he argues that historical, philosophical and practical concerns with the manner in which certain prominent contemporary conceptions of moral agency presume a dichotomy between moral autonomy and subordination to higher authority lead to a paradoxical outcome. The representation of the bureaucrat as a type of subaltern status, as one working to rules and as someone who also exercises moral agency, appears to be fundamentally incompatible when viewed from an ethic of responsibility which sees only those who act with entrepreneurial initiative as being able to be chosen, and thus choose to be responsible. From this background, du Gay's chapter assesses this (re)turn to 'office' in the context of recent management reforms of the public service, most particularly in the UK, and highlights the manner in which the moral agency of public bureaucratic office is constituted by, and not in opposition to, relations of subordination. There is a supposition common to many contemporary moral theories that people should only be subject to moral constraints that they have freely chosen for themselves. In organization theory applied to public office, authentic moral deliberation has traditionally been seen to require detachment from all institutionally given obligations, so that people can 'think for themselves' about right conduct. Bureaucratic roles are thus deployed as an exemplary case of an ethic of responsibility. To be so, a network of duties, responsibilities and concomitant rights of action, as well as necessary attributes, skills and specific virtues (with related vices and failures), that define office cannot be seen as shaped arbitrarily by a central executive bent on securing its own will, regardless of context. Office must provide its own distinctive, if limited, form of liberty. In exploring the notion of office, a key feature of the chapter is its focus on persona as a manifestation and representative of an office, an embodiment of a moral economy.

Olivier Babeau's contribution on 'Granting Disorder a Place in Ethics: Organization's Deviant Practices and Ethics', focuses on the dialectical relationship between rule breaking and rule following as constituting the space in which ethical problems occur. As he argues, a vast literature of the management and human sciences shows how deviance from formal rules provides for well-being and efficiency in a firm. The suppression of gaps through application of the rules and the elimination of hidden practices has a negative impact on productive activity: as strange as it may seem, an enterprise survives thanks to its broken rules. According to common approaches to business ethics, the development of an 'ethical organization' depends on the importance attributed to a generalized transparency that defines all deviance as a clandestine activity by nature. Every single action kept hidden may be suspect as wronging the other actors, or working to foster inequality, as it may develop uncontrolled power relations, or sabotage production processes. Disorder is granted no ethical virtue because only order can enjoy that privilege. In contrast to this mainstream thought Babeau suggests that we think simultaneously of ethics and enterprise by reconciling organization and ambiguity. As he argues, the role of hidden practices in organization has to be rehabilitated. He suggests renouncing simplistic demands for transparency, which favour an exhibited process as always better than one conducted in secrecy. The conclusion of this thought-provoking chapter is that transgression is both an ethical necessity as well as being useful for daily functioning.

In his chapter on 'Being Accountable and Being Responsible', Martin Messner takes up the academic discourse on accounting ethics which has gained particular momentum in the aftermath of recent corporate scandals. Messner shows that the accounting literature features two main approaches to accounting: one which views accounting as a technique, and one which regards it as a social practice. These two 'images of accounting' differ not only in their assumptions about the ontological nature of accounting; they also diverge with respect to how they conceive the moral dimension of accounting. Messner argues that if accounting is viewed as a mere technology, then the question of ethics finds its limits in the notion of accountability. In such a view, one is acting morally rightly if one comes up to the formal or informal expectations which prevail with respect to the giving of accounts and which are assumed to be unambiguous. In contrast, a perspective on accounting as a social practice allows for a different understanding of the moral dimension of accounting. In such a perspective, the moral significance of accounting goes beyond the question whether individuals 'correctly' give and demand accounts according to a certain style of accountability. Rather, responsibility involves that the style of accountability itself becomes subject to reflection and critique, based upon the experience of the limits of accountability in a particular case at hand. To elaborate this argument, Messner draws upon arguments by Jacques Derrida and Judith Butler who both associate responsibility with an experience of and reflection upon the limits of accountability. With respect to financial and management accounting systems, Messner's analysis suggests that there is a need to acknowledge the limits of such systems for guaranteeing a responsible form of accounting. Responsibility will always involve a consideration of the particular case at hand and the reflection upon how the singularity of this case can or cannot be accounted for by drawing upon a given standard or system that is considered right or just.

Carl Rhodes and Bob Westwood's chapter 'Letting Knowledge Go: Ethics and Representation of the Other in International and Cross-Cultural Management', focuses on the ethics of representation in management writing.

Using the discourse on international and cross-cultural management studies (ICMS) as an example they show how theorizing on organizations can (mis-) represent the Other whom the discourses conceive as the cultural agent to be understood, related to and managed. As the authors argue, the world is full of people in organizations that are other to and different from those occupying the global behemoths that bestride the globalized world. Such people, in 'foreign' organizations and as 'foreigners', are the stuff on which ICMS focuses. In their chapter traditional ICMS is critiqued for the way in which it starts from the premise of the normalcy of others being viewed as outsiders or as culturally different. Invoking a postcolonial critique, Rhodes and Westwood suggest that ICMS should be seen in the context of a concern with 'Orientalism' through its use of representational strategies in which the Other is (mis)-rendered in terms of a Western imaginary. From this perspective, those whose culture is not seen as essentially Western become seen in terms of essentialism, exoticism and denigration as something 'other'. Such practices result in the construction of a practice of sameness which erases or silences the radical difference inherent to the other; the other comes to be seen wholly in terms of the categories of those doing the cross-cultural viewing. They draw on work from the humanities writers, Bhabha and Spivak, to recognise the ambivalence, instability and heterogeneity inherent to all Self-Other relations. However, as they note, there is a risk of constructing an unknowable and unbridgeable divide, and thus an ethical chasm. They find salvation from that abyss in the ethical elaborations of Levinas' ideas which assert that the Self-Other relationship is both a primary ethical and a pre-ontological relation. Levinas, Rhodes and Westwood offer suggestions for reconstituting ethics as a means of reconfiguring research practice in ICMS and to related field of organization studies.

The second part of the book focuses on 'Reflexivity and Norms'. The contributions in this section point to the ethical importance of a reflexive attitude and a willingness to engage in dialogue with those affected by the actions or decisions in question. It begins with Martin Müller and Thomas Beschorner's contribution on 'Social Standards: Hybrids in Reflexive Modernity', which explores the relevance of social standards as governance-mechanisms in a global society. The authors argue that social standards result from tensions and conflicts between diverse social sub-systems. They are particularly relevant for the analysis of business ethics because an in-depth understanding of these new institutions reveals different social management mechanisms, which can be illuminated by theories of reflexive modernity. Two central characteristics of effective social standards are reflexivity and stakeholder dialogue. Based on these criteria, the authors discuss two of the most important social standards, SA 8000 and AA 1000, more closely. Although they acknowledge that these two standards are very different in their respective inherent logic they also discuss common features and elaborate on suggestions for further developments of social standards.

In their chapter 'Managing for Compliance and Integrity in Practice', Andreas Rasche and Daniel E. Esser analyse the appropriateness of accountability standards (e.g., SA 8000) for compliance and integrity-driven ethics management. Based on an overview of compliance and integrity as two distinct strategies for ethics management, the authors develop a simple framework with which to analyse the suitability of such standards in terms of the specific requirements of the approaches. By doing so they provide an answer to the practical question of choice of an appropriate standard from the multiplicity of possible standards and clarify the underlying theoretical assumptions and logics that inform both the design of standards and the decision-making process at the organizational level that lead to the adoption or not of specific ethics tools. The chapter also provides practitioners, in the context of the implementation of accountability standards, with guidance as to how they might align targets in the area of ethics management with a compliance or an integrity centred strategy, or – as often found in practice – a mixture of both. Rasche and Esser's conceptual framework is sufficiently flexible to be applied to a variety of ethics tools; however, in their empirical review they focus on SA 8000 since this initiative is one of the most widely used tools for social accounting in practice.

Sue Llewellyn's contribution 'Meeting Responsibilities "On the Stage" and Claiming Rights "Behind the Scenes": The Re-Casting of Companies', argues that the concepts of 'responsibilities' and 'rights' have been developed in the context of individuals and governments – not companies. Only democratically elected governments and expert individuals have been held to be sufficiently responsible to have a mandate to address complex social and political problems. Consequently, only they had rights ascribed to them, enabling them to make discretionary decisions over problems. As the power of companies has increased, their activities have been seen to violate human rights and have an adverse impact on the environment. Recognising this, companies are increasingly urged to accept 'corporate responsibility'. Llewellyn argues that behind the corporate responsibility 'stage' there is something else going on, not yet fully visible, but 'behind the scenes': companies are claiming (or being granted) additional rights, they are being 're-cast'. Her chapter elaborates on this argument and raises awareness of the interrelationships between what is happening 'on the stage' what is going on 'behind the scenes' or 'backstage' in the arena of corporate responsibilities and corporate rights.

The last part of the book focuses on 'Performing Ethics'. The contributions in this section concentrate on tensions and possible reconciliation between the idea of ethics, responsibility and integrity with the reality of everyday organizational life. Wim Vandekerckhove's chapter on 'Integrity: Talking the Walk Instead of Walking the Talk', focuses on a concept of integrity that features prominently in contemporary discussions on business ethics. In fact, integrity is a very popular concept in today's discourse on organizations and especially with respect to the qualities, or absence of them, of the leaders of organizations. Vandekerckhove argues that the concept remains vague. In his chapter he attempts to delineate the concept of integrity as consistent with the demands of today's business environment, and, above all, with the need for flexibility. The chapter reviews a number of possible conceptualizations (at the functional, temporal, spatial and interactive level), but argues that in a discourse on organizations in which flexibility is one of the core concepts only an interactive conception of integrity is tenable. There, integrity designates a wholeness of discernment, action and speaking about action. Such an understanding of integrity opens pathways with which to explore new organizational practices aimed at enhancing integrity. Vandekerckhove discusses the position this delineation takes within the objectivist/subjectivist debate on integrity and points to possible ways of using this conceptualization in the analysis of organizational processes, such as whistle-blowing and storytelling.

In their chapter, 'Practical Wisdom – Integrating Ethics and Effectiveness in Organizations', Matt Statler and Karin Oppegaard respond to the current debate on ethics and performance by arguing for an approach that acknowledges the conflict between ethical normativity and effectiveness and yet which still facilitates action. The authors address this issue at the level of the individual, and they focus on the Aristotelian concept of 'practical wisdom' (*phronesis*) as a way to describe individual decision-making practices that are both ethical *and* effective. Statler and Oppegaard present an interpretative framework that differentiates decision-making practices based on the extent to which they successfully integrate ethics and effectiveness. In conclusion they outline the implications of their framework for future theoretical and empirical research addressing practical wisdom in organizations.

Silke Seemann, Stephan Laske and Martin Kornberger's chapter is entitled 'The Constitution of Ethics: Discourse, Practice and Conflict in a Health-Care Center', and it focuses on how ethics are performed in organizational practice. The context of the study is a relatively large organization in the 'wellness' industry – a large spa-based hotel oriented to wealthy and stressed-out senior executives. Their ethnographic account provides evidence that ethics are not so much explicit but rather implicitly embedded in the organizational context. In fact, rather than understanding ethics as written codes of conduct or explicit discourse, the authors theorize ethics in a way that sees it as a response to environmental challenges and a way of making sense of them. Ethics are not a clear-cut value system that defines 'good' and 'bad' but are constantly negotiated and constructed as organizational members argue for and over resources and responsibilities. As Seemann et al.'s contribution highlights, ethics are used strategically to manage the organization and are, as a means of organizing, necessarily linked to the exercise of power.

In the last chapter of this volume, 'The Guest as a Friendly Foe? Hotel Service Encounters In-between the Face and the Gaze of the Guest', Dirk Bunzel discusses ethics at work and explores the ethical predicament of customer service. The study uses data collected during fourteen months of ethnographic research. The sequences of organization life at the hotel illustrate vividly the consequences of propagating a 'passion for service excellence', when embedded within a context of corporate culture. Bunzel demonstrates how the moral potential of service encounters can be corrupted, as a genuine concern for the other – here, the guest – is instrumentalized for corporate goals. The frame of reference for his analysis is the work of the French philosopher Emmanuel Levinas, whose philosophy attempts no less than grounding all reasoning within a moral obligation to 'care for the other'. His most radical appeal to respect the absolute alterity of the other and to cultivate a 'spirituality of love and charity' provides a stark contrast to the discourse of customer service at the Grand Seaside hotel. As Bunzel concludes, this discourse renders highly ambivalent the status of the guest: potentially an ally, a *friend*, a compatriot, someone to care for; yet, under the spell of corporate culturism, the guest becomes a *foe*.

In conclusion, we can say that each chapter offers a particular perspective on the responsibility of organizations, its members and other stakeholders. In a sense, the heterogeneity of the book is part of its message: ethical issues arise in very different contexts and situations, and cannot be 'solved' by a single formula or theory. To say that ethics exists in practice is to acknowledge its constitutive effect not only for organizations, but also for the individual, their relationships and society at large. Business ethics is always also an ethics of the Self as it is an ethics of the Other who is not directly addressed by a practice. Business ethics therefore point to the way in which individuals, organizations and their environments are connected with each other. From this perspective ethics as practice constitutes, and is constituted by, the interactions and tensions between different rationalities and values. Such ethics are not about prescribing what is right and what is wrong; rather ethics become a practice that allows us to reflect on, negotiate and temporarily resolve the conflicts, tensions and ambiguities that shape our world and, by extension, us.

REFERENCES

Ghoshal, S. (2005), 'Bad management theories are destroying good management practices', *Academy of Management Learning and Education*, **4** (1), 75-91.

PART ONE

ORDER AND REPRESENTATION

2.   Office as a Vocation? The Ethos of Bureaucratic Office and Public Service

Paul du Gay

> But the law is the law, duty is duty, and a man defrauds his own name if he but once neglects his office.
> (Ronan Bennett, *Havoc In Its Third Year*)

In recent years there has been a considerable upsurge of interest in the concept of 'office' within the social sciences, humanities and among scholars of public law and public management (Thompson, 1987; Minson, 1993, 1998; Orren, 1994; Dobel, 1999; du Gay, 2000; Geuss, 2001; Sabl, 2002; Loughlin, 2004). Although there are a number of disparate, often discipline specific factors contributing to this renewed focus, a rather more general aspect of the 'turn' to office stands out. This concerns a rekindled interest in the moral attributes of public agency inspired not only by a number of well publicised political controversies – from the sexual scandals that beset the Clinton administration in the USA, to the Hutton and Butler enquiries in the UK into events surrounding the decision to go to war in Iraq – but also by growing ethical uncertainties attendant upon a rapid and equally controversial series of managerial reforms of a wide range of public institutions.

This chapter seeks to make a case for the continuing indispensability of office-specific conceptions of moral agency in the realm of governmental and political action. Its main focus of concern, however, is with the office of the state bureaucrat, career civil servant, or public administrator. This category of 'person' has been the object of significant practical reform over the last two decades, and serious debate continues concerning whether such incessant reform has undermined key aspects of the role and function of the office to which this persona is attached. Indeed, the rhetoric of office has played and continues to play an important part in framing debates about the status of recent reforms of the public administration as an institution of government.

In seeking to show the continued relevance of office-based conceptions of moral agency to the practice of state administration and to the status conduct of the public administrator, I will have cause to question some of the assumptions underpinning contemporary reforms of state bureaux and the norms of conduct they advocate. In particular, I question whether these reforms have had the effect of undermining the (largely forgotten) 'core business' of public administration: running a state as a state, and operating a constitution. I begin, however, by introducing the idea of the state as a structure of offices and by focusing, in particular, on the purposes and status of the office of state bureaucrat.

OFFICES OF STATE

According to Quentin Skinner (1989), among many others, the idea of the modern state was developed slowly, and with some difficulty, in early modern Europe. This was to facilitate the construction of a single integrated system of authoritative political and legal decision-making over a given territory and subject-population, and to offset the continuing subversive or anarchistic potential of the long-standing viewpoint that derived political authority, in one way or another, from the people over whom it was exercised. At the centre of this novel idea was the concept of sovereignty, of ultimate worldly authority over people and territory, and its firm location within specific institutions and decisions: the right to be obeyed without challenge. 'The entity in which that right inhered', as John Dunn (2000, p. 80) indicates, was no longer envisioned as a particular human being ...

> but as a continuing structure of government, decision-making, legal interpretation and enforcement, which was sharply distinct from its current human incumbents. Such a structure could take in or lose subjects or territory without altering its identity. It could change its system of rule or legal adjudication almost beyond recognition, and yet remain intractably itself.

And, as Udo Wolter (1997, p. 18) has argued, for instance, a central feature of this sovereign entity is the institution of office. According to Wolter the sovereign state is an abstract structure of offices endowed with all manner of powers, warrants and resources which are to be sharply distinguished from the contingent human occupants of these offices. Office is therefore an institution that the state and other juristic bodies of public law make use of in order to accomplish certain purposes. Sovereign and fiscal tasks are delegated to a persona – the 'office-holder' – for a portfolio of responsibilities which is delimited, amongst other things, by norms of competence. These persons – state functionaries or bureaucrats – are subject to official duties which result, inter alia, from legislation, constitutional dictat or official instructions, 'as for example concerning due execution, incorruptibility, or impartiality' (1997, p. 19).

For Wolter (1997, pp. 19-21), the concept of office can be delineated and analysed along two axes. First, organisationally, in terms of the office as instituted competence. Here, the modern state accomplishes its tasks and objectives through a division of labour. Therefore, the idea of office presupposes the existence of a large number of offices which work together in something akin to a 'permanent structure of offices' (ibid., p. 19). The definition and distribution of the functions of an office result from the establishment of specific competencies. In so far as the office fulfils a function of state, it is defined in relation to competencies and therefore made independent in an abstract sense. This requires, first, a fixed definition of responsibilities, and, second, the co-ordination of offices in a hierarchy. Because the office is a function of state, it is also equipped with authority. If the office fulfils duties on behalf of the state, the state has to grant to the office those means which are qualitatively equivalent to those of the state. In other words, the office has the 'official authority' to order and enforce everything that is necessary to fulfil its duties as bound by the limits of its competence (ibid., pp. 19-20).

Secondly, Wolter traces the concept of office in relation to the persona of the office holder, in terms of the regulation of status and duties. The abstract existence of the office, he argues, makes it qualitatively different from any natural person. It is constructed precisely in order to make the activity of the state independent of the insufficiency of any human being, and to achieve substantive effects despite the individual imperfections of any particular office holder (see also Kallinikos, 2004). The office is therefore a fundamentally impersonal institution. This means, negatively expressed, that the office cannot be treated as a personal possession or tradable good. More positively, it means, for instance, that the maintenance of the office holder has to be secured independently of the income of the office, and that the 'depersonalisation' of the execution of official duties has to be ensured through the regulation of official duties.

Thus, in his classic dissection of the vocation of bureaucratic office holding, Max Weber (1978 II, p. 959) writes:

Legally and actually, office holding is not considered ownership of a source of income, to be exploited for rents or emoluments in exchange for the rendering of certain services, as was normally the case during the Middle Ages ... nor is office holding considered a common exchange of services, as in the case of free employment contracts. Rather entrance into an office ... is considered an acceptance of a specific duty of fealty to the purpose of the office (*Amstreue*) in return for the grant of a secure existence. It is decisive for the modern loyalty to an office that, in the pure type, it does not establish a relationship to a *person*, like the vassal's or disciple's faith under feudal or patrimonial authority, but rather is devoted to impersonal and functional purposes ... The political official – at least in the fully developed modern state – is not considered the personal servant of a ruler.

For Weber, the institutional and moral responsibility of the different officers of state – rulers, political leaders, bureaucrats – is to be understood in terms of their quite distinct duties attached to their particular responsibilities of office.

According to Weber (1978 II, p. 958ff), the state bureaucrat or administrative official, on the one hand, and the politician or ruler, on the other, have very different purposes and forms of responsibility. Such differences are not to be deduced from the relative 'interest' or 'complexity' of the tasks each performs, nor from a mechanistic distinction between policy and administration, but rather from the demands made upon them by the distinctive offices they occupy.

'Officials' too are expected to make independent decisions and show organizational ability and initiative, not only in countless individual cases but also on larger issues. It is typical of littérateurs and of a country lacking any insight into its own affairs or into the achievement of its officials, even to imagine that the work of an official amounts to no more than the subaltern performance of routine duties, while the leader alone is expected to carry out the 'interesting' tasks which make special intellectual demands. This is not so. The difference lies, rather, in the kind of responsibility borne by each of them, and this is largely what determines the demands made on their particular abilities (Weber, 1994a, p. 160).

Weber is clearly referring to 'responsibility' in a very specific sense. The term as he deploys it does not pertain to a simple division of organisational labour, in which bureaucratic officials are allocated the sole responsibility for administration, and politicians the sole responsibility for policy. Rather, 'responsibility' refers to a division of ethical labour in which official and political leaders are subject to specific imperatives and points of honour and develop quite different capacities and comportments as a result of the demands of their respective 'offices' – their placement within what Weber describes as different 'life orders'.

In his classic account of the 'persona' of the bureaucrat, Weber (1978, II, p. 978ff) treats the impersonal, expert, procedural and hierarchical character of bureaucratic conduct as elements of a distinctive ethos. According to Weber, the bureau comprises the socio-technical conditions of a distinctive organization of the person. Among the most important of these are, first, that access to office is dependent upon lengthy training, usually certified by public examination, and second, that the office itself constitutes a 'vocation', a focus of ethical commitment and duty, autonomous of and superior to the bureaucrat's extra-official ties to kith, kin or conscience. In Weber's discussions of bureaucratic office-holding as a vocation, these conditions mark out the office as a particular sphere of life and provide the office-holder with a distinctive ethical bearing or status-conduct. In particular, Weber (1978 II, p. 983ff) stresses the ways in which the ethos of bureaucratic office-holding constitutes an important political resource because it serves to divorce the administration of public life from private moral absolutisms. Without the historical emergence of the ethos and persona of bureaucratic office-holding, Weber argues, the construction of a buffer between civic comportment and personal principles – a crucial feature of liberal government – would never have been possible. Indeed, without the 'art of separation' (Walzer, 1984) that the state bureau effected and continues to effect, many of the qualitative features of government that are regularly taken for granted – for instance, reliability and procedural fairness in the treatment of cases – would not exist.

As Weber makes clear, the crucial point of honour for bureaucrats is not to allow extra official commitments to determine the manner in which they perform the duties associated with their office. 'On the contrary, he takes pride in preserving his impartiality, overcoming his own inclinations and opinions, so as to execute in a conscientious and meaningful way what is required of him by the general definition of his duties or by some particular instruction, even – and particularly – when they do *not* coincide with his own political views' (Weber, 1994a, p. 160). Without this 'supremely ethical discipline and self-denial', the whole apparatus of the state would disintegrate (ibid., 1994b, p. 331).

It is the relationship between extra official commitments, broadly defined, and the independent obligations of office that has preoccupied many of the contemporary critics of state and bureaucracy. It is to the work of these critics that I now turn.

CONTEMPORARY CHALLENGES TO STATE AND BUREAUCRACY

As Richard Chapman (2000, p. 4) has reported, the original Society of British Civil Servants had as its motto (when mottoes, as opposed to visions, were in vogue) 'We serve the State'. It is indicative of how far we have travelled that it is impossible to imagine a similar body today choosing to deploy the 'S' word to frame its 'core business'. A document produced by the UK Cabinet Office (1999a) entitled 'Vision and Values' provides the more appropriate contemporary comparator. Here we find the Civil Service's mission defined thus: 'to make the UK a better place for everyone to live in, and support its success in the world. We want to be the best at everything we do'. A more vacuous statement it is hard to imagine, but a more telling example of the eclipse of the state in contemporary public management discourse it would be difficult to find.

Given the contemporary obsession with 'society' as the source of public policy, most notably in contemporary theories and programmes of 'network governance' (Rhodes, 1996, 2000; Stoker, 1998, 2000a, 2000b), it seems that reasons of state are always bad reasons (Kriegel, 1995). This gradual occlusion of the concept of the state in recent political and public management thought, most especially, but not exclusively, its ethical component, has condemned a whole body of practical thinking concerning the problems, purposes, techniques and comportments appropriate to the responsible running of a state, if not to oblivion, then certainly to a shadowy existence in the interstices of various machineries of government adopted by many actually existing states (Geuss, 2001; Minson, 1998). In particular, it has consigned the ethos of bureaucratic office to the dustbin of history, representing it not only as morally bankrupt but also as organisationally redundant.

Exactly why the state and bureaucracy find themselves in this position is not too difficult to discern. After all, opposition to the idea of 'the state', and to 'bureaucracy', has long been a feature of a wide variety of political discourses. Over the last thirty years or so, however, it has enjoyed a remarkable resurgence in popularity. One of the most prominent of the many recent criticisms directed at the 'cold monsters' of state and bureaucracy concerns their presumed negative consequences for personal liberty. Whether couched in predominantly managerialist or economistic terms – states and their bureaucracies hinder the unique virtue and efficacy of a capitalistic organisation of production – or in relation to populist criteria of political right – only governments that are responsive to, and thus accurately and sensitively express, the opinions and judgements of their own citizens can be fully entitled to their obedience – states and bureaucracies are seen as undermining freedom.

Underlying the first of these conceptions, we might contend, is the assumption that economic freedom, and the efficiency of governmental policy, is a function of the state's subordination to the laws of the 'free' markets. For the second, the guiding assumption is that the justness of governmental policy is directly related to the degree of the bureaucracy's subordination to the popular will. Both strands of critique can be easily traced in recent and ongoing experiments in reforming state bureaux, most particularly, but not exclusively, in their Anglo-American variants. So, for instance, contemporary demands for more 'responsive' public management and the mechanisms devised to achieve this end frequently contain two distinctive elements. On the one hand, the 'unresponsiveness' of which many democratic populists complain often appears to be based upon the assumption that it is impossible to justify substantial governing power being allotted to unelected officials. Thus the ceaseless demands for 'modernisation' and 'reinvention' of state bureaux made by advocates of enhanced democratic rule are often based on the belief that bureaucracies should be more 'responsive' to the wishes of their political superiors and/or to the people they ostensibly serve. When applied to machinery of government, this understanding of 'responsiveness' is thought, for instance, to entail the development of policies and practices that remove 'obstacles' between government and governed ('sunshine' laws requiring that governmental deliberations be conducted in public; increasing 'deliberative democracy' and 'client participation' in agency decision-making).

On the other hand, the 'unresponsiveness' of which many managerialist or economistic critics of state bureaucracy complain centres on the presumed 'inefficiency' of grant-income state bureaucracies as compared with organizations exposed to the vicissitudes of market competition. When applied to the machinery of government, this understanding of 'responsiveness' entails, *inter alia*, the development of market-type mechanisms ('internal-markets', quasi-autonomous agencies, and Public-Private Partnerships (PPPs) that will help stimulate efficiency, competition and profitability (no matter in how opaque a manner) in and among state bureaux or, bypassing those bureaux altogether, in the name of vitalising the state service to provide what some advocates have termed 'entrepreneurial governance' (Osborne and Gaebler, 1992; Osborne and Plastrik, 1997). In contrast to the democratic impulse, this approach to responsiveness highlights the need for managerial autonomy from political control so that services can be delivered to customers with maximum efficiency, as in any other business context.[1]

As indicated earlier, both strands of critique can be traced in recent and ongoing experiments in reforming state bureaux. The question that arises, though, concerns the effects of such demands on the character of bureaucratic office. What impact have attempts to institute more 'responsive' forms of government had upon the capacity of state bureaucrats to live up to the obligations of their office? In particular, what effects have programmes designed to enhance 'responsiveness' had upon what Weber characterised as the separation of office and self?

POPULIST DEMOCRATIC CRITIQUES AND THE ETHOS OF BUREAUCRATIC OFFICE

There are, of course, many different forms of populist democratic critique of state bureaux. Some critics approach the issue of enhanced 'responsiveness' by stressing the bureaucrat's independent obligation to act on the basis of their sense of individual and/or social responsibility. Here, bureaucrats are represented as influential participants in the policy process, who should be encouraged to act more freely on the dictates of their own consciences to ensure socially equitable outcomes (for a discussion see Uhr, 2001). Others encourage the adoption of relatively direct ways for members of the public to influence the behaviour of public bureaucrats, through the deployment of citizen-consumer charters for instance, or through associated devices such as the creation of various user groups that function as virtual boards of directors for public organizations (for a discussion, see Peters, 2000). Yet others propose the enhanced use of political appointees and special advisers in an increasing number of government positions, thus ensuring that the will of the government can be enthusiastically promoted and its priorities enforced in the face of the perceived inertia represented by the 'forces of conservatism' inherent in state bureaucracies (for a discussion, see Jones, 2002).

What each of these critiques shares is an assumption that the justness of bureaucratic policy and practice is a function of the degree to which it is subordinate (i.e. 'responsive') to a conception of the 'popular will'. On the one hand this may be achieved through mechanisms such as the increased use of political appointees, in which the 'popular will' is effectively mediated through political elites of some sort. Responsiveness here is conceptualised as being to political leaders as representatives of 'the people'. On the other hand, mechanisms such as 'citizen-consumer' charters or client 'virtual boards of directors' suggest a more direct – though still mediated – form of popular control.

The idea of the bureaucrat acting on his or her own conscience in the service of individual moral and/or social responsibility appears at first sight to sit uncomfortably with either of these notions. However, the inculcation among bureaucrats of an office-independent, socially responsible muscle of the spirit, suggests that the bureaucrat is in some sense reimagined as a representative of the people, continually conducting an inner moral audit, measuring their conduct not so much against the demands of their office, as against a wider conception of moral principle and socially beneficial outcomes. The 'responsiveness' here is to the bureaucrat's own conscience as evidenced in their moral conception of 'socially responsible' conduct. Only insofar as role – or office – based obligations are represented in terms of morally justifiable higher purposes – engendering social justice and civic renewal – should public bureaucrats regard them as an altruistic 'personal' responsibility (Minson, 1998).

While it often seems difficult to argue against populist, democratic mechanisms for holding bureaucrats to account – however they are understood – given the normative power associated with the democratic signifier, nonetheless there may be some significant problems with the practical operation of such mechanisms when it comes to maintaining the separation between 'office' and 'self' that Weber characterised as a fundamental component of the operation of the state as a state. As we saw earlier, Weber's understanding of bureaucratic office is framed in opposition to theological or otherwise pre-modern understandings of office as divine right, personal possession or private property. It is also clearly distinguished from certain doctrines of popular sovereignty. As he makes clear, in *Economy and Society* and *The Profession and Vocation of Politics*, for instance, when you have a state as your form of political organization, and especially if you are living in a world of basically competitive states, the preservation and flourishing of your state gives rise to an independent set of reasons for action: those pertaining to the security of the state as its own *raison d'être*. Or what we have come to know as *raison d'état*. If, in certain forms of populist democratic thought, 'public' means all that pertaining to the concerns of all the people, then when state officials come to take care of these public concerns it is clear that a transmutation of meaning and ethos is effected that is of fundamental significance (Geuss, 2001). For under these circumstances the term 'public' comes to refer to the offices themselves rather than the 'common concerns' or more specifically, the latter come to be seen exclusively in terms of the former. It is precisely a reversal of this development that I argue can be seen at work in the contemporary populist democratic critique of bureaucratic office.

An example will assist. The last three decades have witnessed a concerted attempt by governing parties in many different political contexts to strengthen their control over state bureaux. These moves have been framed in terms of enhancing the responsiveness of the bureaucracy to the political will of those with a democratic mandate. One aspect of this particular trend has been the erosion of the powers of centralised staffing agencies which safeguarded public service recruitment and promotions from political or official interference; strengthening ministerial control of top departmental appointments by removing the need to consult an independent staffing agency; substituting short-term contracts for security of tenure in top official posts, and generating the general attitude that party-political governments should not have to tolerate obstruction or inertia from conservative bureaucrats, and should instead surround themselves with enthusiastic, committed leaders who would champion their policies and ensure they were 'delivered' (Chapman, 2004). In attempting to achieve these ends, however, politicians and their advisers have arguably weakened the legitimate role of officials in government by undermining the ethos of bureaucratic office (Parker, 1993; du Gay, 2000; Chapman, 2004).

The increasing use of external appointments to senior civil service positions and, in particular, the appointment of those with known prior policy enthusiasms, gives rise to two particular problems.[2] The first is that of ensuring that standards in state service are maintained – that the obligations of office are lived up to; the second is that distinctions between office and self are not so blurred that the state service becomes a politically partisan institution.

In the United Kingdom, for instance, the political neutrality, or party political impartiality, of the British Civil Service has flowed in no small part from its career basis (Bogdanor, 2001; Chapman, 2004). Career civil servants are expected to serve successive governments of differing party political hues. The key to being able to do this, as Weber indicated, is to cultivate a degree of indifference to the enthusiasms of all political parties; to display, in effect, party political impartiality. Traditionally, at least, civil servants have been trained to conduct themselves in such a manner. Indeed, in Britain, as elsewhere, people with strong party political or single issue interests have – until recently – been unlikely to be appointed to senior Civil Service positions, or to present themselves for consideration as candidates in the first place (Chapman, 1988). As a result, civil servants have been likely to greet the panaceas of all political parties with caution, if not scepticism. Inevitably, this leads them to embrace party political programmes with less fervour than party political enthusiasts would like. But this is part of their job; one assigned to them by the constitution. And in fulfilling this role they may be seen as servants of the state. It is precisely this *étatiste*/constitutional role – an obligation of office – that is being affected by the appointment of political enthusiasts or loyalists to senior positions in the bureaucracy. New recruits coming from outside – whether from commercial organisations or social enterprises, will generally lack the traditional patterns of experience, such as those gained by being a private secretary to a minister, which help inculcate in civil servants those very conducts of impartiality. Moreover, someone recruited from outside the service by virtue of relevant knowledge and approved commitments is likely to arrive with all sorts of partisan baggage derived from their previous situation. That is almost inevitable, if 'new' civil servants are expected to be cheerleaders for government and act as committed champions of specific policies. It is not easy, however, for those same people to both fulfil such a role and at the same time conform to traditional practices of subordination and lack of constitutional personality, their views not being individually held but those of their minister.

As Bogdanor (2001, p. 296) has suggested, it is not clear, therefore, how far outside recruitment to senior policy positions in the Civil Service can avoid the dangers of politicisation or at least a degree of prior policy commitment, incompatible with traditional notions of 'political neutrality'. The problem here, in effect, is that office and self become blurred, with the committed champions coming to see the office as an extension of themselves, thereby effecting a confusion of public and private interests and identities. Dobel (1999, p. 131) calls this 'zealous sleaze', a process whereby individuals come to see public office as an extension of their own will and ideological commitments. The introduction into state bureaux of too many people with prior policy commitments and enthusiasms sympathetic to the government of the day could therefore easily undermine the traditional obligations of office framing the conduct of the Civil Service as an institution of government. Similar objections can be made concerning the increased use of special advisers, especially when, as in some well known cases in the UK, this category of actor has been allotted extraordinary powers to issue orders to civil servants or has, through its gatekeeper role with ministers, effectively been able to negate the influence of civil servants in the area of advising on policy issues (Jones, 2002; Oliver, 2003).

THE ETHOS OF BUREAUCRATIC OFFICE AND STATE INTEREST

Clearly, political circumstances change, and so should the machinery of government. After all, too narrow a focus on the inviolability of a set of pre-existing commitments can be just as problematic, politically and administratively, as too abstract a fixation on the imperatives of epochal change. Institutions must be allowed to adapt from their original purposes if the circumstances in which they operate have changed. This, though, begs a very large question. Have political circumstances changed so fundamentally that we can do away with office-based conceptions of ethical agency?

To judge by the comments of some advocates of entrepreneurial government, or social governance, for example, many of the problems the state evolved to address have been solved; the only issues left to deal with concern better management of contracts, or how to make decision-making more 'deliberative' or 'participative'. These may be the 'parish pump' concerns of what has been characterised as a fundamentally 'anti-statist' age (Mulgan, 1994; Gamble and Wright, 2004), but are such assumptions warranted? Has the state and its hierarchically structured domain of offices been transcended?

We have been here before. Early in the twentieth century we find Max Weber railing against the various political romanticisms – anarchists, socialists, armchair litterateurs – who would do away with bureaucracy, law and other detritus of the liberal state in pursuit of their own radical 'visions'. Weber was quite clear that the ethos of bureaucratic office constituted a virtue that a liberal regime, with a parliamentary democracy and market economy, could not do without. As we saw earlier, he was adamant that 'without this supremely ethical discipline and self-denial the whole apparatus would disintegrate' (1994b, p. 331).

To reiterate: for Weber, the state bureau comprises the social and cultural conditions of a distinctive and independent comportment of the person, one that is basically non-sectarian in character. Among the most important of these conditions is that the office constitutes a 'vocation' (*Beruf*) – a focus of ethical commitment and duty, autonomous of and superior to the holder's extra-official ties to kith, kin, class or conscience. For Weber, this marks out the bureau as a specific *Lebensordnung* or 'life-order', and provides the bureaucrat with a distinctive ethical bearing and status-conduct. The ethical attributes of the good bureaucrat – strict adherence to procedure, acceptance of sub- and superordination, *esprit de corps*, abnegation of personal moral enthusiasms, commitment to the purposes of the office – are to be seen as a positive moral achievement requiring the mastery of a definite ethical techniques and routines – declaring one's 'personal' interest, developing appropriate professional relations with one's colleagues, subordinating one's 'self' to the dictates of procedural decision-making – through which individuals come to acquire the disposition and ability to conduct themselves according to the ethos of bureaucratic office (Weber, 1978 II; Minson, 1993; Hunter, 1994; du Gay, 2000).

In addressing the different kinds of responsibility that particular 'offices' make on those subject to their demands, Weber is insisting on the irreducibility of different orders of life and on the consequent necessity of applying different ethical protocols to them. Forged in the party system and tempered by the organisational adversarialism of the parliament, the politician belongs to an order of life quite unlike that of the state bureaucrat. The party leader possesses the political abilities and ethical demeanour required by the unremitting struggle to win and regain power. As Weber makes clear, it is not the trained expertise and impersonal dedication of the official that equips the politician to pursue the worldly interests of the state in the face of hostile and unpredictable economic and political environment. At the same time, however, those very same capacities that enable the bureaucrats to live up to the demands of their office and, in their different but no less essential way, serve the interests of the state. The key to the 'self denial' that Weber recognised as a crucial feature of the performance of bureaucratic office, was a trained indifference – *sine ira et studio* – to party or partisan creed, combined with an attachment to the authority of the state, political order or regime. In other words, official indifference meant not being committed, by convictions guiding one's official actions, to the creed and platform of a political party, while being able without a crisis of conscience to further the policies of any current governing party. In this way, state bureaucrats were likely to greet the panaceas and enthusiasms of all political parties with caution. This was part of their job and in performing that role they could be seen as servants of the state. As Weber makes clear, it is the honour of bureaucrats not to allow extra official commitments to determine the manner in which they perform the duties associated with their office.

More recently, Michael Lind (2005, p. 34-37) has described how the bureaucratic 'mandarinate' – that other governing profession – having helped to deliver the state from the dangers of 'mobocracy' in the early twentieth century now finds itself scapegoated by a range of powerful forces that are managerialist, populist, libertarian and religious. To the managerialist, the bureaucrat is an amateur; to the libertarian, a statist; to the populist, an elitist, and to the religious fundamentalist, a heathen. Lind (2005, p. 37) asks the rhetorical question: 'What could be worse than a society run by such people?' His answer is simple: 'a society without them'. The contemporary US, and to a lesser extent Britain, shows the consequences of turning a modern polity into a 'mandarin free zone'. Lind is referring, in particular, to the vast social experiment with responsiveness that has taken place in these and other liberal regimes, an experiment 'as audacious, in its own way, as that of Soviet collectivism' (2005, p. 37). Referring explicitly to developments in America Lind (ibid.) writes:

The US ship of state veers now in one direction, now the other. From a distance, one might conclude that the captain is a maniac. But a spyglass reveals that there is no captain or crew at all, only rival gangs of technocrats, ideologues, populists and zealots devoted to Jesus Christ or Adam Smith, each boarding the derelict vessel and capturing the wheel briefly before being tossed overboard.

For both Weber and Lind, in their rather different ways, something important is being registered: the crucial role of the ethos of bureaucratic office as a sort of 'gyroscope of state', helping to provide, for example, the stability, continuity and institutional memory that were once deemed crucial to the realisation of responsible and effective government. It is precisely this *étatiste* role and status-conduct that constitutes the distinctiveness and virtue of the ethos of bureaucratic office, and yet is also exactly this which cannot be registered in the pervasive languages of managerialism or democratic populism. As John Rohr (1998, p. xi), for instance, has argued, this is a 'forest and trees problem of the first order ... and underscores one of the most fundamental problems with the public management movement', namely its diminution of the statist and constitutional character of public bureaucratic office through the substitution of a language of political administration by a managerialist lexicon.

In seeking to recast bureaucratic office-holders as generic managers, for instance, managerialist critics arguably constrict their role in governance. They do so by evacuating the bureaucratic role of much of its determinate content. By conceiving of state bureaux as predominantly 'delivery' mechanisms, for instance, some of the crucial *étatiste* responsibilities of office become literally 'inconceivable'. In Britain, for example, the Blair government's informal 'all on one team' approach, combined with its singular focus on 'delivery' and its experiments with fostering a 'just do it ethic' among civil servants, has had some unfortunate consequences for the ethos of bureaucratic office.

The revelations elicited by the Hutton Inquiry in the UK into the events surrounding the death of the government weapons expert, Dr David Kelly, of the extent to which, under the 'New' Labour administration, the traditional bureaucratic practices of careful and precise note-taking and writing of minutes had fallen into abeyance, were both striking and deeply worrying. It was revealed most vividly when Jonathan Powell, the Prime Minister's (partisan) Chief-of-Staff, disclosed to Hutton that of an average seventeen meetings a day in Downing Street, only three were minuted. When role-specific differences between politicians, special advisers and career state bureaucrats, for example, are elided, then detailed record keeping, it would appear, can be deployed more flexibly; perhaps because it is assumed that everyone is obviously singing from the same hymn sheet, the need for things like minutes is less obvious – what the Butler report into the use of intelligence in the lead up to the invasion of Iraq famously described as 'the informality and circumscribed character of the Government's procedures' seriously risked 'reducing the scope for informed collective political judgement'. As a former Cabinet Secretary (Lord) Richard Wilson (2004, p. 85) commented in relation to this point, formal meetings and minute-taking, for instance, might seem overly 'bureaucratic' and thus very un-modern technologies, yet they play a crucial practical role in ensuring good government and provide a necessary underpinning for the realisation of constitutionally sanctioned accountability requirements – of ministerial responsibility to parliament, for example – by ensuring a proper record of governmental decision-making exists and that agreed actions are clearly delineated.

Linked to this, Michael Quinlan (2004) has indicated how the government's zealous managerialist focus on 'delivery' has occurred at the expense of attention to bureaucratic due process. As he puts it, a singular focus on delivery can easily 'slide into a sense that outcome is the only true reality and that process is flummery. But the two are not antithetical, still less inimical to one another. Process is care and thoroughness; it is consultation, involvement ... legitimacy and acceptance; it is also record, auditability and clear accountability. It is often accordingly a significant component of outcome itself; and the more awkward and demanding the issue – especially amid the gravity of peace and war – the more it may come to matter' (ibid., p. 128). Too exclusive a focus on delivery can therefore have the effect of undermining other aspects of the role that an official is charged with undertaking.

What we see here is a managerialist agenda constitutionally incapable of registering the statist – non-partisan – character of public bureaucratic office holding. By casting reasons of state and public administration in term of its own 'business' model, managerialist reforms have assisted in the politicisation of state service. In focusing exclusively – and simplistically – on 'delivery', such managerial reforms have enabled the governing political party to buttress its own power and influence at the expense of the proper exercise of sovereignty. The managerialist approach to government can therefore have deleterious consequences for the maintenance of the 'independent' state oriented obligations of office, and for what Dobel (1999, p. 41) describes as a 'prized accomplishment' of modern political existence, the separation of public office and 'self'.

CONCLUDING COMMENTS

In this chapter I have sought, rather too briefly, alas, to make a case for the continuing indispensability of office-specific conceptions of moral agency in the realm of governmental and political action. In particular, I have attempted to provide a number of arguments in support of the continued relevance of the ethos of bureaucratic office to the practice of state administration. In so doing, I have suggested that many of the audacious experiments in public management – whether couched in populist democratic or overtly managerialist terms – that have been foisted upon state bureaux over the last two-three decades have had the effect of undermining the 'core business' of public administration: running a state as a state. Slogans about the state being the servant not the master of 'the people' (Mulgan and Wilkinson, 1994) or those that espouse the managerial line of 'businesslike is best', have a way of trapping minds. And for such trapped minds, state bureaux can only be viewed as a profound disappointment, ripe for transcendence or radical reform.

How one seeks to deal with such disappointment is the crucial question. For democratic populists and managerialists this involves imagining the state and its offices as something other than they are. In particular, they want the state and its bureaux to conform to or express some sort of principle. In so doing, as I have attempted to show, they serve to evacuate state or public administration of its determinate content. The work of Max Weber offers an alternative way of dealing with such disappointment. At heart, this means coming to terms with the state's imperfection and accepting it as an inevitable part of its positivity. After all, 'the state is born imperfect, for to be born it had to renounce perfection, its own and that of its subject population, making do instead with its capacity to enforce social peace and their capacity to act civilly' (Hunter, 2005, p. 9). It is also imperfect because it is nothing more than a bundle of offices – political, legal, bureaucratic, military, police – reliant on contingent funding, fallible (or, as we have seen, worse) management, and prone to varying degrees of dissolution arising from a host of sources (corruption, incompetence, ideological conflict, military disasters etc.) (ibid., p. 5). And yet, what else can do its job? Certainly nothing sketched in the dreams and schemes of populist democratic critics and/or their managerialist counterparts. So while they and the advocates of other visions – of global cosmopolitanism, or of religious fundamentalism, for instance – seek to move beyond the state and its structure of offices, for others it might be useful to follow in the footsteps of John Dewey for whom it was 'always important to rediscover the state'.

NOTES

1. Interestingly, though, while both conceptions of 'responsiveness' are distinctive and non-reducible, they have often fed off of one another in specific programmes of administrative reform. Thus proponents of increased democratic control have often advocated managerialist measures to achieve their desired ends, while managerialist critics have themselves cited enhanced consumer choice as one of the 'democratic' outcomes of their favoured reform measures (du Gay, 2000; Peters, 2004).

2. In the United Kingdom, the current government has indicated its desire to open up more and more senior public positions to external competition. It wants to do this not only to attract the requisite talent able and willing to deliver its reform agenda, but also because an 'open' civil service is deemed to be preferable to a 'closed' civil service. As Bogdnaor (2001, 295) puts it, '[T]his argument would seem at first sight to be unanswerable. Yet, if the Civil Service is, as some former heads such as Warren Fisher and Edward Bridges believed, a genuine profession, ought it not in fact to be closed? It would not, after all, be very sensible to suggest to someone who objected to unqualified doctors or lawyers that he or she favoured a "closed" medical or legal profession. For professions are, almost by definition, closed'. The big issue is whether the Civil Service as a profession devoted to running a state and operating a constitution, based on its own particular expertise and obligations of office, is to survive or whether it is simply set to become a politicised vehicle for enthusiastically delivering the government's agenda.

REFERENCES

Bennett, R. (2004), *Havoc in Its Third Year*, London, UK: Bloomsbury.

Bogdanor, V. (2001), 'Civil service reform: A critique', *The Political Quarterly*, **72** (3), 291-299.

Cabinet Office (1999a), *Vision and Values*, London, UK: Cabinet Office.

Chapman, R. A. (1988), *Ethics in the British Civil Service*, London, UK: Routledge.

Chapman, R. A. (2000), *Ethics in Public Service for the New Millennium*, Aldershot, UK: Ashgate Publishing.

Chapman, R. A. (2004), *The Civil Service Commission 1855-1991: A Bureau Biography*, London, UK: Taylor Francis Routledge.

Dobel, P. (1999), *Public Integrity*, Baltimore, USA: The Johns Hopkins University Press.

Du Gay, P. (2000), *In Praise of Bureaucracy*, London, UK: Sage.

Dunn, J. (2000), *The Cunning of Unreason*, London, UK: Harper-Collins.

Gamble, A. and T. Wright (eds) (2004), *Restating the State?*, Oxford, UK: Blackwell.

Geuss, R. (2001), *History and Illusion in Politics*, Cambridge, UK: Cambridge University Press.

Hunter, I. (1994), *Re-Thinking the School*, Sydney, Australia: Allen & Unwin.

Hunter, I. (2005), 'Security: the default setting of the Liberal state', accessed at http://www.apo.org.au/webboard/results.chtml?filename_num=42404

Jones, N. (2002), *The Control Freaks,* London, UK: Polticos.

Kallinikos, J. (2004), 'The social foundations of the bureaucratic order', *Organization*, **11** (1), 13-36.

Kriegel, B. (1995), *The State and the Rule of Law*, (trans. M. LePain and J. Cohen), Princeton, NJ, USA: Princeton University Press.

Lind, M. (2005), 'Red-state sneer', *Prospect*, January, 34-37.

Loughlin, M. (2004), *The Idea of Public Law*, Oxford, UK: Oxford University Press.

Minson, J. (1993), *Questions of Conduct*, Basingstoke, UK: Macmillan.

Minson, J. (1998), 'Ethics in the Service of the State', in M. Dean and B. Hindess (eds), *Governing Australia: Studies in Contemporary Rationalities of Government*, Melbourne, Australia: Cambridge University Press, 340-363.

Mulgan, G. (1994), *Politics in an Anti-Political Age*, Cambridge, UK: Polity Press.

Mulgan, G. and H. Wilkinson (1994), *Politics in an Antipolitical Age*, Cambridge, UK: Polity Press.

Oliver, D. (2003), *Constitutional Reform in the UK*, Oxford, UK: Oxford University Press.

Orren, K. (1994), 'The work of government: Rediscovering the discourse of office in Marbury v. Madison', *Studies in American Political Development*, **8** (1), 60-80.

Osborne, D. and T. Gaebler (1992), *Re-Inventing Government*, Reading, MA, USA: Addison-Wesley.

Osborne, D. and P. Plastrik (1997), *Banishing Bureaucracy: The Five Strategies for Reinventing Government*, Reading, MA, USA: Addison-Wesley.

Parker, R. (1993), *The Administrative Vocation*, Sydney, Australia: Hale and Iremonger.

Peters, B. G. (2000), 'Is democracy a substitute for Ethics? Administrative Reform and Accountability', in R. A. Chapman (ed.), *Ethics in Public Service for a New Millenium*, Aldershot, UK: Ashgate.

Quinlan, M. (2004) 'Lessons for Governmental Process', in W. G. Runciman (ed.), *Hutton and Butler: Lifting the Lid on the Workings of Power*, Oxford, UK: British Academy/Oxford University Press.

Rhodes, R. (1996), 'The new governance: governing without government', *Political Studies*, **XLIV**, 652-667.

Rhodes, R. (2000), 'Governance and Public Administration', in J. Pierre (ed.), *Understanding Governance*, Oxford, UK: Oxford University Press.

Rohr, J. (1998), *Public Service, Ethics and Constitutional Practice*, Lawrence, KS, USA: University of Kansas Press.

Sabl, A. (2002), *Ruling Passions*, Princeton, NJ, USA: Princeton University Press.

Skinner, Q. (1989), 'The State', in T. Ball, J. Farr and R. L. Hanson (ed.), *Political Innovation and Conceptual Change*, Cambridge, UK: Cambridge University Press.

Stoker, G. (1998), 'Governance as theory: five propositions', *International Social Science Journal*, **155**, 17-28.

Stoker, G. (2000a), 'The Challenge of Urban Governance', in J. Pierre (ed.), *Debating Governance*, Oxford, UK: Oxford University Press.

Stoker, G. (2000b), 'The Three Projects of New Labour', *Renewal*, **8** (3), 7-15.

Thompson, D. (1987), *Political Ethics and Public Office*, Cambridge, MA, USA: Harvard University Press.

Uhr, J. (2001), 'Moderating Ministerial Ethics: Putting Political Ethics in its Place', in J. Fleming and I. Holland (ed.), *Motivating Ministers to Morality*, Alndershot, UK: Ashgate Press.

Walzer, M. (1984), 'Liberalism and the art of separation', *Political Theory*, **12**, (3), 315-330.

Weber, M. (1978), *Economy & Society* (2 Vols.), Los Angeles, US: University of California Press.

Weber, M. (1994a), 'Parliament and Government in Germany under a New Political Order', in P. Lassman and R. Speirs (eds), *Weber: Political Writings*, Cambridge, UK: CUP.

Weber, M. (1994b), 'The Profession and Vocation of Politics', in P. Lassman and R. Speirs (eds), *Weber: Political Writings*, Cambridge, UK: CUP.

Wilson, R. (2004), 'Issues of Evidence: Discussion', in W. G. Runciman (ed.), *Hutton and Butler: Lifting the Lid on the Workings of Power*, Oxford, UK: British Academy/Oxford University Press.

Wolter, U. (1997), 'The *Officium* in Medieval Ecclesiastical Law as a Prototype of Modern Administration', in A. Padoa-Schioppa (ed.), *Legislation and Justice*, Oxford, UK: Clarendon Press.

3. Granting Disorder a Place in Ethics: Organization's Deviant Practices and Ethics

Olivier Babeau

INTRODUCTION

Ancient Greeks had the odd and genial custom of celebrating the law and its transgression on the same day. As paradoxical as it may seem, the Dionysian feast, which took place in March, celebrated Dionysos, god of drunkenness and excess, but also celebrated the law. During this feast, the choir sang the hymn to the god, and an actor told the legend of his life. A goat, the beast associated with Dionysos, was sacrificed, hence the name 'tragedy' given to the spectacle: τραγος–οδη, 'goat's song'. Tragedy is literally a tale of the mythic life of Dionysos. Like the god it celebrates, tragedy is a dramatization of transgression: 'Norm is only given in Greek tragedy *in order* to be transgressed or *because* it is transgressed; Greek tragedy is dependent on Dionysos, god of confusion and god of transgression' (Vidal-Naquet, 1982, p. 27).

Greek civilization was skilled in the conciliation of opposites, and the acknowledgement of the world's ambiguities. Human and divine rules, as the Greeks knew, were deeply linked in their transgression. Moral life did not mean necessarily abiding by the rules but rather the practice of the *metis*, 'circumspect wisdom'. First wife of Zeus or, according to the orphic theogonia, primitive goddess, *Metis* symbolizes the art of catching the *kairos*, the 'right moment'. She refers directly to the notion of *ruse*, which is not always pejorative for a Greek mind: Hermes is at the same time the god of honest endeavours (such as trade) as well as dishonest tricks (robbery).

It seems today that this ambiguity has been somewhat forgotten and replaced by a strong belief in dualism: rule and transgression are now strongly separated. Maybe Immanuel Kant had the most important influence on the dualism rule/deviance? It is in fact surprising to note how Kant's conception of morals has penetrated minds over the last two centuries. His famous categorical imperative seems to be the unconscious collective measure of ethics: 'Act so that the maxim [of your action] may be capable of becoming a universal law for all rational beings' (Kant, 1785). It is known that *unconditional respect of law* is the corollary of it: transgressing a rule, even only once, would imply that it is possible to make an universal law of deviance, that is to say suppressing all rules, which would end in chaos.

Rawls develops the same idea in his *Theory of Justice*, arguing that abiding by rules is a duty: 'Our natural duty to uphold just institutions binds us to comply with unjust laws and policies or at least not to oppose them by illegal means as long as they do not exceed certain limits of injustice' (Rawls, 1971, p. 353). The diffusion of this idea explains that the respect for rules, whether formal or informal, is generally understood as the *sine qua non* condition of ethical organization. According to this general opinion, thinking of ethics in organization involves searching how the system of norms could be perfected in order for everybody to abide by it. The general respect for rules would bring about harmony, efficiency and employees' satisfaction. Such a conception is the enemy of all clandestine arrangements with rules, the opponent of all deviancy. The main reproach is that made to transgressions: they introduce a disastrous exception in the equality of everybody in terms of the norm; they violate normalcy. Adopting the Kantian point of view makes every rule transgression a pathological and harmful phenomenon which wisdom and moral command demand should be eliminated. Does not the liar 'corrupt the social link' according to the Professor of Königsberg?

Before going any further, let us make precise two points of vocabulary. First, we do not find it necessary here to distinguish between 'rules' and 'norms'. While the distinction is possible, we regard these two words as referring to the same phenomenon: the common reference to what is supposed to be done or forbidden in a social group. Such a definition is broad ranging, it encompasses all types of rules, obligations and injunctions of things to do, or more often what not to do. The common point of these obligations is that everyone chooses to abide by them or not. In other words, there is no essential difference between the two words, even if we could surely state that rules may be only a part of norms, which encompass both formal and informal types of obligations. From the point of view of transgression, norms and rules are the same.

There is a second distinction, which establishes the difference between transgression and deviance, which we do not find necessary to make. The work of Becker (1963) and Goffman (1963) demonstrate that nobody is deviant before being *branded* so by an observer. Deviance qualification implies a social judgement, whereas transgression seems to be only a factual statement. These results are not being disputed here but in this chapter the distinction is not relevant: the question of the branding is set apart, as we choose to stay at the level of mere individual actions. For the purposes of this chapter, the word 'deviance' is therefore not to be understood in terms of the meaning attributed to it by sociologists of deviance but as synonymous with transgression.

The purpose of the present chapter is not to discuss questions of right and wrong, or the existence of natural morals, but rather it is to underline the difference between the common representation of what ethics should be and their reality in practice: this gap, in our opinion, merits serious attention by theorists of business ethics.

Rather than concerning ourselves with the ethical rules for business relations as a whole, we focus instead on ethics in organizations themselves. We are interested in exploring how different groups live together within organizations. In particular, the co-habitation between management and employees is a focus of this chapter. A progressive organization seeks to reconcile two necessities: the autonomy of its employees and the coordination of their actions. Rules are the mechanisms which manage the equilibrium. As organizational insiders are often aware, condemning rule transgression often seems like a mistake, or perhaps to put it more bluntly, an act of ignorance. Many scholars have shown the importance of deviance and the part it plays in the 'normal' functioning of a company over the past decades. The goal of absolute rules respect is always reaffirmed but as an idle horizon that seems not only unrealistic but also aporetic.

How would it be possible to impose ethical behaviour? Such an exercise, would exclude a gamut of deviant behaviour. Yet as disturbing as it might seem, we realize that organizations rely on deviance. Thinking of organization's ethics imposes a realization of the extent to which they can be compatible with deviance. More precisely, we have to think about how justice in a firm – conceived as the establishment of fair relations between its members – can derive not from transparency but from the fuzziness produced by slack around the rules. In a nutshell, we invite the reader to a reasoned praise of transgression in organizations.

To be more specific, the suspicion which grounds this chapter is that rule transgression is not innocuous, but plays an essential part in social functioning. Our fundamental argument is that rule transgression 'says something'. It is evidence of an underground functioning of coordination. In other words, rules would indeed be a tool allowing coordination, but through an original mechanism. It is because it is transgressed that a rule allows coordination. Deviance ceases to be a dysfunction which should be suppressed and becomes the necessary response to the fundamental contradiction of every organized action: conciliating coordination and autonomy.

THE ROLE AND IMPORTANCE OF TRANSGRESSIONS IN ORGANIZATION

In this first part, we are going to show how transgressions are spread widely across the organizational world. We will suggest that these deviant practices do not necessarily hamper organizations from functioning effectively.

Deviance's Omnipresence: From Prescribed Task to Real Work

The existence, beside formally prescribed behaviours, of a whole world of informal life is certainly not a recent discovery. Taylor was troubled by the amount of control workers had and he saw this as resulting in the workplace being little more than an unbearable and counterproductive space of liberty. Taylor developed scientific management as a means of seizing control of the organization from – as he saw it – recalcitrant workers. Informal work organization historically pre-exists the great normalization of production process which was set up in manufactories during the nineteenth century. Domestic fabrication of goods was deeply linked with familial and daily life. The distinction between private and professional life had not been established. Production processes were entirely made of informal arrangements.

The hegemonic domination of rules and procedures is a fiction which owes its verisimilitude to a century of frantic inhibition. The cursed part of work which is *informal* was pursued and eventually denied until Harvard's *Western Electric* experiments began to rediscover it. As Dejours writes, the main contribution of ergonomics is 'to pinpoint the relentless gap between prescribed task and real work' (Dejours, 1993, p. 66). Ergonomists have shown that 'all orders are re-interpreted and re-built: real work organization is not prescribed organization. It is never so: it is impossible to foresee and control everything' (ibid., p. 231).

Contrary to the traditional representation of the firm, deviance can exist permanently. The coexistence, on the one side, of a representation system which excludes all deviance from the rule and, on the other side, of deviant practice, is the commonplace of industrial observation: 'Fictions are very powerful in factory. Some rules are never abided by, but are perpetually enforced. Contradictory orders are not contradictory according to factory logic. Through all this, work has to be done. The worker has to sort it out himself, or is fired. And he does it' (Weil, 1951, p. 243).

Modernity and Uncertainty

Many factors explain the existence of a growing gap between normative and concrete systems. Let us briefly evoke what we think are the most decisive among them: the development, during the twentieth century, of task complexity and the fast evolution of business environments. The replacement of pure execution tasks by synthesis and reflection tasks and the growing tertiary industry made untenable the Taylorian scheme of definition of movements and actions for a given postion.

Tasks complication is such that no one can completely prescribe the work to be done. Increasingly more actors control an *uncertainty zone* (Crozier, 1963) because they are the only ones to have the specific knowledge of their job (a computer scientist for example), or because of the nature of the task makes control very difficult. What is more, the fast and erratic evolution of environments makes any mid-term prevision uncertain. Consequently, it is futile to establish rules and to believe in their strict application.

Should a manager be appalled by the statement that transgression is a common place part of organizational life? In other words, is transgression only a symptom of malfunction or organizational pathology? We do not think so, as some types of deviances do have a positive effect on the daily functioning of the firm. It is to this, that we now turn.

Deviancy Serving the Firm

Among the variegated types of deviance, 'useful deviance' is the one that merits special attention as it aims to deliver a more effective organization. Those 'useful' deviances are not the ivy that uses the tree in order to grow but are part of organization and contribute to its survival. Like bacteria that pollute every living organism, deviance contributes to the proper functioning of the entity it lives in.

In the context of an organization, a rule is a means to try to structure the behaviour of individuals, and any subsequent transgression is seen as pathological in terms of its marginality. One can hardly understand how coordination remains possible in the wake of constant transgression.

Paradoxically, the only explanation is to assume that deviance plays a role in actors' coordination in an organization.

If, as we have said, the gap between the prescribed and real task has been identified for so long, deviant practices have continued to be considered as being only a space of liberty for the worker, without any other interest for organization. The real revolution will be to regard transgressions as participating in 'normal' and efficient production processes:

> Informal activity was only seen from the point of view of the individual, as a means of saving him from his job's monotony and disinterest. Managers only considered it seriously as helping individual. When it appeared that firms could not work without those informal adjustments, and that they were necessary to production, they began to be taken into account (Bernoux, 1999, p. 189).

An absolute respect for rules seems, in many cases, to be an inhibitory obstacle to the realisation of a task. Often, the successful accomplishment of a work task requires a degree of deviance – work 'is never reducible to a pure application of planning. When they keep close to prescribed tasks, as in work to rule strikes, workers paralyse organization; order transgressions allow performances and suppress planned organization's countless failures' (Périlleux, 2001, p. 27; Chateauraynaud, 1991).

The case of air traffic controllers is a good example of collective permanent rule transgression in order to allow the realization of the job. Air traffic controllers are in charge of traffic regulation in airports. Their responsibility is tremendous: a single mistake can cost the lives of hundreds of persons. While security norms ruling this activity are numerous, they are also ignored on a routine basis, for instance, in the case of the regulations outlining aircraft traffic control and so forth. Controllers flout the security norms in order to reconcile two contradictory needs, which are traffic flow and safety. Given that the reference frame is not imposed by the administration, but rather the norm of the group (Périlleux, 2001, p. 27), the Traffic Controllers do not see themselves as engaging in deviant behaviour.

It is important to note that deviance does not mean an *absence of norms*. A parallel norm exists, which is abided by: 'Those norms are not formalized or written by controllers. They are at the same time secret and visible, implicit in front of administrative rules ..., explicit between them. They are orally transmitted (...). Those rules are codified and ritualised' (Poirot-Delpech, 1996, p. 45).

Interestingly, an industrial relations action, such as working to rule, can undermine the ability of an organization to function. For instance, if the Traffic Controllers were to adhere to their formal work norms, it would paralyse air traffic, and become nothing but a strict application of the norms. Paradoxically, the act of abiding by air traffic control rules would mean that airports would become inoperable. There are numerous other examples that illustrate this phenomenon. For instance, Bernoux (1999, p. 189) reports the case of a bank where the formal bureaucratic work model was replaced by a more flexible initiative, in which employees would learn part of a colleagues' job so that they could perform it if necessary. The superior principle which justifies deviance is the accomplishment of the given task: 'their reference frame overflows the strict frame of the job to embrace a horizon of task realization on the position and team work scale' (Bernoux, 1999, p. 338).

If we turn to the case of a hospital, Guy Vallancien, chief of the urology department at the Montsouris Institute, recently argued that 'probably not one hospital in France fits with the directives of the Direction of Hospitals or medical agencies, not even when they admit a patient in the operating theatre' (Vallancien, 2001). Every medical operation begins with the deviance from the rules, as they are so numerous and constraining.

It is useful to refer to Alter's (1992, 2002) work which establishes the necessity of disorder in the innovative process. Without this exploration out of the regular path of actions, change in firms would be impossible. Deviance is the compulsory element of innovation, which is itself the necessary energy of firms' adaptation and survival.

We have shown that transgression may be useful. But is it sufficient to say that transgression is desirable in firms? From the traditional ethical point of view, ethics and rule-following are two merged concepts. So, is the statement of the omnipresence of deviances the final demonstration of the unethical nature of the firm? We do not think so, because the link ethics/rule needs to be re-examined. Given that we have established the permanence and necessity of some types of deviances in organization, it is time to consider the ethical implication of deviance's omnipresence.

DEVIANCE AND FREEDOM: SHADOW ZONE OF TRANSPARENCY

John Rawls' influential *Theory of Justice* reactivated debate around social contract theories and has tried to answer their main question: 'how should we live together?' In other words, what is the power repartition system which allows the best cohabitation of people? It is impossible to sum up in a few words the answers given by Rawls and his followers. Let us recall nevertheless that, according to Rawls, a society cannot exist without the freedom of its members (Rawls, 1997, p. 237).

Translated to an enterprise – a community of a special kind organized around production – the theme of liberty appears to be the touchstone of ethics in firms: how can we maximize actors' freedom, considering the production constraints which reside in the firm? Obviously, norms have a fundamental role to play in individuals' freedom preservation in a social group. According to philosophers writing on social contracts, law is firstly a way of reducing arbitrary power decisions by means of constraint homogenization.[1]

The republican system inaugurated in France by the 1789 revolution is entirely based on this principle: law, which is the same for everybody, frees all from arbitrary monarchical power. It guarantees liberty from the abuses of a centralized power; it guarantees equality of treatment for everyone, and it creates a fraternity amongst these equals undivided by the rigid estates. The uniform constraint which applies to every citizen, without any consideration of wealth or rank, is the nodal point of a system which intimately links liberty and equality. Democratic law is a device of constraint homogenization which is frontally opposed to the traditional system grounded on an *intuitu personae* treatments of classification. How, in these conditions, could we understand every stretch to regulation as anything other than a surreptitious return of the arbitrary, a default which endangers the whole system's efficiency? How could we clear irregularity from the heavy accusation of dysfunction? What moral status shall we grant to disorder? Here we are at the very node of our reflection.

Ethical enterprise respects employees, creates the conditions for the equality of treatment, and a certain liberty of its members. Rule, as we have just seen, is supposed to be the necessary adjunct of this liberty, and consequently, of the ethics of organization. But the first part of this chapter has shown how deviance is necessary for companies. Reducing this deviance can destroy the organization. What, then, could an 'ethical company' be?

First proposition: a pessimistic position according to which the organization is deeply sinful. In other words, enterprise and morals would be irreducibly dissociated. Being ethical would be for a manager a choice which would necessarily imply a loss of efficiency, or even bankruptcy. A win-win game between ethics and firm efficiency would be impossible.

Second proposition: rehabilitating the role of disorder in organization, the win-win game becomes possible if we break the ethics/rules relation. We have already evoked the beneficial part of deviance. Let us show now, *a contrario*, how transparency, which includes a suppression of deviances, may be harmful for individuals' well-being.

Foucault's Criticisms of Transparency

Transparency, that is to say external and internal consistency of organization, is often described as an essential part of ethics. In fact, an organization could not be qualified as 'ethical' if it did not assure the consistency of its different faces, if it did not harmonize *discourses* and *practices*. The demand for complete disclosure is often regarded as the preliminary to every ethical progression. Alter (1992, p. 188) notes that a belief inherited from scientific work organization survives today, according to which every uncertainty should be reduced. Similarly, we could add, very few express doubts about the belief in a necessary universal transparency.

Michel Foucault shows how the demand of *avowal* can be the pernicious tool of a false liberation and the cause of an all the more radical alienation of the individual. Foucault shows how the multiplication of discourses about sex, the demand of expression of everything that refers to it is a *de facto* alienation with totalitarian consequences. After having described the disciplinary mechanisms at work in our society in *Surveiller et Punir* (1975), Michel Foucault tried, in *La Volonté de Savoir* (1976), to pinpoint the role of sexuality in the diffusion of power mechanisms. The unexpected presence of the latter is shown in the former. Moreover, Foucault underlines that power acts even in what is commonly identified as a battle *against* power.

Foucault firstly evokes the common thesis concerning sexuality: the *Ancien Regime* would have been a relatively permissive period concerning sexuality. From the Revolution on, interdictions would have multiplied, to culminate in the nineteenth century with an era of Puritanism and global repression. If this hypothesis is true, disciplinary mechanisms would only be the cynical expression of a coercion that dares to show itself. But Foucault develops another hypothesis: would it not rather be the ultimate ruse of coercive mechanism to make believe that it naively shows its techniques when it exists even in the criticisms that it has itself produced? Dreyfus and Rabinow note: 'Foucault wages war against the repressive hypothesis that is to say against the idea that truth always plays the role of liberator' (1984, p. 186). As a matter of fact, Foucault develops a radically different interpretation of the relations between sex, truth, power, body and individual (he calls this new synthesis *bio-power*).

Foucault disputes the hypothesis according to which "industrial societies have inaugurated an age of increased repression against sex" (1976, p. 67). On the contrary, he explains that discourses on sex have never been so numerous since the classical age, and especially the nineteenth century. This period has known totally new discourses, in fact an inflation of discourses, an unprecedented will of telling and showing everything. It is necessary at that time not to leave anything in the shadow, to put sex under light, to know it entirely: 'sex ... has become something to say and to say thoroughly with discursive devices which are diverse but which are all constraining. ... It is an immense prolixity that our civilization has demanded and organized' (ibid., pp. 45-46).

Once repression is denied, does it imply that liberty has increased since the classical age? Certainly not! This 'general discursive erethism' (ibid., p. 45) is in fact the most efficient way to control sexuality, namely, discourse sees 'government take charge of sexuality' (ibid., p. 61). Foucault's argument is simple: power cannot control what is hidden, subterranean and private. Thus, it must constrain the individual to publicize the private aspect in order to control totally. Avowing is 'among the major rituals of production of truth' (ibid., p. 78).

Sex is 'the means of controlling the individual' (Foucault, 1994, p. 194). One can then understand why in schools, in the eighteenth century, 'the sexuality of adolescents became a medical problem, a moral problem ...', because through (and under pretext of) this control of sexuality, one could invigilate children and adolescents lives at each moment, even during sleeping' (ibid.).

The greatest ruse of power is to make believe that it only exists under the 'repressive-judiciary' (Foucault, 1975, p. 109) form. Why this ruse? Because 'it is under the condition of masking an important part of itself that power is tolerable' (ibid., p. 113). In other words, by making believe that discourses on sex are a means of opposition to a power busy repressing it, power efficiently hides its omnipresence. Contrary to common opinion, the goal of power is not to repress instincts: this apparent repression is often 'a manner of stimulating, of exciting by irritating, tormenting them, in order to lead them where we want, by making them functioning in such way' (Foucault, 1994, p. 396).

In the middle of the twentieth century, a stream of revolt against power has wanted to make of sexual liberation the sign and the medium for setting the individual free from power. But it only resulted in an accentuation of the latter's pressure: 'all this sex revolution, all this anti-repressive fight was nothing else than a moving and a tactical turning in the great sexual device' (Foucault, 1975, p. 173). Foucault shows how the repeated proclamation of liberty and the liberation of individuals by transparent practices is only a perverse ruse of power in order to dominate. The modern era of so-called individual liberation is in reality an era of accentuation of repressive order. The imposition of transparency which is supposed to be the guarantee of a recovered freedom is actually a domination mechanism. Telling, acknowledging, expressing and clarifying are just many ways of disclosing the totality of human actions under the eye of the state, which brings to light formerly hidden practices, even those judged to be part of private life. In this society of equals, all interpersonal links are put under the eye of authority.

The demand for transparency is a perverse injunction which destroys what it unveiled. Some things are to be left hidden. Certeau establishes a direct link between the negation of this *metis* we mentioned in the introduction and the dogma of transparency: 'our scientificity, by substituting his own places to the complex field of social ruses and its "artificial languages" to ordinary languages, has permitted and imposed to reason a logic of mastering and transparency' (1990, p. 40). That which is secret is hated by a modernity grounded on the perfect equivalence of individuals in front of the state. On secrecy hangs an unbearable suspicion: it creates inequality between those who know it and the others. It must be suppressed, publicized, in order to recreate everybody's equality before information. If this much is true of sexuality may it not also be true of other central life spheres, such as those organizations in which we work? Can we, perhaps, review business ethics through the Foucauldian lens we have been preparing in this section?

Ambiguity and Transparency in Post Taylorian Firm

The mechanism denounced by Foucault is identified by Périlleux (2001) in today's firms. He describes the perverse consequences of the demand for the unveiling of every single action and process. The contemporary firm is characterized by its flexibility: people, structures and processes are supposed to be able to adapt themselves permanently, as the price for the survival of a company in a competitive environment. The corollary of flexibility is *rule imprecision*. What use would it be to fix precise norms to what may change tomorrow? Ambiguity is then made a principle of organization in firms.

In Taylorism, 'a techniques and formalist orientation forbids recognizing that infractions to rules can be efficient: it rejects in illegality or secret the arrangements invented by actors to palliate deficiencies of operative plans' (Périlleux, 2001, p. 26). The new flexible firm diverges from this opinion. The criticism of Taylorism denounces a *staging* of reality in this dichotomy between official normative order and the universe of practices. The paradox is that new practices of flexible organization will institute a new staging: over implication, over motivation and, paradoxically, disinterestedness. Ethical charters which are supposed to be proofs of transparency are seen by Le Goff as 'an imaginary realization of homogenous firm' (1992, p. 108). The discrepancy between official discourses and reality is all the more blatant in those organizations where worker participation and transparency are said to reconcile diverging interests among actors.

Deviance is recognized, but this does not signify that the distortion between prescribed task and real work is accepted. Flexibility is only a form of annihilation of this latter. The proclamation of openness to creativity and personal autonomy comes along with a will of suppression of every parallel practice and exposition of every traditionally disclosed part. General transparency is the aim of this new organization: 'The development of the modern state and its capitalist-industrial substructure is characterized by a tremendous extension of supervision. Nowadays, by its very nature, supervision demands transparency, divulging' (Giddens, 1984, p. 182).

Deviance from norms is only accepted when it is public, exposed. In modern firms, light is shed on all disclosed practices. Management methods such as participative management make communication fluidity and individual appraisal a priority goal for the firm (see for example Hermel, 1988). Showing everything, knowing everything, and bringing every part of the activity to light are the main concern of post-Taylorian firms.

One can understand the pernicious functioning of this system. Deviance is encouraged and exposed, but stays deviance: in case of failure, creativity will be punished. The worker, deprived of the security of clandestineness, can no more hide mistakes, and is condemned to success. What actually could be the rule that one can transgress? What force may it have if it is not officially inviolable? A system of sanction must necessarily exist for those who have transgressed uselessly: risk and fear of doing wrong is present more than in traditional planned enterprise. Everybody is encouraged to transgress, to be autonomous from rules, but this does not suppress sanction in case of failure. There is an obligation of *results* where planned enterprise had only a demand for *means* (rule respect). The system grounded on contestation of Taylorian organization suppressed secret margins of action, which were the only acknowledged advantage of this old system: 'From the persons' point of view, the demand of autonomy becomes a kind of trap when it signifies that everybody has to make do with more and more pressured merchant and techniques constraints without having the means to face them' (Périlleux, 2001, p. 37).

Suppression of strict norms and clandestine arrangements, total transparency of processes and flexibility only reproduce and increase the defaults of Taylorian systems: arbitrariness, uncertainty, ambiguity and suffering are all the more present. Managers exploit this uncertainty as they did before but workers no longer have the refuge of obscurity! The declination of the themes of liberty, workers respect, theoretically 'ethical' intentions, leads to an all the more radical alienation:

It is impossible to suppress all uncertainty in work organization and ambiguity may be a good thing when its recognition shows the limits of planning. But it can not be maintained for long when it erases frontiers of professional implication. Temptation is strong for managers to act as if ambiguity did not exist, while benefiting from this growing fuzziness in appraisal criteria. This might produce new kinds of arbitrary in professional relations (Périlleux, 2001, p. 129).

CONCLUSION: VIRTUE OF DISORDER

An easy distinction between rules, respect (moral action) and deviance (immoral action) is, alas, impossible. The binary conception of law, with an objective threshold separating legal and illegal, is only an intellectual construct. The thin and clear line which marks the frontier is in reality a *grey zone* where *tolerated* cohabitates with *permitted*, and even with *forbidden*. Following circumstance and the state of mind of the appraiser, a given act could be qualified as legal or not. It is impossible to establish a permanent parallelism between, on one side, deviance and lack of ethics, and on the other side, regular action and ethics. Rule and deviance stand in a dialectical relationship. Transgression is the cathartic element of the affirmation of order. Georges Balandier states 'no society can be rid of disorder; then it has to use trickery with it instead of eliminating it' (1988, 35). Curiously, the challenge for organizations is to encourage a place of disorder as a means to protect order.

In summary, in this chapter we aimed to demonstrate that the rationale of creating a space for transgression is twofold. First, the insight that no organization can function properly without a gap between its prescriptions and consequent actions makes transgression an unavoidable feature of organizational life; the fast paced nature of the world precludes dealing with it through the strict application of laws. The actor has to adapt his practice to reality, and therefore often has to drift from the rules. Second, transgression appears as an ethically necessary response to the inherent risks of abuses of power in an organization. By creating liberty spaces characterized by their fuzziness and ambiguity, transgression provides the means to balance the relationship between different actors. Transgression is a tool for de-centring power, in other words, deviance is not only good because rule-following is less productive, but also because it contributes to reconciling autonomy and liberty in organizations.

The notions of *honesty* and *frankness*, which express the demand for transparency, and are part of ethics, are hardly usable in organizations. It is not possible for a firm to *put clearly* all its processes, and an employee cannot be asked to stop all his clandestine practices without losing a great deal. The virtue of fuzziness in organization may be hard to conceive for minds like ours, used to a strict and binary understanding of morals. It is this *ethics of ambiguity* that we have to adopt in order to continue believing in enterprise though. Parallel arrangements also have their part in what is Right and Good; was not *Loxias* ('the devious') the surname of Apollo, god of beauty, measure and light, as his oracles were always abstruse?

A special type of rule may illustrate this idea: *vague rule*. On a building site, for example, orders are given with what Duc and Faïta (1996) call 'vague prescriptions'. They are 'global rules given by the chief which contain the conditions of their own contradiction' (ibid., p. 65). The chief establishes a planning of tasks which have to be done during the day, but he has 'few illusions on his chances to see this planning become during the day the real scheme of collective action' (ibid., p. 78). Norms produced in this instance are not abided by. They are only a canvas, an *a priori* structure with which workers will be able to act and which will evolve during the day and its chances. This example helps us to think of a rule which it *would not be done for it to be followed*, a kind of 'orientation-rule'. This rule lays on this 'vague logic', evoked before, according to which one has at the same time to follow a rule and to transgress it.

All organizations have in themselves contradictory practices and norms. These contradictions can be *permanent* and not only *transitory,* as they are too often described by unconscious reference to the 'equilibrium' model, introduced by Leon Walras in economics. In a way, the organization which meets contradictions *is balanced*, as it succeeds in conciliating contradictions, like a human being is in good mental health when s/he makes various desires cohabitate peacefully.

For the worker, deviance resides in this space of freedom where humanity is given back to him or her. But this freedom remains deeply ambivalent. The *uncertainty zone* created by this tolerance to deviance has two opposite faces, like the roman *Janus*. On the one side, the face of managerial agreement when confronted by transgressions which make things easier and even increase production, thus allowing autonomy to the worker. On the other side, it is a pernicious mechanism of social control, of pressure on life reducing freedom.

The dangerous ambiguity of deviance has scarred many; this is why their sheer suppression has often been recommended as a solution. But we have shown that the desire to eradicate ambivalence exposes organizations to the violent back draft of a stronger ambiguity. It is out of the question to deny that disorder can favour the arbitrary and, eventually, unfairness. But we have shown that exposition is neither the infallible way of suppressing this arbitrariness, and that uncertainty and constraint already exist in management methods which refer to autonomy and transparency. The sociologist Maffesoli (2002) writes that the classical representation of *homo oeconomicus* leads to the evacuation of imperfection. In order to pass beyond the economic representation of organization's functioning, management sciences must abandon their 'fear of darkness'. They must recognize the existence of this 'devil part' and know 'how to use it to prevent it from submerging society' (Maffesoli, 2002, p. 16).

Of course, it would be interesting to further this reflection to the "external" face of the firm and its stakeholders (customers, suppliers, competitors, etc.). Would it be possible to draw the same conclusion about the virtue of ambiguity? We think so. But this would obviously be too long a demonstration. Let us just say that it would be relatively straightforward to show how in contemporary practice the kind of slight deviance from the rules that we described exists in every business relation. Asserting then that the 'right' business relations would necessarily exclude this common practice would be the same strange negation of reality's complexity; the same simplistic statement we have denounced in this chapter.

What kind of relation can we establish between ethics and norms in enterprise? Let us finish with a reflective sketch on this matter. Morals, much as wisdom, are always to be found in middle ways. Lipovetski (1992, p. 17) pinpoints that the manager must permanently arbitrate between efficiency and fairness, profit and employee retribution, autonomy and directivity. A company survives thanks to a temporarily established equilibrium between opposed interests. How shall we determine this equilibrium? Which measure shall we use to find this middle way, if unconditional respect for the rule cannot be the reference? In the manner of a *da capo* ending, let us come back to Kant and his *categorical imperative*. We have said that, too strictly applied, this demand of constant submission to moral law was hardly applicable. We can keep the principal idea though – acting with constant regard to morals – and turn to antiquarian wisdom, which was especially one in which the human condition was one of tragic acceptance and contrarian conciliation. In one of his letters to his friend Lucilius (11, p. 8), Seneca quotes this epicurean sentence: 'We must choose a good man and keep him constantly in front of us in order to live under his eyes, and to rule our actions as if he was watching us.'

Telling right from wrong, knowing in each case the right action is difficult. This is why we should take an example of wisdom, and strive to act according to what seems right. This does not exclude mistakes or deviances from a necessarily imperfect rule. This method seems the most pragmatic though, perfectly meeting then the very definition of ethics, 'wisdom of action'.

NOTE

1. We deliberately exclude Marxist criticism which understands norms as class domination stratagems. We prefer to follow philosophers of social contract such as Locke, Rousseau or Rawls.

REFERENCES

Alter, Norbert (1992), *La Gestion du Désordre dans l'Entreprise*, Paris, France: l'Harmattan.
Alter, Norbert (ed.) (2002), *Les Logiques de L'innovation*, Paris, France: La Découverte.
Balandier, Georges (1988), *Le Désordre, Eloge du Mouvement*, Paris, France: Fayard.
Becker, Henry (1963), *Outsiders*, translated in Henry Becker (1985), *Outsiders*, Paris, France: Métailié.
Bernoux, Pierre (1999), *La Sociologie des Entreprises*, Paris, France: Seuil.
Certeau, Michel (de) (1990), *L'invention du Quotidien, 1, Arts de Faire*, Paris, France: Gallimard.
Chateauraynaud, F. (1991), *La Faute Professionnelle : Une Sociologie des Conflits de Responsabilité,* Paris, France: Métailié.
Crozier, Michel (1963), *Le Phénomène Bureaucratique*, Paris, France: Seuil.
Dejours, Christophe (1993), *Travail et Usure Mentale. Essai de psychopathologie du travail*, Paris, France: Bayard.
Dreyfus, Hubert and Paul Rabinow (1984), *Michel Foucault, un Parcours Philosophique*, Paris, France: Gallimard.
Duc, Marcel and Daniel Faïta (1996), 'Savoir-faire d'Encadrement et Prescription Floue', in Jacques Girin, *La Transgression des Règles au Travail*, Paris, France: l'Harmattan.
Foucault, Michel (1975), *Surveiller et Punir*, Paris, France: Gallimard.
Foucault, Michel (1976), *Histoire de la Sexualité I, la Volonté de Savoir*, Paris, France: Gallimard.
Foucault, Michel (1994), *Dits et écrits 1954-1988*. Paris, France: PUF.
Giddens, Anthony (1984), *The Constitution of Society*, translated in Anthony Giddens (1987), *La constitution de la société*, Paris: PUF.
Goffman, Erving (1963), *Stigmate*, translated in Erving Goffman (1975), *Stigmate,* Paris, France: Minuit.
Hermel, Pierre (1988), *Le Management Participatif*, Paris: Editions d'Organisation.
Kant, Immanuel (1785), *Grundlegung zur Metaphysik der Sitten*, translated in Emmanuel Kant (1969), *Fondements de la Métaphysique des Mœurs*, Paris: Delagrave.

Le Goff, Jean-Pierre (1992), *Le mythe de l'entreprise, critique de l'idéologie managériale*, Paris: La Découverte.

Lipovetski, G. (1992), 'Les noces de l'éthique et du business', *Le Débat in Problèmes Economiques*, **2276**, pp.1-12.

Maffesoli, Michel (2002), *La Part du Diable, Précis de Subversion Postmoderne*, Paris, France: Flammarion.

Périlleux, Thomas (2001), *Les Tensions de la Flexibilité*, Paris, France: Desclée de Brouwer.

Poirot-Delpech, Sophie (1996), 'Règles Prescrites et Règles Auto-instituées dans le Contrôle du Trafic Aérien', in J. Girin et al., *La Transgression des Règles au Travail*, Paris, France: l'Harmattan.

Rawls, John. (1971), *A Theory of Justice*, Cambridge, MA, US: Harvard University Press.

Rawls, John (1997), *Théorie de la Justice*, Paris, France: Seuil.

Sénèque (1992), *Lettres à Lucilius, livre I*, Paris, France: Les Belles Lettres.

Vallencien, Guy (2001), 'Hôpital: tareset retards', 20 April, Paris, France: Le Figaro.

Vidal-Naquet, Pierre (1982), 'Preface', in Eschyle, *Tragédies*, Paris, France: Gallimard.

Weil, Simone (1951), *La Condition Ouvrière*, Paris, France: Gallimard.

4. Being Accountable and Being Responsible

Martin Messner[*]

INTRODUCTION

Accounting academics are now increasingly discussing the moral significance of accounting practice, not least because of the prominent role that accounting representations have played in recent corporate scandals (Humphrey, 2005). While the examples of Enron, Parmalat, Worldcom and others have strikingly demonstrated that moral issues may well arise within accounting practice, there are at the same time quite diverging perspectives on the moral significance of accounting. In short, different images of accounting have resulted in competing notions of accounting ethics, accountability and responsibility.

In this chapter the discourse on accounting ethics is taken up and it is argued that the moral dimension of accounting is grounded in the difference between responsibility and accountability. To elaborate on this argument, accounting will be regarded not as a mere technology but as a social practice that consists, at its core, of the giving and demanding of accounts. While such a perspective has been proposed before (e.g. Francis, 1990; Nelson, 1993; Schweiker, 1993; Munro and Mouritsen, 1996; Shearer, 2002), this chapter seeks to offer an original contribution by linking the image of accounting as a moral practice to the question of how the notions of accountability and responsibility relate to each other. It thereby uses arguments by Jacques Derrida and Judith Butler who both associate responsibility with an experience of and reflection upon the limits of accountability. In such a perspective, the moral significance of accounting goes beyond the question whether individuals 'correctly' give and demand accounts according to a certain style of accountability. Rather, responsibility involves that the style of

---

*The author would like to thank Bernadette Loacker for helpful comments on this paper.

accountability itself becomes subject to reflection and critique, based upon the experience of the limits of accountability in a particular case at hand.

The structure of the chapter is as follows. The next section will explain how financial and management accounting relate to the everyday phenomenon of accountability. This is followed by a discussion of the existing literature that has addressed the moral dimension of accounting. Here, two main approaches to accounting will be distinguished: one which views accounting as a technique, and one which regards it as a social practice. These two 'images of accounting' differ not only in their assumptions about the ontological nature of accounting; they also diverge with respect to how they conceive of the moral dimension of accounting. Analysing the two key approaches identified above, this chapter will compare and contrast the notions of accountability and responsibility. Drawing upon the image of accounting as a social practice, responsibility will finally be related to the limits of accountability.

ACCOUNTING AND ACCOUNTABILITY

In its broadest sociological meaning, an *account* may be defined as a statement made by a social actor in order to explain his or her actions or beliefs to others. To give an account, in this sense, is to provide reasons for one's conduct or character (Garfinkel, 1967; Orbuch, 1997). Often, accounts are provided in order to render intelligible unexpected or deviant behaviour. In such a case, the giving of an account serves to 'prevent conflicts from arising by verbally bridging the gap between action and expectation' (Scott and Lyman, 1968, p. 46). Social communities feature norms which regulate such 'repair work' by defining who is expected to account for what, to whom and in which manner. The sum of these implicit or explicit expectations regarding the provision of accounts is usually referred to as 'accountability' (Lerner and Tetlock, 1999). To be 'account-able' for something means not only to be *expected* to account but also implies that one is *able* to account, which is why, in order to be stable, expectations will need to be realistic and legitimate.

Accountability is an intrinsically social phenomenon, since it refers to an '*exchange*, in that one side, that calling for the account, seeks answers and rectification while the other side, that being held accountable, responds and accepts sanctions' (Mulgan, 2000, p. 555). The existence of accountability usually implies negative consequences for those who do not provide satisfactory explanations, while it promises rewards for those who do (Lerner and Tetlock, 1999, p. 255). In this sense, accountability is part of the normative social order of a community which is maintained by positive and negative sanctions.

Forms of accountability will vary among social communities and contexts. Different social contexts imply different ways in which an actor is expected to account for his or her behaviour. This, in turn, means that what people deliver and accept as justification for their behaviour can tell us, to some extent, how they think and live (Wittgenstein, 1975, p. 325). Referring to organizations, Ahrens (1996) speaks of different 'styles of accountability', that is, distinguishable ways of giving and demanding accounts. Styles of accountability 'rely on certain representations of organisation. They test ideas for action against certain variants of financial, strategic, economic, operational, or bureaucratic concepts' (ibid., p. 153). Different images of an organization will shape the way in which organizational behaviour is rationalized and justified. As Ahrens points out, such rationalizations will often refer to discourses in the institutional environment of the organization, merging organizational concerns with more generally available postulates of 'good management' (ibid., p. 140). Organizations also provide their members with particular systems and mechanisms which serve as resources for the practice of giving and demanding accounts. Accountability can be realized, for example, by resorting to reporting routines, systematic assessment procedures, or formal meetings. Accounts may, however, also be exchanged more informally, in everyday discussions or coffee-break talks. Different 'styles of accountability' refer to both content and form, defining the type of arguments that are provided in accounts as well as the way in which these arguments are put forward. In most organizations, the style of accountability will be influenced to a considerable degree by financial and management accounting practices.

Financial accounting is a particular way to manage the accountability relation between the organization and its environment, while management accounting refers to accounts exchanged within the organization. In the first case, one may speak of a means to realize 'public accountability', while the second form refers to 'managerial accountability' (Sinclair, 1995). In financial accounting, an organization portrays itself in the form of accounts to external share- and stake-holders. It provides others with information about past actions, the current situation and possible future states. The accounts provided by the organization are an important source of information for the public. They are not the only one, but they are certainly crucial inputs for the decision-making of key stakeholders such as investors, customers, creditors, prospective employees, or politicians. The same is true for the accounts produced within the organization. Managers and employees are made accountable in terms of costs, profits, returns or other categories that are supposed to convey relevant information about their behaviour. Again, accountability within the organization will not rely exclusively on such categories, but will also assume forms that do not build upon 'conventional' accounting information. Still, one may speak of a form of 'accounting', as people give and demand reasons for conduct.

From a sociological point of view, the notions of accounting and accountability may therefore be used interchangeably. To practise accounting, in its broad sense, is to give and demand accounts and thus to engage in mutual accountability. If one wants to uphold the distinction between a more narrow sense of (financial and management) accounting, on the one hand, and accountability in general, on the other hand, one therefore needs to restrict the term 'accounting' to a particular type of accounts. What is often referred to as 'accounting representations' (e.g. Roberts and Scapens, 1985; Roberts, 1991; Ahrens, 1996) obviously alludes to such a specific type of accounts. This notion usually denotes a set of categories such as profits, costs, revenues, value added and other numbers-based concepts that serve as inputs for various 'calculative practices' (Miller, 2001). Roberts (1991, p. 359), for example, contends that '[a]ccounting's central values are those of profit and rate of return on capital to which both producers and the activity of production are merely instrumental'. If accountability builds upon accounting representations, it may assume a particular quality. For if such categories loom large in the giving and demanding of accounts, then there is a risk that accountability becomes constrained by the 'impoverished language' of accounting representations (Roberts, 1991, p. 367). A focus on the 'single-minded medium of money' may, in other words, impede actors' ability to 'hear the distinctive voices of others' (Nelson, 1993, p. 226).

Ahrens (1996), however, alerts us that such 'an accounting constrained style of accountability' cannot be explained by the accounting numbers themselves, but only by the way in which these numbers are used. He therefore suggests studying 'the style in which accounting information is mobilized and functions within processes of accountability' (ibid., p. 154). A particular style of accountability may privilege accounting knowledge over other types of organizational expertise, possibly resulting in a practice of accountability that is constrained by the focus on accounting numbers and only marginally takes into account other explanations and justifications for action. A given style of accountability may, however, also feature a definition of 'acceptable accounts' that favours other types of content, such as bureaucratic rules, customer demands, or political agendas. In all such cases, the practice of giving and demanding accounts will follow a certain 'order of discourse' (Foucault, 1981) in which some explanations and rationalizations of action are acceptable, while others are not. Accounts which are in accordance with this order will usually be honoured, while those which do not meet the prevalent rules of accountability will qualify as '*illegitimate* or *unreasonable*' (Scott and Lyman, 1968, p. 54).

In general, an inquiry into the restrictive nature of a given system of accountability will have to consider the 'degrees of freedom' that this system entails. Such an inquiry will only be feasible, however, if one chooses a perspective on accounting that is sensitive to the constructive quality of accounts. For only then will it be possible to acknowledge the difference between the 'reality' (in singular) constructed by a given practice of accounting, on the one hand, and the 'realities' (in plural) that could potentially be accounted for, on the other hand.

The next section discusses two different approaches to accounting as they can be found in the existing literature. Only part of this literature fully acknowledges the constructive quality of accounting practice, which, furthermore, implies diverging perspectives on the moral dimension of accountability.

ACCOUNTING: TECHNIQUE OR SOCIAL PRACTICE?

It has been argued that accounting is 'an ensemble of devices and ideas' (Miller, 1998, p. 608) without any 'essence or core' (ibid., p. 619), such that there is 'no invariant object to which the name "accounting" can be attached' (Miller and Napier, 1993, p. 631). Nevertheless, it seems that some parts of the literature hold a rather stable idea of what accounting is or should be. Although accounting can take many forms, '[m]ore often than not, accounting theorists subscribe to a favored image as if it were the one best way of getting at accounting truth' (Davis *et al.*, 1982, p. 308). Particular images feature certain ontological assumptions about the nature of the phenomenon and usually imply particular methodological approaches for its empirical study.

In what follows, I will apply a classification of the accounting literature that has been repeatedly used in similar form before (e.g. Nelson, 1993; Scapens, 1994). Acknowledging that any classification simplifies at the expense of appreciating detail, I shall distinguish between two broad approaches to accounting: one treating accounting as a technique or technology, and one treating accounting as a social practice. The former group is mainly represented by authors who draw upon economic theory and the corresponding scientific model of the natural sciences (see Zimmerman, 2001). Economics-based approaches to accounting tend to regard accounting as a matter of technical expertise and as an instrument to effectively manage principal-agent relations. In financial accounting research, this approach might take the form of an inquiry into the effects of accounting disclosure on the capital markets. In management accounting research, it could, for example, mean looking at transfer-price arrangements in different settings and exploring whether they come up to the criterion of optimal resource allocation. Economics-based accounting research is thus mainly interested in the usefulness of *systems of accounting* for the management of scarce resources.

Social theory approaches to accounting, on the other hand, have suggested that in order to understand accounting *as it happens* in organizations, one needs to go beyond a focus on accounting *systems* and consider the social *practices* involved in applying these systems. Accounting practice, it is argued, is not absorbed by the model-like application of techniques, but takes place in the context of various power relations, norms and interpretive frames which potentially impact the way in which accounting is carried out (Roberts and Scapens, 1985). As a consequence, accounting is regarded as a social practice that may be subject to various rationalities other than the straight pursuit of organizational goals (Baxter and Chua, 2003, p. 102).

Accounting as a Technique

The overly technical and economic perspective on accounting that dominates much contemporary accounting research has resulted in a relative lack of concern with moral issues in this part of the literature (Williams, 2004). To say that 'this stems from a research paradigm focusing on descriptive as opposed to prescriptive research, in addition to a belief that ethical issues are not conducive to economic modeling or empirical research' (Ayres and Ghosh, 1999, p. 335) reveals only part of the truth, however. On the one hand, some accounting researchers have shown that moral issues can also be dealt with based on a dominantly descriptive interest (e.g. Macintosh, 1995; Lambert and Sponem, 2005), and not only by offering prescriptions concerning how to make accounting more ethical. On the other hand, the methodology applied in economic research on accounting does indeed make it difficult to gain valuable insights into the moral issues of accounting, for this methodology often fails to capture the social context in which moral issues become relevant (Macintosh, 1995, p. 296). Much more than being just a methodological issue however, the absence of ethics seems to be directly linked to the way in which accounting is substantially conceived, namely as a technical system providing objective information and decision making support and, as such, value-free in character (Nelson, 1993). As a consequence, accounting does not appear as a moral practice except in a very narrow sense, according to which accounting practice is taken to be morally valuable if it is performed correctly, i.e. in line with a given and unquestioned set of rules.

To illustrate the implications of such a perspective for an ethical inquiry into accounting, I shall briefly discuss the argumentation of a seminal paper (Benston, 1982) which takes an explicitly economics-based perspective on accounting. Benston examines the question of whether corporate accounts should be designed to contain information about social responsibility issues rather than being formulated in purely financial terms. He approaches this question by making clear that corporations need to be seen, primarily, as accountable to their shareholders, such that the usefulness of social responsibility accounting needs to be assessed, first and foremost, against the end of shareholder value creation. Pointing to various control mechanisms at work, Benston argues that corporate managers in general 'have little discretion to act other than in the interests of shareholders', such that the 'principal implication ... for corporate social responsibility accounting is that, if concern for shareholders is the motivating factor behind this accounting, there is no reason to require its inclusion in public reports', since this would only impose costs on shareholders without giving them extra benefits (ibid., pp. 92-3).

Throughout his essay, Benston takes a purely instrumental perspective on accounting, being mainly concerned with the question whether certain forms of accounting have a positive net information value for shareholders. Given complete and perfect markets, shareholder wealth creation is the only criterion against which to judge the 'morality' of accounting practice. In making this claim, Benston 'fails to consider the possibility that shareholders' interests may not serve the greater good, except to the extent that incomplete ownership rights or market imperfections are to blame' (Shearer, 2002, p. 562). For him, corporate accountability is fully absorbed by shareholder accountability.

Acknowledging that there can be externalities in a market such that self-interested behaviour might not lead to optimal allocation of resources, Benston turns to the question whether, in these cases, social responsibility accounting could be valuable. He remains quite sceptical of such accounting, however, since 'the required measurements are beyond the ability or province of accountants' (Benston, 1982, p. 97). Social costs and benefits are impossible to measure objectively, and would thus most likely 'misinform and mislead readers and impose unnecessary costs on shareholders' (ibid., p. 100). Benston thus sees no place for social responsibility accounting, since such an accounting would not come up to the ideal of objective and unambiguous accounts. For what cannot be measured without subjectivity does not correspond to the (implicit) claim of accounting to deliver true and value-neutral information. Hence, in Benston's argumentation, accounting becomes visible only as a technical accomplishment which can only be performed sensibly when all ambiguity is discussed away. But to deny any ambiguity that can arise within financial and management accounting makes it hard to conceive of accounting as a moral practice at all. If there were no discretion in the production of accounts, if accounting revealed truth rather than creating it, then accounting could indeed not be considered as a moral practice. But such an image of accounting is problematic. Accounts contain images of reality which can be, and often are, questioned on many grounds, precisely because they are ambiguous, i.e. allow for multiple interpretations. Without doubt, this ambiguity is often covered in practice, such that accounts appear as objective and unambiguous representations of reality (Francis, 1990). This does not mean, however, that accounting theory should join in this ideology of objectivity, for this would obviously restrict the scope of ethical inquiry into accounting.

I will now turn to a perspective on accounting which questions some of the presuppositions that economic theory takes for granted and thereby opens the discussion of accounting for socio-political and ethical issues.

Accounting as a Social Practice

That a 'strictly "technicist" view can inhibit accounting scholars and immunize practitioners from ever having to contemplate the ends being served by their technology (Williams, 2002, p. 5) has motivated many authors to study accounting practice in its recursive relationship with the institutional and social context in which it is embedded. Instead of viewing accounting as a 'mere collection of techniques' (Burchell *et al.*, 1980, p. 6), these authors are concerned with accounting 'as a *social and institutional practice*, one that is intrinsic to, and constitutive of social relations' (Miller, 1994, p. 1). In making transparent how accounting both shapes and is shaped by other social practices, these contributions also promise a more encompassing perspective on the moral dimension of accounting.

Central to a social theory approach to accounting is the distinction between accounting systems and accounting practice. While the former refer to a body of available rules and resources, the latter notion designates the actual way these systems are drawn upon in practice (Roberts and Scapens, 1985). According to Giddens (1979, 1984), social practices are regular patterns of action in which structural rules and resources are enacted and thus reproduced. The rules and resources which structure the site of the social can thereby be distinguished into three dimensions. All social practices are, at the same time, practices of signification, legitimation and domination, i.e. they reproduce the structure of meaning and language, the structure of morality and structural power relations. Applying this perspective to accounting, one can analyse how accounting has an impact on particular structures of meaning, legitimation and power, and as such, shapes organizational reality and individual identities. Of particular importance for an ethics of accounting would be the moral dimension, since

> the practice of accounting can be seen to involve the communication of a set of values, of ideals of expected behaviour, of what is approved and disapproved. The practice of accounting involves communicating notions of what *should* happen, and it is only on the basis of these notions that sense is made of what has happened' (Roberts and Scapens, 1985, p. 448).

To acknowledge this powerful role of accounting opens up an ethical perspective which is not confined by the language of economics but which critically examines the creation of such a language and its reproduction in accounting practice (Shearer, 2002; Williams, 2004). The individual thus no longer appears as a moral agent only with respect to whether he or she plays by the established rules or not. Rather, it is these rules, and the role that accounting plays in defining and carrying them, which come under scrutiny. Accounting is regarded as a moral practice, as it participates in the reproduction of specific structures of legitimation, both at the micro (organizational, interpersonal) and at a more macro (inter-organizational, socio-political, economic) level.

With respect to the latter, consider, for example, Macintosh's (1995) analysis of profit manipulation in multi-divisional organizations. When business divisions are assessed on the basis of their reported profits, managers of these divisions may be inclined to make self-beneficial choices regarding accounting methods, which could be seen as unethical from the perspective of others. Macintosh stresses that an ethics approach to profit manipulation cannot sensibly be undertaken in a de-contextualized way, but needs to consider the social and institutional context in which moral behaviour is performed. Since questions of morality cannot be separated from issues of signification and domination, profit manipulation must be assessed in conjunction with the power and meaning structures at work in the organization. Macintosh shows that both top management and department managers can in principle make legitimate claims as to whether profit manipulation should be considered right or wrong. There will thus be 'no rational way to settle the debate', since '[t]here are no established, untarnished, logical ways of deciding between the rival claims' (Macintosh, 1995, p. 300). It is then up to accounting ethics to look at how such debates are settled in practice and to highlight the way in which a certain moral order 'is deeply implicated in the struggle and conflict over domination structures as well as determining which meanings and discourses are paramount' (ibid., p. 309).

Although both (global) top managers and (local) division managers have a stake in this game, Macintosh stresses that the former will often be in a better position to mobilize accounting systems to extract profits from their business divisions. That this can happen is in part because accounting is 'disguised as a neutral and objective enterprise and so has become a major non-violent means by which meganational conglomerates, invoking the profit motive ethic, extract profits from their business components strung around the globe' (ibid., p. 310). In this respect, the role of accounting is not only relevant within the organization but spans wider economic and socio-political issues as it helps to 'appropriate profits to the already affluent parts of the advanced Western capitalist world from nations facing crushing poverty, internal political turmoil and, more often than not, ruthless and corrupt governments' (ibid.).

In claiming that an ethical approach to accounting needs to consider the wider institutional and social context of accounting, Macintosh echoes a view taken by many critical accounting scholars. Such an approach can free ethical considerations from too narrow a stress on the agency of individuals and reconnect a concern for ethics with a concern for politics (see Parker, 2003). While economic theory approaches tend to focus on the question of optimal resource allocation and bracket out questions of welfare distribution (see Noreen, 1988; Keller, 2006), a critical perspective on accounting explicitly addresses the issue of distributive justice. What comes to the fore is thus the way in which particular systems of accountability help reproduce organizational or societal structures that favour some at the expense of others (see Baxter and Chua, 2003, p. 99).

The moral dimension of accounting can also be addressed at a more local level, however, by pointing to the implications that a particular type of accounting has on individual actors and their relations to each other in situations of 'co-presence' (see Giddens, 1984, p. 64). Here, the focus is on how a particular system of accountability has an impact on the way in which we approach, identify and recognize each other as accountable and responsible selves. Roberts (1991, 1996, 2003), for example, has argued that conventional accounting practice produces a sense of the self that is detrimental to our moral attitude towards each other. He sees accounting as representative of a *hierarchical form of accountability*, where individuals learn that their value and worth is expressed by their position within the organizational hierarchy, which in turn depends upon the fulfilment of given norms or targets. In striving for acceptance and recognition, individuals are drawn 'further and further into conformity with the standards of utility upon which "success" depends' (Roberts, 1991, p. 360). Internalizing these standards, individuals come to see themselves as solitary and singular, being dependent in their self-esteem on impersonal principles and rules. 'These standards are "taken over" and become the lens through which we judge ourselves, and compare ourselves with others' (ibid., p. 362). Hierarchical forms of accountability have an individualizing character, since they promote a sense of the self that is preoccupied with achieving certain norms and standards and at the same time induce the self to relate to others only through the lens of these categories. The concepts provided by accounting – costs, profits, returns, etc. – become the focal point for individual efforts and for structuring the relations with others. They become the reality on the basis of which communication and organizational life is built.

Drawing upon Habermas' distinction between instrumental and communicative action, Roberts contrasts the individualizing form of accountability with the more socializing forms which cultivate dialogue and openness instead of calculation and instrumental reason. A socializing relation to others is characterized by a quest for mutual understanding which goes beyond the giving and demanding of accounts through formal categories, as provided by accounting. Such socializing talk will be possible in the relative absence of asymmetries of power and in the context of face-to-face contact of the persons involved. In these circumstances, people can relate to each other informally, openly and without the need to rush to a certain result. Socializing forms of accountability thus foster a recognition of the self and of others that is free from distortion by any imposed formal definitions of the situation.

While in organizations both forms of accountability will necessarily co-exist, Roberts (1991; and others such as Boland and Schultze, 1996; Laughlin, 1996; Shearer, 2002) warn against too much reliance on conventional accounting techniques based on formalized and quantitative measures. Such techniques are considered to be detrimental to the moral climate, since they produce a very selective image of reality and a very limited sense of one's social responsibilities. Viewing the world through the lens of accounting, it is argued, is accompanied by a loss of sensibility for what is not captured in the accounts. As Roberts contends, there is an inherent risk in accounting

> that we will only ever discover here what we think to look for, and even then we will only be able to 'see' with such technologies in the way of seeing that they make possible. So only what is amenable to quantification can be seen; I have to identify and then count and measure what can only ever be proxies for what I am looking for .... Looking at accounting representations will always be a seeing robbed of sensibility (Roberts, 2003, p. 261).

From such a perspective, accounting representations fuel the 'attraction to abstraction' (Nelson, 1993, p. 222) that is characteristic of modern management in general (Townley, 2002). Accounting comes to be seen as 'a profoundly normalizing activity' (Miller and Napier, 1993, p. 645) that provides an oversimplified image of a complex social reality, while simultaneously reducing sensibility for appreciating this complexity. An inquiry into this 'distinctive morality' of accounting (ibid.) will need to question a given system of accountability with respect to the selectivity of the 'truth' that it produces. It is quite obvious, then, that such an inquiry will require a different idea of responsibility than one that equates responsibility with accountability.

ACCOUNTABILITY AND RESPONSIBILITY

In the above discussion, I distinguished between two main images of accounting and demonstrated that these imply different perspectives on how the moral dimension of accounting is conceived. If accounting is regarded as a mere technology, i.e. a means to serve certain predefined ends, then the moral character of accounting practice 'as such' does not really come to the fore (Nelson, 1993). Accounting is not regarded as a moral practice, for it is supposed to be plainly a matter of technical effectiveness and efficiency. At the same time, the individual behaviour of accountants or managers may well be subject to discussion in moral terms. Individuals are often deemed to act morally wrongly when they breach the letter of accounting standards or the 'spirit' behind this letter. Such an attribution of moral wrongdoing builds upon the idea that accounting procedures are *truth-revealing*, i.e. that they are 'privileged ways of representation'; as a consequence, a violation of an accounting rule is deemed to have an ethical implication (Williams, 2002, p. 6). This, however, turns the question of ethics into a question of lawful behaviour, such that responsible action is equated to action that conforms to a given system of accountability. This has two major implications which became apparent in the discussion of Benston's (1982) paper. First, such an approach implies that questions about the desirability of a given system of accountability do not come to the fore, for the system itself is not subject to moral inquiry. Only individual actions which deviate from the rules become objects of moral discourse, while the 'styles of accountability' (Ahrens, 1996) which define these rules stay outside. Second, it portrays individual decision-making as a question of either/or: either one decides to follow the law and act morally rightly, or one decides to do otherwise. What is left out in such a dichotomous view is the fact that the application of a rule always entails the exercise of discretion and judgment. Individuals not only have to decide whether or not they want to apply a rule but also need to judge how to apply it (responsibly) in a given situation.

To sum up, one could say that if accounting is viewed as a mere technology, then the question of ethics finds its limits in the notion of accountability. In this view, one is acting in a way that is morally right if one comes up to the formal or informal expectations which prevail with respect to the giving of accounts and which are assumed to be unambiguous.

The moral dimension of accounting appears in a different light if accounting is regarded as a social practice which both shapes and is shaped by wider structures of signification, legitimation and power. Such a view acknowledges the constitutive role that accounting plays with respect to reality, as the process of accounting for reality actually constructs a *particular* reality (Hines, 1988; Lukka, 1990). As any account is selective with respect to what could, in principle, have been accounted for, there will always be some sort of 'otherness' that is not captured in the account but that, one could claim, nevertheless needs to be accounted for *in some way* in order to act responsibly. An inquiry into the moral dimension of accounting that builds upon this constructivist notion of accounting will therefore address the question of how the selective visibility produced by accounting also implies the production of invisibility. As shown above, this can refer both to a macro level with a focus on the socio-political or economic reality at large (e.g. Cooper and Sherer, 1984; Macintosh, 1995), and to a more micro level, where the concern is the construction of human subjectivity and identity (e.g. Miller and O'Leary, 1987; Roberts, 1991).

When a given system of accountability is questioned with respect to what it excludes, then the notions of *responsibility* and *accountability* can obviously no longer be equated. What is considered responsible action will then go beyond established forms of giving and demanding accounts. But what could responsibility mean if it does not simply correspond to coming up to one's accountability? One way of how to draw a distinction is offered by Sinclair (1995) who explored notions of accountability among Australian executives. Sinclair identifies a 'structural' and a 'personal' discourse of accountability. Although she speaks of 'accountability' in both cases, the 'personal' notion of accountability actually seems to point to the *limits* of (structural) accountability:

> Accountability in the structural discourse is spoken of as the technical property of a role or contract, structure or system. Territories are clear and demarcated, accountabilities uncontested .... In contrast, the personal discourse is confidential and anecdotal. In this discourse, accountability is ambiguous, with the potential to be something that is feared or uplifting .... The personal discourse functions to

admit the risks and failures, exposure and invasiveness with which accountability is experienced (ibid., p. 224).

Sinclair describes personal accountability as a 'matter of judgement' (ibid., p. 231) and associates it with a sense of morality that goes beyond structurally defined duties and rights. While the realm of structural accountability is the basis for responsible action, there are likely to be situations in which the given duties and rights turn out to be indeterminate, ambiguous, or contradictory, or when they are challenged by a more personal "feeling" of accountability' (ibid., p. 233). In such cases it becomes apparent that a given system of accountability cannot offer sufficient guidance to act in a responsible way. Once the limits of accountability come to the fore, responsible action cannot be warranted unless these limits will in some way be accounted for.

I would argue that this experience of the limits of accountability corresponds to the experience of the *impossible* or *undecidable* as described by Derrida (1992). Derrida sets forth that a 'real' decision always takes place within the space of the undecidable, in which no rule or law can tell us how to proceed appropriately. 'A decision that didn't go through the ordeal of the undecidable would not be a free decision, it would only be the programmable application or unfolding of a calculable process' (ibid., p. 24). Justice or responsibility, however, are not matters of pure calculation. If one follows a law *blindly*, we may say that he has acted according to the law, but we cannot really say that he has applied the law in a responsible way.

> To be just, the decision of a judge, for example, must not only follow a rule or a general law but must also assume it, approve it, confirm its value, by a reinstituting act of interpretation, as if ultimately nothing previously existed of the law, as if the judge himself invented the law in every case .... In short, for a decision to be just and responsible, it must, in its proper moment if there is one, be both regulated and without regulation: it must conserve the law and also destroy it or suspend it enough to have to reinvent it in each case, rejustify it, at least reinvent it in the reaffirmation and the new and free confirmation of its principle (ibid., p. 23).

In order to act responsibly, one has to experience the aporetic moment of having 'to calculate with the incalculable' (ibid., p. 16), of having to decide that which cannot be decided by simply drawing upon a rule. The undecidable 'is the experience of that which, though heterogeneous, foreign to the order of the calculable and the rule, is still obliged ... to give itself up to the impossible decision, while taking account of law and rules' (ibid., p. 24).

Hence, responsibility requires that one operates at the limits of what is (im-)possible. To *account for* something in a responsible way thus cannot be absorbed in accounting for something according to a set of rules or a given system of accountability. A responsible form of giving or demanding accounts will have to be prepared to take into account what cannot *yet* be accounted for, i.e. what exceeds the possibilities of accountability.

Importantly, there are two dimensions of such a responsibility, which one may call a *private* and a *public* one. The former relates to the decision that one has to take in the situation at hand. It is part of the aporetic nature of a just or responsible decision that it is 'always required *immediately*, "right away"' (Derrida, 1992, p. 26). '[T]he moment of decision, as such, always remains a finite moment of urgency and precipitation ... it always marks the interruption of the juridico- or ethico- or politico-cognitive deliberation that precedes it, that *must* precede it' (ibid.). Hence, the situation in which one is required to account is always a *private* situation, involving only those who are present in that situation. No public deliberation can replace the need to decide in that situation. Even if one decides not to decide and to wait for a public discourse to take place, one clearly has taken an ethically relevant decision.

While a responsible decision is always warranted in the given situation, responsibility, at the same time, involves going beyond that situation. If the limits of a norm come to the fore in a concrete case, then a responsible reaction will also include a reflection upon the *general* value of this norm. Otherwise, each situation would be dealt with only on its own and without regard to how it may relate to other, similar situations. There would thus be no chance to learn from the experience of the particular case.

While Derrida clearly accounts for this connection between the particular and the universal (see e.g. Derrida, 2005), we may also turn to the work of Judith Butler where we can find an even more explicit concern with the *public* dimension of responsibility. Butler (2005) recognizes that the act of giving an account is a social endeavour that cannot do without an addressee and without the norms that mediate this address. Whenever we give or demand reasons for conduct, we are subject to a given system of accountability that defines what it means to give an adequate account. 'There is the operation of a norm, invariably social, that conditions what will and will not be a recognizable account, exemplified in the fact that I am used by the norm precisely to the degree that I use it' (ibid., p. 36). If, in this sense, my account (of myself or of somebody or something else) is not fully mine, but mediated and made possible by social norms and the prevailing 'regime of truth' (Foucault, 1995), then my efforts to *account in a responsible way* will necessarily involve a critical reflection upon these norms. For if responsibility, as Derrida argues, entails an experience of the impossible, then it also entails a critical reflection upon the norms which define what is possible. This is why Butler contends that 'ethical deliberation is bound up with the operation of critique' (2005, p. 8). Referring to Foucault and Adorno, she argues that a confrontation with the limits of social conventions in a given situation allows us to 'raise the question whether a good life can be conducted within a bad one, and whether we might, in recrafting ourselves with and for another, participate in the remaking of social conditions' (ibid., pp. 134-5).

It is, in other words, the experience of the limits of accountability *in a given situation* that may motivate an actor to reflect upon the rules of accountability *in general*. Such a critical reflection by the individual can be extended into a public discourse on the appropriateness of the prevailing rules. It is then part of the responsibility of the individual to consider whether such a discourse will be necessary. For there is a responsibility also to account for those that are not present in the given situation and this responsibility requires the critical voice to be raised in public.

CONCLUSION

I have argued in this chapter that any 'style of accountability' (Ahrens, 1996) favours some types of accounts at the expense of others and construes responsibility as a particular form of accountability. This becomes particularly visible when processes of accountability draw upon formal systems of financial and management accounting. As other authors have shown (e.g. Roberts, 1991; Shearer, 2002), it is the pervasive influence of accounting numbers and concepts on practices of accountability that raises important ethical concerns regarding the selectivity of the accounts produced.

To grasp this moral dimension of accounting is to make a distinction between accountability and responsibility. While accountability refers to the recognition of certain rules and conventions that may, for example, emerge from systems of financial and management accounting, the practice of drawing upon such rules potentially reveals the limits of such systems of accountability. To experience these limits is to realize that one cannot rely on the inherited rules of accountability if one wants to give or receive accounts *in a responsible way*. It is here, 'precisely at the limits of our schemes of intelligibility', where the question of ethics can emerge; when 'we ask ourselves what it might mean to continue in a dialogue where no common ground can be assumed, where one is, [as] it were, at the limits of what one knows yet still under the demand to offer and receive acknowledgment: to someone else who is there to be addressed and whose address is there to be received' (Butler, 2005, pp. 21-22). At the same time, it is this experience of the concrete situation which may help us reflect critically upon a given system of accountability in general and, by way of social critique, expose those characteristics of such a system which run counter to our sense of responsibility and justice.

With respect to financial and management accounting systems and the practice of accountability building upon them, there is a need to acknowledge the limits of such systems for guaranteeing a responsible form of accounting. While it is certainly true that formal and informal rules, standards, and laws have a moral importance as they enable a consistent accounting across different cases and situations, it is also important to recognize that treating each and every situation or individual like the other does not automatically ensure responsible action. Rather, responsibility will always involve a consideration of the particular case at hand and the reflection upon how the singularity of this case can or cannot be accounted for by drawing upon some universal standards that are considered right or just.

REFERENCES

Ahrens, T. (1996), 'Styles of accountability', *Accounting, Organizations and Society*, **21** (2-3), 139-173.

Ayres, F. L. and D. Ghosh (1999), 'Research in ethics and economic behavior in accounting', *Journal of Accounting and Public Policy*, **18**, 335-338.

Baxter, J. and W. F. Chua (2003), 'Alternative management accounting research – whence and whither', *Accounting, Organizations and Society*, **28** (2-3), 97-126.

Benston, G. J. (1982), 'Accounting and corporate accountability', *Accounting, Organizations and Society*, 7 (2), 87-105.

Boland, R. J. and U. Schultze (1996), 'Narrating accountability: Cognition and the production of the accountable self', in R. Munro and J. Mouritsen (eds), *Accountability, Power, Ethos and the Technologies of Managing*, London, UK: Thomson Business Press, pp. 62-81.

Burchell, S., C. Clubb, A. G. Hopwood, J. Hughes and J. Nahapiet (1980), 'The roles of accounting in organizations and society', *Accounting, Organizations and Society*, **5** (1), 5-27.

Butler, J. (2005), *Giving an Account of Oneself*, New York, US: Fordham University Press.

Cooper, D. J. and M. Sherer (1984), 'The value of corporate accounting reports: Arguments for a political economy of accounting', *Accounting, Organizations and Society*, **9** (3-4), 207-232.

Davis, S. W., K. Menon and G. Morgan (1982), 'The images that have shaped accounting theory', *Accounting, Organizations and Society*, 7 (4), 307-318.

Derrida, J. (1992), 'Force of Law: The Mystical Foundation of Authority', in D. Cornell, M. Rosenfeld and D. Gray Carlson (eds), *Deconstruction and the Possibility of Justice*, London, UK: Routledge, pp. 3-67.

Derrida, J. (2005), *Rogues: Two Essays on Reason*, Stanford, US: Stanford University Press.

Foucault, M. (1981), 'The Order of Discourse' (I. McLeod, Trans.), in R. Young (ed.), *Untying the Text: A Post-Structuralist Reader*, London, UK and New York, US: Routlede & Kegan Paul, pp. 48-78.

Foucault, M. (1995), *Discipline and Punish: The Birth of the Prison* (A. Sheridan, Trans.), New York, US: Vintage Books.

Francis, J. (1990), 'After virtue? Accounting as a moral and discursive practice', *Accounting, Auditing & Accountability Journal*, **3** (3), 5-17.

Garfinkel, H. (1967), *Studies in Ethnomethodology*, Cambridge, UK: Polity Press.

Giddens, A. (1979), *Central Problems in Social Theory: Action, Structure and Contradiction in Social Analysis*, Berkeley and Los Angeles, US: University of California Press.

Giddens, A. (1984), *The Constitution of Society*, Cambridge, UK: Polity Press.

Hines, R. (1988), 'Financial accounting: In communicating reality, we construct reality', *Accounting, Organizations and Society*, **13** (3), 251-261.

Humphrey, C. (2005), 'In the aftermath of crisis: Reflections on the principles, values and significance of academic inquiry in accounting: Introduction', *European Accounting Review*, **14** (2), 341-351.

Keller, C. (2006), 'Smith versus Friedman: Markets and ethics', *Critical Perspectives on Accounting*, in press.

Lambert, C. and S. Sponem (2005), 'Corporate governance and profit manipulation: A French field study', *Critical Perspectives on Accounting*, **16**, 717-748.

Laughlin, R. (1996), 'Principals and Higher Principals: Accounting for Accountability in the Caring Professions', in R. Munro and J. Mouritsen (eds), *Accountability, Power, Ethos and the Technologies of Managing*, London, UK: Thomson Business Press, pp. 225-244.

Lerner, J. S. and P. E. Tetlock (1999), 'Accounting for the effects of accountability', *Psychological Bulletin*, **125** (3), 255-275.

Lukka, K. (1990), 'Ontology and accounting: The concept of profit', *Critical Perspectives on Accounting*, **1**, 239-261.

Macintosh, N. B. (1995), 'The ethics of profit manipulation: A dialectic of control analysis', *Critical Perspectives on Accounting*, **6** (4), 289-315.

Miller, P. (1994), 'Accounting as Social and Institutional Practice: An introduction', in A. G. Hopwood and P. Miller (eds), *Accounting as Social and Institutional Practice*, Cambridge, UK: Cambridge University Press, pp. 1-39.

Miller, P. (1998), 'The margins of accounting', *The European Accounting Review*, **7** (4), 605-621.

Miller, P. (2001), 'Governing by numbers: Why calculative practices matter', *Social Research*, **68** (2), 379-396.

Miller, P. and C. Napier (1993), 'Genealogies of calculation', *Accounting, Organizations and Society*, **18** (7/8), 631-647.

Miller, P. and T. O'Leary (1987), 'Accounting and the construction of the governable person', *Accounting, Organizations and Society*, **12** (3), 235-266.

Mulgan, R. (2000), 'Accountability: An ever-expanding concept?', *Public Administration*, **78** (3), 555-573.

Munro, R. and J. Mouritsen (1996), *Accountability: Power, Ethos and the Technologies of Managing*, London, UK: International Thomson Business Press.

Nelson, J. S. (1993), 'Account and acknowledge, or represent and control? On post-modern politics and economics of collective responsibility', *Accounting, Organizations and Society*, **18** (2-3), 207-229.

Noreen, E. (1988), 'The economics of ethics: A new perspective on agency theory', *Accounting, Organizations and Society*, **13** (4), 359-369.

Orbuch, T. L. (1997), 'People's accounts count: The sociology of accounts', *Annual Review of Sociology*, **23**, 455-478.

Parker, M. (2003), 'Introduction: Ethics, politics and organizing', *Organization*, **10** (2), 187-203.

Roberts, J. (1991), 'The possibilities of accountability', *Accounting, Organizations and Society*, **16** (4), 355-368.

Roberts, J. (1996), 'From discipline to dialogue: Individualizing and socializing forms of accountability', in R. Munro and J. Mouritsen (eds), *Accountability: Power, Ethos and the Technologies of Managing*, London, UK: International Thomson Business Press, pp. 40-61.

Roberts, J. (2003), 'The manufacture of corporate social responsibility: Constructing corporate sensibility', *Organization*, **10** (2), 249-265.

Roberts, J. and R. Scapens (1985), 'Accounting systems and systems of accountability – understanding accounting practices in their organisational contexts', *Accounting, Organizations and Society*, **10** (4), 443-456.

Scapens, R. W. (1994), 'Never mind the gap: Towards an institutional perspective on management accounting practice', *Management Accounting Research*, **5** (3-4), 301-321.

Schweiker, W. (1993), 'Accounting for ourselves: Accounting practice and the discourse of ethics', *Accounting, Organizations and Society*, **18** (2-3), 231-252.

Scott, M. B. and S. M. Lyman (1968), 'Accounts', *American Sociological Review*, **33**, 46-62.

Shearer, T. (2002), 'Ethics and accountability: From the for-itself to the for-the-other', *Accounting, Organizations and Society*, **27**, 541-573.

Sinclair, A. (1995), 'The chameleon of accountability: Forms and discourses', *Accounting, Organizations and Society*, **20** (2-3), 19-237.

Townley, B. (2002), 'Managing with modernity', *Organization*, **9** (4), 549-573.

Williams, P. F. (2002), 'Accounting and the moral order: Justice, accounting, and legitimate moral authority', *Accounting and the Public Interest*, **2**, 1-21.

Williams, P. F. (2004), 'You reap what you sow: The ethical discourse of professional accounting', *Critical Perspectives on Accounting*, **15**, 995-1001.

Wittgenstein, L. (1975), *Philosophische Untersuchungen* (Third edition), Frankfurt am Main: Suhrkamp.

Zimmerman, J. L. (2001), 'Conjectures regarding empirical managerial accounting research', *Journal of Accounting and Economics*, **32** (1-3), 411-427.

5. Letting Knowledge Go: Ethics and Representation of the Other in International and Cross-Cultural Management

Carl Rhodes and Robert Westwood

Writing social science is a practice of writing about other people – whether they are real, or imagined … or even a little of both. This is an act of inscription where the person who writes imagines a self that is capable and author-ative of representing others. Writing, in this sense, is not a matter of the trained skills of constructing sentences, paragraphs and so forth – it is about the institutional location of the authors and the privileges that they seek to exercise. In the social sciences this posits some people as the tellers and others as the told. Here, the tellers seek (and sometimes find) the power to define the character of other people. When this is achieved, the tellings come to be regarded as knowledge … truth even. In this chapter we are concerned with the ethical status of such knowledge as it relates to the way that people who study management write about people from cultures other than their own. In such a post-colonial context the writing of international management has, as we shall see, participated in reproducing culturally distributed power inequalities as a means to enable the management and control of western business interests. Our aim in this chapter is to engage with some philosophical ideas so as to consider the ethics of 'writing the Other' in relation to such forms of knowledge.

The relationship between the writer and the written-about in international management is one where institutional author-ity is located in the Western academy and where the written-about are located as 'Other', usually outside the developed West. As the authors of this chapter, 'we' (Bob and Carl) are implicated in such relationships. We appear here before you in this book because we have drunk deeply from the cultural well of the academy; it fills us, sustains us and at times intoxicates and consumes us. We cannot escape the tradition of privilege that enables us to write – this is the case no matter how much concern, unease (or even guilt) that we express for it. Given what we take to be our self-knowledge as authors, in writing this chapter we want to move towards some understanding of what it might mean to be responsible for 'writing the Other'. As a device to enable this, we (Bob and Carl) have decided to write the chapter as a first person narrative. The 'I' of the text below is a fictional 'I' whom we have created in order to tell one possible story of how to consider the relationship between Self and Other in the study of international management. We have separated the identity of the narrator from that of the authors to highlight the fact that our knowledge is one that is actively narrated by *us* – and for which we are responsible. In summary, please be on notice that what we write here is a work of fiction … and that is why we take it so seriously.

I look across your desk, across its fastidious neatness of compulsively composed piles of files and papers. I look at your face. It is the face of a stranger. It is the face of a middle-aged Chinese business man – or at least these are the words I conjure up most inadequately to describe your face. I cannot prevent the word 'inscrutable' from entering my mind. Why? I don't know you. I am projecting things onto your face from my reservoir of thoughts, ideas and images that some might call 'knowledge'. Included are elements from the repertoire that some label 'Theory'. But these are jumbled with other elements differently labeled and unlabelable. I am asking you questions in a style that some might call 'interview' and I write down what you say. You tell me things that appear to be about how you do business...

[sometime later]...

I look across my desk at my computer screen. On it is displayed a transcript of the interview I had with the 'Chinese business man'. His face is no longer there – not even in my memory. I just have 'his' words. What do they mean? I look at the words on the screen. My reservoir of thoughts, ideas and 'theories' direct my attention to certain words and certain phrases. I extract these. Later I will order them in a particular manner. Then I will write a text of my own because I am supposed to account for this 'Chinese business man'. I will presume to represent him and his words in my text. What can I say about him? What do I know about him and his world – this stranger? Are we connected? Yes/No. I am uneasy and uncertain. How wide and how deep is the abyss that separates me from this other person?

I go in search of knowledge, of authority. I go in search of textual reassurance to relieve my anxiety. How do people, labelled 'international management scholars', account for people from different places and cultures? How do they make their representations? In the 1959 book *Management and the Industrial World* (Harbison and Myers, 1959), I locate the following passage discussing management and industrialization in Israel:

> The Arab and Sephardic elements are technically and culturally less well advanced, in fact some authorities feel that the European and Asiatic groups are centuries apart culturally ... For the analysis in this essay, this implies that the two former groups, with some few exceptions, constitute the unskilled and semiskilled labor force and currently, from a standpoint of potential management base, are of less significance (p. 188).

I find this unsettling. Arabic people are mentioned only on this one occasion, Palestinians not at all. In talking about Egypt, they declare indigenous management 'primitive' and enterprises managed by a 'strong willed individual or family clique' where 'one finds a personal rather than a functional type of organization, a complete absence of rational management procedures, and a dearth of competent professional and supervisory personnel" (p. 158). They further assert that Egypt's greatest current asset is those people with overseas training or experience – since this makes them 'sophisticated' (p. 162). Elsewhere, there is reference to British 'aristocratic values', German 'authoritarianism', the 'unquestioning loyalty' of the Japanese subordinate, the 'patrimonial', 'thrusting and unscrupulous' Indian businessman (p. 153). I could go on.

This is not an obscure book – it is a foundational text for international and cross cultural management studies (ICMS). Harbison, Myers and others were there (see also Kerr et al., 1960) at the start when ICMS emerged as an academic discourse in the United States just after World War Two. As US international trade burgeoned, there was a perceived need to confront Soviet global incursions through the bulwark of US international investment and business practice. It was also desirable to have representations of other cultures' business and management practices so that the world could be managed through a knowledge that embraced the injunctions of normal science, realist ontology, neo-positivist epistemology and the methodological colours of structural functionalism, as exemplified by Parsons in sociology and Radcliffe-Brown in anthropology.

What I also found in this early discourse of ICMS was a universalistic tendency deploying the rhetoric of modernization, development and industrialization that tied US business interests to those projects and to US foreign policy ambitions. There is an accompanying belief that to modernize and develop, other countries must traverse the same kind of industrialization process the West had already successfully negotiated. It used a language that represented non-industrialized countries in relation to the pre-modern, undeveloped and underdeveloped world and the need for Western intervention to bring development and modernity to it. It is a continuation of an exploitative imperial project in that it involves a colonization of indigenous people through a 'truth' that sustains the colonizing culture (see Diprose, 2002) – the culture that sustains both my life and my anxieties.

Like a bastard social Darwinism, ICMS demanded nothing less than progress – progress built behind a veneer of positivistic theories and methods deployed to scrutinize and represent the management and organization practices of the non-West. It was an appropriation strategy that constructed representations of non-Westerners refracted through a Western theoretic-ideological lens and devoid of any input from them: of their understandings, interests and knowledge systems. With the rise to dominance of contingency theory in organization studies with its 'culture-free' hypothesis (Hickson et al., 1974), weaponry kept being added to the armoury.

Fearing that I was misled by these dusty and sacred texts from the dawn of the discipline, I looked for something more contemporary. After all, most of this was written in the 1950s and, culturally enamoured by the notion of temporal progress, I hoped for more. I looked into Redding's *The Spirit of Chinese Capitalism* (1990) and found an intriguing account of contemporary business and management among the overseas Chinese based upon a carefully constructed Confucian heritage. However, not only are a divergent and dispersed set of people collected up and homogenized, but their contemporaneousness is denied by anchoring all they do to the glories of China's past. Essentialisms flow like the Yellow River: 'compliance and conservatism are widespread characteristics to a degree where they might be taken as central parts of the ideal-type Chinese personality' (Redding, 1990, p. 52); 'Chinese workers are notable for their "trainability". They have traditions of diligence and disciplined education, and also a high level of manual dexterity' (p. 222); 'Chinese people "see the world" differently to others' (p. 72); 'cause for the Chinese is a matter of "connectedness", of understanding the mutual, reciprocal interplays between a large array of forces' (p. 76), and so on.

Despite my concerns, I know that Redding's is a sympathetic attempt to portray another culture's business systems emically. But still, the core theme is that the contemporary East is only made meaningful either by reference to the legacies of a faded civilization, or to the West's modernity and progression. This is a text written by a Westerner for a Western audience, yet one that presumes to have gazed upon, apprehended and accurately represented the East. But I don't want to single out Redding – such practices are apparent in almost every ICMS text. The one that really grabbed me, even astonished me, was *Comparative Management: A Transcultural Odyssey* (Gatley et al., 1996). Replete with its Homeric eponym, the book divides the world's cultures into four 'paradigm views', making a central contrast between Western 'atomism' and Eastern 'holism'. This is oddly linked to theories of the dual hemisphericity of the brain: 'These two orientations [atomism and holism] have been attributed to the relative dominance of the two brain hemispheres, the analysing reductive left brain, which seems to dominate the Western world and the synthesising, visio-spatial right brain which seems to dominate in the East' (p. 13). My hopes for proper knowledge of other cultures began to wane.

If I did come to a point of knowing something, it was that ICMS, like all research practices, is embroiled in the problematics and politics of representation. But there seemed a particular acuity in ICMS given its express encounter with difference and the presence of differential power structures and relationships inevitably framing any research. ICMS offered itself to me as a practice of appropriation and representation where Western scholars (my own image keeps creeping back, despite my protestations) subject other countries'/cultures' management and organizational practices to the machinery of northern science so they can construct representations that stand as 'knowledge' all the better to engage with, manage and control them. Simultaneously, the West's management systems and managers are conjured up and valorized in relation to the represented Other. This is a white man's knowledge spoken with an authority and universalism of egological narcissism. It requires no conspiracy theory to see this authority as handmaiden to Western dominance in international business.

It was clear by now that the answers and solutions I was looking for were not located in ICMS. In fact, ICMS made my problems worse. I did find, though, that my problems resonated with the philosophical investigations of postcolonial theory. I turned to it for guidance. Initially I considered the detailed examination of the representation of the colonial Other by the West in Said's discussion of *Orientalism* (1978). For Said 'orientalism is a style of thought based upon an ontological and epistemological distinction made between "the Orient" and (most of the time) "the Occident"' (p. 5). Orientalism understands difference in relation to the primacy of a western Self. Indeed, this notion of the Other, for Said, is a means through which the Oriental is positioned as not only being different from the West but also as inferior. The Orient is used to reinforce a sense of Western supremacy, such that the Orient is only ever an image of what is non-Western, and therefore lesser. Orientalism constructs, appropriates and represents the Oriental Other through a complex and networked set of practices that are less about a genuine attempt to see, understand and explain any actual other people and more about providing a representation meaningful to the West. Through Orientalism the Other is understood in the language of the Same (i.e. the occident), it is an assimilation of the Other to the Self. Said meticulously unravels the multitude of representations and representational practices and reveals their interdependence with the institutions and practices of colonialism. This was a 'knowledge' of the orient that came to be regarded as 'fundamentally stable' (p. 32). But the Oriental never spoke for him-or her-self.

Comparing what I read in ICMS to Said, I provisionally concluded that Orientalism and northern science were twins enabling and legitimating discourses that continue to serve the neo-colonial, imperialist project of which ICMS is a component. These representations are not accurate or real, they were never required to be; as Said says, Orientalism is 'entirely distinct and unattached to the east as understood within and by the east' (p. vii). There is no genuine desire to know other people or cultures in their own specificity. I was not the first to realize these connections – they have recently been documented in the margins of organization and management theory (see Westwood, 2001; Prasad, 2003). In ICMS, as in Orientalism, the Other is that which is constructed by a Western discourse that claims to speak authoritatively and definitively. Along the way, non-Western people are silenced through not being able to self-represent. Silenced through being homogenized. Silenced through having their knowledge systems derided, obliterated, ignored or marginalized. Silenced through the West's control and policing of the discourse and the machineries of knowledge production and dissemination.

Said was pessimistic. He thought Westerners were incapable ontologically of a 'true' or even sympathetic representation of others. This made me shudder.

So what is my relationship to my Chinese businessman and how can I relate to his difference from me? How do I deal with cross-cultural research when my knowledge and culture are rooted in the West? What might my (subject) position be? Who is my Western Self that is in relation to that which I find different? What are my responsibilities? Should I presume to speak about/of/for this person, or remain silent? If I speak, by what right do I do so? My questions remain unanswered, reinforced by the belief that all our confrontations with difference are fraught with danger.

Whilst Said focuses almost entirely on the discourse(s) of the colonizer, reading Bhabha (1994) took me in a different direction: towards a different idea of the Other. Bhabha imagines a complex and negotiated interplay between the colonized and the colonizer. He does not accept that colonial discourse is monolithic or that the colonized is merely captive of that discourse. This seems more respectful and less pessimistic – I like it. The West, he argues, has an ever-present ambivalence towards the Oriental Other informed in part by its own psychic uncertainties and anxieties. The Orient is, for example, at once both completely knowable through the 'scientific' gaze of the colonizer, but at the same time it is an object of desire, a danger and threat that is mysterious and unknowable. The relationship is essentially unstable, mobile and conflictual; structured 'by forms of multiple and contradictory belief' (Bhabha, 1994, p. 75). Bhabha's Other cannot be apprehended as having a set of fixed, pre-given characteristics inscribing a predetermined cultural identity. Nor can all colonizers be seen as coming to the Other with a fixed and homogenous set of ideas and categories with which to affix to the Other in a monological imposition.

For Bhabha cultural identities are negotiated, and cultural differences and their representations are 'performed' in a liminal space, a space of hybridity, since neither Self nor Other sustains an independent and untrammelled identity at the interface. Bhabha sees the homogenization and monolithic tendencies of colonial and Orientalist discourse as akin to fetishism – an attempt to construct a fixed, arrested and stable imaginary Other to satisfy the desires of Self. It is a fetishism constituted by the oscillation, the 'play', between the desire for affirmation of the Same or sameness and the anxiety associated with difference and a sense of lack in self in the face of that difference, that Otherness. However, the meanings slip and disperse and the would-be monolithic discourse loses coherence. It fractures to reveal the uncertainties, ambiguities and fetishes of the colonizer. Colonial discourse is always 'less than one and double' (Bhabha, 1994, p. 97). The discourse is unstable because of the 'translation' as the West's ideas and theories get ensnared in the dynamics of interface, of the space between Self and Other, and become hybridized. Even if the Other is seduced into a self-identification with the identity offered by the colonizer, this mimicry turns back to the colonizer as a deformation, challenging the coherence and fixity the colonizer aspires to. The mimic's not-quite-sameness destabilizes the regime of the stereotype and the coherence of the identity of the Self seeking definition in a fixed and knowable Other.

In terms of my own problems as a Western ICMS researcher, reading Bhabha shows that I cannot assume a stable identity in the Other that I could find, know and then write. It also tells me that my own identity is at stake. The other person that I confront is already soaked in the (neo)colonial experience, in the serried representations proffered by the (my) West, and in his/her reactions and hybridizations of those strategies. More complexly, any sense of this other person available to me can only emerge in the performance of the interaction, in the interstices of a cultural encounter, the constitution of which cannot be determined *a priori.*

I cannot see any way back from these recognitions to the old assurances of univeralizations or even limpid humanistic pluralizations. But then I recognize that I am a hybrid too, a mongrel diasporized 'Englishman', a constructed identity at the interstices of all manner of historical and cultural confluences and confusions. Furthermore, is not the ethos of the United States based upon hybridity and does not the field of ICMS actually celebrate hybridity as a feature of globalization – itself presaging a dissolution of those tricky cross-cultural differences that beset international business encounters? The construction of the mimic man was, after all, a colonial device of control. If we are all hybrids, where is the difference that differentiates and where is the divide that we have to negotiate?

If compelled to reject any essentialist view of identity and the epistemic violence by which colonial discourse constructs universalist categories, stereotypes and codings of difference, am I left with complete heterogeneity and particularism? Am I doomed to only speak about *this particular* 'Chinese' 'businessman' (even those categorizations may be troublesome essentialisms).

Looking further, I approach the work of Spivak and find her using the term *toute autre* to ward off assimilation and sustain heterogeneity. The Other, in Spivak, remains an absolute alterity, akin to Bhabha's notions of the completely Other, the 'untranslatable' element of identity (Bhabha, 1994, p. 74), and the incommensurability of cultural differences. This absolute Other cannot be assimilated to the sameness of Self, cannot be recuperated in the codes and categories of the West. Spivak seems to advise that the absolute Other be considered as an 'inaccessible blankness' revealing the limits of the West's knowledge and representational systems.

But, where does all that leave me? What can I say about the differences I encounter – am I silenced, unable to represent at all? But, pragmatically, difference is spoken, whether that results in appropriation, misrepresentation or other violations. But can I make representations of those seen as Other *responsibly and ethically*, given that if I speak I cannot step outside my own particular, historical, cultural, ideological subject-position. I cannot step outside the interestedness of my need to so represent, I cannot assume innocence.

In the 'Politics of Translation', Spivak (1993) acknowledges my concerns stating that 'it is not possible for us as ethical agents to imagine otherness or alterity maximally. We have to turn the Other into something like the self in order to be ethical.' She invokes Derrida's notion of the inner voice of the Other in us. As Spivak notes 'Derrida does not invoke "letting the other(s) speak for himself" but rather invokes an "appeal" to or "call" to the "quite-other" (*toute autre* as opposed to a self-consolidating other), of "rendering *delirious* that interior voice that is the voice of the other in us"' (Spivak,

1988, p. 89). This 'Self-in-the-Other' echoes Bhabha's insistence (via Lacan) that a sense of self and identity is dependent on the Other. In 'Remembering Fanon', he says that 'to exist is to be called into being in relation to an Otherness' (Bhabha, 1986), Self-Other as ineluctably relational and the notion of a totally independent Self is as untenable as an absolute Other.

Spivak retreats from the abyss of complete heterogeneity by acknowledging it to be an idealization. The construction of collective identities is allowable as a pragmatic strategic essentialism necessary to achieve full decolonization. Essentialisms are permissible provided we remain conscious of their expedient, strategic status and do not imagine a real, accurate representation has been created, and provided it contributes to a liberatory, not repressive, practice. So, I am not condemned to silence or solipsism with respect to difference, I can speak, but I need to do so brutally aware of my own commitments, motives and subject positions, of my responsibilities, and of the brutality of language.

I am still groping towards an ethic of my relationships to those different others I encounter in my research practice and am not fully persuaded that Said, Bhabha and Spivak have given me the answer. Given the intellectual connections and lineage between Spivak and Bhabha to Derrida, I was drawn back to Emmanuel Levinas. It is hoped that some inspiration might be found there. Upon reading Levinas I was encouraged when I found that he not only dealt specifically with an ethics of the Self-Other relationship, but also directly addressed this in terms of work.

Levinas expressed both grave concerns and hope about the way others are understood in relation to work. Here, other people are 'already merchandise reflected in money' – a mode of representation which renders people as substitutable such that there is an attempt to rob them of any true difference – any true particularity. Despite such force the absolute difference of the other person does not submit entirely. This is the 'the en-ergy of the vigilant presence which does not *quit* the expression' even when the will withdraws from work. The defect that Levinas identifies is 'the unrecognition of the worker that results from this essential anonymity ... a humanity of interchangeable men, of reciprocal relation' (Levinas, 1978/1991, pp. 297-298).

Levinas' expression of the humanity of interchangeable persons speaks directly to my experience with ICMS – in fact it could be said that ICMS exacerbates this interchangeability in a context where these persons are from elsewhere. Whether in relation to work or culture, the worker is already positioned both as 'merchandise reflected in money' and as having his/her particularity rendered into cultural anonymity. As Levinas argues, there is a gaping abyss between work, as production for the consumption of others, and the expression of an irreplaceable self – an abyss wrenched wider in those international management practices where it is the east that produces and the west that consumes. Indeed, for Levinas work is a matter of 'actions, gestures, manners, objects utilized and fabricated' (Levinas, 1978/1991, p. 175), a relationship of exteriority in the sense that workers are always interchangeable so as to render them subjects of the 'anonymous field of economic life' which 'reduces to the same what at first presented itself as other' (p. 176). Such a reduction to the same echoes Bhabha's concerns, but presents the possibility of another Other – one whose absolute difference from the Same is not irredeemable. This is an Other whose 'will' might not be violated by regarding him/her only in terms of belonging to categories which anonymize particularity. When Levinas writes of 'political life', understood as rules and institutions for the governance of people, humanity is little more than the interchangeability of people. Such work is a betrayal of the self – a masking and dissimulation of the self (see pp. 176-178) involving a 'primal disrespect' that enables the exploitation and Orientalization of the Other that I noted in ICMS.

At this point, my problems seem to be getting worse. Is there no hope for a solution to the ethical problems of representing the Other in ICMS or organization studies? Levinas does, however, provide a proviso, one that might help me out. He is specific in claiming that the political renders people anonymous *only* if it goes unrebuked. It is within this fissure in the politics of work where such a rebuke, such a critique, is rendered possible. But I am starting to realize that the real difficulty is the way that my problem is articulated as being one of a search for knowledge. Levinas' attestation to a rebuke is not based on the desire for knowledge of an object (e.g. the objectified worker) but a form of knowing that is 'able to put itself in question'. It is the Western desire to have secure knowledge of the Other that engenders ICMS' post-colonial predicament. My starting question needs to be questioned, not answered. Answering would mean 'elaborating a psychology' which involves 'the determination of the other by the same'. Questioning would mean 'the act of unsettling its own condition'. This is an attestation to the Other that 'eludes thematization' while being shameful of 'the consciousness of [its] own injustice' in refuting the identity of the Other by representing it (Levinas, 1978/1991, p. 86).

But I have elided the crucial question that haunts all statements so far and that informed the anxiety of the anecdotes I opened with. This is the question of the *ethics* of the representational practices of ICMS. The ethics of how people denoted as different are constructed in Western systems of knowledge – of how other people are rendered as Other. It is here that a conception of the Other reaches its full potential in Levinas.

For Levinas, ethics requires the Other be considered as radically different from the same – it needs to account for the absolute particularity, strangeness and *unknowability* of the Other. As Levinas describes it, this is an Other irreducible to the I, irreducible to me – an Other radically separated from oneself and one's knowledge rather than a subject of it. Levinas makes the telling point that comprehension, intelligence and knowledge are a 'way of approaching the known being such that its alterity with regard to the knowing being vanishes' (Levinas, 1969/1991, p. 42). I take this to mean that recognition of the Other places it outside such knowledge systems and into the realm of ethics. So, must I address the Other from a point that might be located outside of knowledge itself?

I started with a problem of how to understand difference without falling into the trap of that difference being rendered as an Orientalist Other. Now my problem seems to be less about the specific knowledge of ICMS, than about knowledge itself, about the presumption of the knowability of difference and the presumption of a righteousness of the quest for such knowledge. What Levinas adds is that rather than being premised on a pre-occupation with knowledge, subjectivity *starts* with ethics in the sense that the self is 'hostage' of the Other *not a knower* of it – this is the very Other in relation to which the self exists. This relationality suggests that a self is always one from which a response to the Other is demanded and to which the self is responsible. This is not a relationship whereby difference is subsumed into or known by the self (as in ICMS), but rather one of 'infinite responsibility' to the Other – an Other who can never be known in the intensity of its own particularity and to whom one is responsible without the expectation of reciprocity. As Davis, commenting on Levinas, says 'the Other lies absolutely beyond my comprehension and should be preserved in all its irreducible strangeness' (Davis, 1996, p. 3). It is with such a Levinasian concept of the Other that ICMS' treatment of difference can be fully appreciated as being unethical.

But dealing with such an absolute and infinite conception of the Other is not about knowing nothing, but about being prepared to revoke the primacy of knowledge of the Other in the name of ethics. It is not an ethics that can be applied to solve my ethical crisis of representation. More radically, the relationship between Self and Other *is* ethics. This is a relationship of exteriority entailing being open to 'the existence of the separated being' (Levinas, 1969/1991, p. 302). Responsibility, or ethics, is not something achieved by a particular way of dealing with other people but is rather a condition of the self that can never be achieved. The anxiety that provoked my questions must remain unresolved if this ethics is to remain alive. If I thought I had solved my initial problems of wanting to know how to capture difference, then those problems would have been multiplied. My question does not provoke a knowledge-based solution, it provokes affect and sensibility: 'Knowledge would be the suppression of the other by the grasp, or by the hold, or by the vision that grasps before the grasp' (ibid.).

Naiveté is always inviting – an invitation to take up easy positions that assuage guilt and uncertainty, that remove anxiety. I am not immune. I am a doer of knowledge. I *do* represent other people who are different from me, and I do so both as professional researcher and as everyday user of language. These representations are 'knowledge', the very knowledge that tries to cast the unknowability of the Other asunder. So given the antipathy of knowledge and ethics, yet the impossibility of not doing knowledge, a new question begins its irritation: 'how might ICMS take responsibility for its representations of the Other?' Let's not be glib – this 'taking responsibility' is no simple matter, it is one we face everyday as we choose how we represent other people by writing and talking. In Derrida's (1992) terms this puts the 'representor' squarely in a position of undecidability. Derrida describes this undecidability as 'the experience of that which, though heterogeneous, foreign to the order of the calculable and the rule, is still obliged – it is obligation that we must speak – to give itself up to the impossible decision, while taking account of law and rules'. For Derrida, there is no free decision without the experience of the 'ordeal of undecidability'; an ordeal that is never calculable but always open to a future that cannot be located or predicted in the present or the past. And this ordeal is not overcome by deciding:

> [t]he undecidable remains caught, lodged, at least as a ghost – but an essential ghost – in every decision, in every event of decision. Its ghostliness deconstructs from within any assurance of presence, any certitude or any supposed criteriology that would assure us of the justice of a decision, in truth of the very event of a decision (Derrida, 1992, pp. 24-25).

The ethical issue for ICMS that this implies is one of taking up responsibility for the representation of those that have hitherto been subsumed as Oriental Others and accepting that such representations be regarded as a matter of decision rather than of neutral, objective or mimetic representation. This is clearly relevant to any practice of representing the Other, but is particularly salient to ICMS on account of the colonial legacy of exploitation on which so much of its representational practices depend. In a sense this calls for a post-colonial ICMS that takes its colonial legacy as being central both to the problem of representation and to the decisions that might be made in the present when choosing (or choosing not to) study people from other cultures and in making particular representations of them. Such decisions, as Derrida points out, are always particular and always require some ordeal of undecidability: '[e]ach case is other, each decision is different and requires an absolutely unique interpretation, which no existing, coded rule can or ought to guarantee absolutely' (Derrida, 1992, p. 23). In a Levinasian sense 'not knowing how to respond in the face of the call from the Other ... involves undecidability, a clear and certain recognition that one is drawn in [at least] two irreducible directions but still must decide in order to act' (Jones, 2003, p. 239). Moreover, as Derrida proposes, deciding in the face of the undecidable is a form of madness, rather than of knowledge or rationality. It is an immersion in this madness that might bend towards the impossible demands of an ethics of the infinitely Other.

From Levinas to Derrida, a new ethics of ICMS seems imaginable (but not easy). This imaginability emerges when the representation of the Other in ICMS is regarded as a site of undecidability, even though the reality of ICMS has been born from a desire to remove the undecidability of the Other by rendering it knowable in an absolute and universalistic fashion. The radicalness of this aporia weighs heavy, especially since 'management thought has returned again and again to the suggestion that there might be a solid ground ... that would remove uncertainty' and that 'the disappearance or management of political and ethical quandaries in the face of some great calculating machine would indicate not ethics but rather then *end* of ethics' (Jones, 2003, pp. 238-239). The problem then is that the desire for certainty in *knowing* the Other (as many) has been at the very centre of ICMS as a project whose intention was to render the cultural Other knowable such that s/he can be managed. An ethicalization of ICMS would entail, at very least, abandoning this quest as both futile and wrong.

Discussing Levinas' ethics in relation to the multitude of Other people, Hansel notes the political imperative that '[the] institution ... can in turn pervert itself, forgetting its justification and oppressing human beings in an impersonal totality. We must remain vigilant to prevent human rights – or, more precisely, the rights of the other man [sic] in his uniqueness – from being flouted by the abstraction of the system' (Hansel, 1999, p. 122). If we regard ICMS as having been a handmaiden to the modern institution of the western corporation, then the political implications of Hansel's comments to ICMS are palpable. In one sense this is relevant to all confrontations with difference in organizations, however, ICMS' colonial and Orientalist legacy makes it particularly salient to, and exaggerated in, that discourse. At very least, this involves Levinas' awareness that 'we' or 'them' can never be the plural of 'I' or 'you'.

Diprose (2002) has written the provocation that

Decolonization, the opening of modes of living beyond the imperialism sustained by the truth of colonization, rests on the ability of the colonizers to respond to [the] contestation of their 'truth' generously, in Levinas' sense. This is a generosity born of an affective corporeal response to alterity that generates rather than closes off cultural difference (p. 146).

To try and get at such an affectivity, I turned to Levinas' distinction between the *said* and the *saying* in *Otherwise than Being*. If I've come to a provisional conclusion from these deliberations, it is about how the knowledge of the said might be replaced by the affect of the saying as a means of cultivating a necessary undecidability for an ethical ICMS. For Levinas (1978/1991), the said is that which is signified – it is the ontological function of language that seeks to represent and objectify; it is that which would:

idealize the identity of entities ... [it] ... would constitute that identity, and recuperate the irreversible, coagulate the flow of time into a 'something', thematize, ascribe a meaning. It would take up a position with regard to this 'something', fixed in a present, re-present it to itself, and thus extract it from the labile character of time (p. 37).

In these terms, ICMS, in its representation of the Oriental Other, is a particular and extreme instance of the objectification that is enabled by the said – one that fails to acknowledge its limits or the potency of that failure. *Saying*, on the other hand, is that 'which signifies prior to essence, prior to identification' (ibid., p. 46). The saying precedes the said, such that the said can never be reduced to saying (despite the most ardent protestations). Levinas' comments point to the very limits of language as a means of signifying the ethical relation with the Other. It is in the saying that language is not reduced to an objective knowledge but involves that *activity* of knowing difference. Saying is a matter of responding to the Other – one that 'weaves an intrigue of responsibility' (ibid., p. 6), it is sincerity, an openness to the Other rather than closing off the Other in the said. Saying is not 'the communication of a said, which would immediately cover over and extinguish or absorb the said, but saying holding open its openness, without excuses, evasions or alibis, delivering itself without saying anything said" (ibid., p. 143). The saying is the ethics of language that constitutes the condition of the possibility of the said, yet an exclusive focus on the said overlooks the 'essential exposure to the Other'; the quandary that results is that 'Saying is never fully present in the Said, yet the Said also constitutes the only access we have to it; it leaves a trace on the Said but is never revealed in it' (Davis, 1996, pp. 75 and 76).

Levinas' distinction between the saying and the said does not 'solve' any (of my) epistemological problems, it more importantly suggests a reconsideration of those problems, a reconsideration that I have been trying to work through here. The saying points towards an ethics requiring a certain humility in relation to the knowledge structures that I might be seduced by – structures that are inevitably in the realm of the said. As Ronell has convincingly argued, the most dominant form of stupidity is not that which lacks knowledge, but rather than which 'doesn't allow for questions about the world' or for doubt, relying instead on the demand for knowledgeable answers. This is a stupidity that manifests in forms of knowledge (including ICMS) that 'demand an answer and instrumentalize the moment of the question, they escape the anguish of the indecision, complication, or hypothetical redoubling that characterizes intelligence' (Ronell, 2002, p. 43). Speaking against such knowledgeable and contained moments there is a call for responsibility that 'must always be excessive, beyond bounds, viewed strictly as unaccomplished' such that the ethical being 'can never be grounded in certitide or education or lucididy or prescriptive obeisance' (ibid., p. 19).

ICMS has been a practice aimed at *knowing* difference – in Ronell's terms it is guilty of a dominant stupidity. Ethically, this stupidity has resulted in a practice that has failed to be open to the otherness of the Other; instead, it has always sought to render it in relation to the same or self. As a form of knowledge ICMS fails to take responsibility for the undecidabilities (and un-knowabilities) of its own epistemic practice, and it fails to leave open those questions that might sustain its own ethicality in relation to the difference it tries to know. What this has left me with is the idea that ICMS, as a post-colonial knowledge system used to categorize difference such that it be made manageable, is one that at best privileges knowledge over ethics and at worst destroys ethics with knowledge.

REFERENCES

Bhabha, H. (1986), 'Remembering Fanon: Self, Psyche, and the Colonial Condition', Foreword to F. Fanon, *Black Skin, White Masks*, Minnesota, US: Pluto Press, pp. vii-xxvi.

Bhabha, H. K. (1994), *The Location of Culture*, London, UK, and New York, US: Routledge.

Davis, C. (1996), *Levinas: An Introduction*, Notre Dame, France: University of Notre Dame Press.

Derrida, J. (1992), 'Force of Law: The "Mystical" Foundation of Authority', in D. Cornell, M. Rosenfeld and D.G. Carlson (eds), *Deconstruction and the Possibility of Justice*, London, UK: Routledge, pp. 3-67.

Diprose, R. (2002), *Corporeal Generosity: On Giving With Nietzsche, Merleau-Ponty and Levinas*, Albany, NY: SUNY Press

Gatley, S., R. Lessem and Y. Altman (1996), *Comparative Management: A Transcultural Odyssey*, London, UK: McGraw-Hill.

Hansel, G. (1999), 'Emmaunel Levinas (1906-1995)', *Philosophy Today*, **43** (2), 121-125.

Harbison, F. and C. A. Myers (1959), *Management in the Industrial World: An International Analysis*, New York, US: McGraw-Hill.

Hickson, D. J., C. J. McMillan, C. R. Hinings and J. Schwitter (1974), 'The culture-free context of organisation structure: A tri-national comparison', *Sociology*, **8** (1), 59-80.

Jones, C. (2003), 'As if business ethics were possible, "within such limits"...', *Organization*, **10** (2), 223-248.

Kerr, C., J. T. Dunlop, F. H. Harbison and C. A. Myers (1960), *Industrialism and Industrial Man: The Problems of Labor and Management in Economic Growth*, London, UK: Heinemann.

Levinas, E. (1969/1991), *Totality and Infinity*, Dordrecht: Kluwer.

Levinas, E. (1978/1991), *Otherwise Than Being or Beyond Essence*, Dordrecht: Kluwer.

Prasad, A. (2003), *Postcolonial Theory and Organizational Analysis: A Critical Engagement*, New York, US: Palgrave.

Redding, S. G. (1990), *The Spirit of Chinese Capitalism*, New York, NY, US: Walter de Gruyter.

Ronell, A. (2002), *Stupidity*, Chicago, US: University of Illinois Press.

Said, E. (1978), *Orientalism: Western Conceptions of the Orient*, New York, US: Random House.

Spivak, G. C. (1988), 'Can the Subaltern Speak?', Reprinted in P. Williams and L. Chrisman (eds), (1994), *Colonial Discourse and Postcolonial Theory*, New York, US: Columbia University Press, pp. 66-111.

Spivak, G. C. (1993), 'The Politics of Translation', in *Outside in the Teaching Machine*, London, UK: Routledge, pp. 179-200.

Westwood, R.I. (2001), 'Appropriating the Other in the Discourses of Comparative Management', in R. I. Westwood and S. Linstead (eds), *The Language of Organisation*, London, UK: Sage, pp. 241-262.

PART TWO

REFLEXIVITY AND NORMS

6. Social Standards: Hybrids in Reflexive Modernity

Martin Müller and Thomas Beschorner

INTRODUCTION

Over the past few years, businesses have been under the spotlight of a critical general public, particularly when it comes to the activities of multinationals in developing countries. Poor working conditions, unhealthy work environments, dumping of wages, child labor, absence of work councils and labor unions, discrimination due to gender or religion, (implicit) support of dictatorial regimes through economic activities, and enormous environmental damage are just a few examples that attracted negative attention through non-governmental organizations, media and consumers. For example, apparel distributors such as Nike, Disney, Levi Strauss, Benetton, Adidas or C&A were blamed in recent years for questionable production practices. Inhumane working conditions (Preuss, 2001; Graafland, 2002) or the contamination of the (local) environment were frequently mentioned as problems.

Social standards are not political or scientific discoveries; they emerge from very concrete problems faced by businesses within a society increasingly critical of business practices. One very early social standard has been developed by the chemical industry: the 'Responsible Care Program' can be regarded as the reaction of this sector to the disasters of Bhopal, Basle and Seveso. In 1991 the International Council of Chemical Associations established a code of conduct with respect to health, environment, safety, and community relations (Crane and Matten, 2004, p. 420).

Following Pearson and Seyfang (2001, pp. 49-50), we wish to distinguish between norms such as the International Labour Organization conventions, which are binding on countries rather than on individual firms, and social standards as 'codes of conduct', which could be understood as 'voluntary self-regulatory tools that are applicable to specific firms, or group of firms, and thus certain groups of workers at certain times'. Currently, about 25 different social standards exist worldwide. One can differentiate them according to their initiators (e.g., NGO, state, worker or industry associations), their regional origin (e.g., global, North, South, North America, Europe), their geographical coverage (e.g., global, EU firms), sectoral coverage (e.g., all industries, clothing, football), and workforce coverage (e.g., subcontractors, home workers) (Pearson and Seyfang, 2001). They are valid either in specific sectors, such as the Responsible Care Program in the chemical industry or the FIFA CLP standard in the soccer industry, or are universal, such as SA 8000, AA 1000, the Global Compact, the OECD Guidelines for Multinational Enterprises, Global Reporting Initiative (GRI), the Caux Round Table Principles for Business, etc.

Hence, there are two important points to note. First, social standards are *directly addressed to businesses* and not to national governments. In other words, they deal with the moves of players (businesses) and not with the rules of the game (set by national states). More precisely, they can be understood as voluntary rule settings through the players themselves. Second, social standards attempt to address issues of the social responsibility of businesses *beyond mere profit maximization* (in the sense of Friedman, 1970). They regard responsible business actions as the voluntary integration of social and environmental concerns into business practices and as an 'obligation to constitute groups in society other than stockholders and beyond that prescribed by law or union contract' (Jones, 1980, pp. 59-60; see also Beschorner, 2006). In this sense 'the most important function of these standards is to identify indicators of social performance as well as methodologies for measuring and auditing performance along these indicators' (Norman and MacDonald, 2004, p. 243).

In this chapter, we are interested in the *potential* of social standards to foster active ethical behavior of businesses. We should make it clear that we are not asking the important question of how individual businesses empirically apply social standards. We focus instead on the different kinds of governance capabilities of social standards in times of globalization. In other words, we investigate social standards from a social theory perspective to clarify their functions as institutional support for business ethics measures.

This chapter considers social standard initiatives as being self-regulating governance mechanisms, which are characterized by a process of voluntary adherence on the part of firms to certain mechanisms or principles that seek to promote a 'good society'. Two specific internationally established standards are discussed: SA 8000 and AA 1000. These institutionalized approaches are described and then contrasted with respect to a number of different factors, particularly the degree to which they foster 'reflexivity', in terms of how businesses think about these issues, and dialogue, in terms of how businesses interact with stakeholders. Such questions are relevant to the ways in which these standards might be introduced and implemented, and which of these institutionalized approaches are the most promising for international businesses in developing countries.

BUSINESS ETHICS IN THE ERA OF GLOBALIZATION

Approaches to business ethics are based on explicit or implicit theories of individual and social behavior. In contemporary economics, it is widely assumed that the economic system has is to separate from ethical concerns: the economy is a result of historical processes which separated economy and ethics, leaving as a consequence the economy as an *autonomous* sphere (Homann and Blome-Drees, 1992, p. 11). From this perspective, it is argued that the *logic of the economic system* is the driving force of modern societies. Face-to-face-interactions are no longer the central form of coordination of social interactions. In a large, anonymous society, coordination is replaced by the market. Consequently, ethical issues will only be truly relevant when they affect the cost-value calculation of economic agents (Beschorner, 2004b).

We share the opinion that such an economic perspective is both legitimate and important. However, we consider this perspective as only *one* possibility based on a specific (economic) methodology that relies on certain assumptions regarding individual and collective behavior. Any scientific theory consciously disregards certain aspects of a complex reality. This is unavoidable, since theories do not represent a facsimile of reality, but rather they unearth *certain* structural elements of reality that act as an important orientation guide. This leads us to a pluralism of theories, illuminating different aspects of reality through a prism of changing perspectives.

Addressing ethical issues differently and increasing the number of possible explanations through new methodological approaches become increasingly important for very practical reasons, since orthodox economic theories assume a world in which market economies can be regulated through the regulative power of the national state. This, however, does not reflect the construction of reality in a world society, as we know from the debate on globalization. The entire internalization of negative external effects through national regulation is increasingly difficult. Four arguments explain our point: first, national regulations *do not address every social and ecological deficit* due to the complexity of economy and society. Second, state-controlled intervention is, for the most part, *reactive* only correcting undesirable phenomena after they occur. Third, global markets are becoming more interdependent and global society is developing more dynamically. This has created a need for *legal regulations in a shorter period of time*, which are difficult to follow up. Finally, in times of globalization, the actors (in particular international actors) can easily ignore or escape the *rules of the game as set by the state.*

With respect to firms, these arguments underline their social responsibility which, apart from legal and regulatory obligations, require additional internal rules and mechanisms of control. The crucial question is: can social actors such as companies, associations of companies, consumers, and non-government organizations be educated to become *active* members of a fair social policy in time of globalization? (Beschorner, 2004c; Crane and Matten, 2004, p. 413).

In the following sections we would like to present our arguments for a modified theoretical framework in which the autonomy of the economic sphere is strongly disputed; however, we also acknowledge certain logics inherent to sub-social systems. We argue that differentiated societies are characterized to a high extent by *tensions and conflicts between diverse sub-social systems* such as economic policy, science, religion etc. (Weber, 1915/1988). As a result of these tensions, new social institutions arise and become relevant in terms of questioning economic and business ethics. As a result of the antagonism between different spheres of value, modern society displays new forms of institutions that cannot be located exclusively within a single sphere of value. A resulting 'competition' between different 'social logics' persists. We call these types of institutional forms 'social hybrids' (Beschorner, 2004a, p. 142) since they are not exclusively related only to one societal sphere but at least to two spheres. Social standards are examples of such hybrids: a firm, an actor located in the economic sphere, relates itself to social issues that are not primarily part of the economy (as a neoclassical economist would see it). In the following section, we will develop the scope of this fundamental idea more precisely by referring to theories of reflexive modernity (Beck et al., 1995).

We are going to show that social standards can be complementary to the traditional regulation of a nation state, which is of major importance given the lack of regulating mechanisms on an international level. Social standards can therefore represent a crucial regulative element in international cooperation, particularly between industrial and developing countries. We assert that the factual range of social standards is determined by two central factors which are (a) the reflective capacity of the actors, and, (b) the *involvement of stakeholders*. These two elements serve as a means of analysis and constructive criticism of Social Accountability 8000 and Accountability 1000, both of which are recognized currently, as two critical social standards.

REFLEXIVE MODERNITY

Approaches in the field of law stress that traditional legal instruments are not useful for managing increasingly differentiated sub-social systems (Teubner and Willke, 1984, p. 1; Beck, 1991; Giddens, 1997). Increasing complexity, increasing development of lateral systems (in particular in the fields of economy, technology, ecology and culture), social, ecological and economic problems, the public outcry for a sustainable development and the shifting view of time from an operational to a strategic perspective account for new governance mechanisms. Due to these factors, internal processes in social sub-systems and the interaction between them become long-term, increasingly complex and caught up in networks leading to non-linear consequences.

In this context, a debate on the modernization process of management instruments is taking place (Beck et al., 1995). This relates directly to the theory of 'reflexive modernity' as developed by Beck et al. Giddens defines reflexive modernization as the way that modernity becomes a subject unto itself; it modernizes and rationalizes itself. Consequently, changes come from within: reflexivity of life in modern society consists of social practices whose character constantly changes through incoming information relating to these practices, as they are being questioned and improved (Giddens, 1997, p. 42). In reflexive modernization this is not only part of its program, but it also becomes manifest in its content as side effects are formulated as a central sociological issue. The 'expectation of the unexpected' (Beck and Bonß, 2001, p. 41) as a postulated criterion contains the consideration of side effects in decision-making processes. Side effects are the result of ignorance and add to the process of increased knowledge when matters of application are subject to clarification. An adequate principle of management which includes ignorance and side effects as potential problems is called *reflection* (Teubner and Willke, 1984, p. 24). It is a principle that is used in newer approaches to law (Amstutz, 1993, p. 79).

How does reflexivity express itself? The reflexive orientation of an individual or of a collective actor means having empathy, understood as the capacity to place oneself in the role of an actor, and from this perspective to come to an understanding of one own's role (Teubner and Willke, 1984, p. 24). Reflexivity, as in the definition given by Orts (1995, p. 1281), can be seen as a continuous process of self-reflection and self-reform in light of information pertaining to social practices (Teubner and Willke, 1984, p. 27).

Reflexive structures can only exist under the condition of a democratization process in each sub-social system. In this way, each subsystem's discursive structures can be constructed autonomously (Teubner and Willke, 1984, p. 57; Teubner, 1989; Wolf, 1996, p. 87). In other words, reflexive norms ought to facilitate actively self-regulating, self-educating social systems while simultaneously attempting to eliminate their negative external side effects by compensative corrections. Market participants are requested to reflect upon external effects of their actions on their environment and consider the results of these actions as a parameter of their decision-making. This presupposes that the actors receiving regulations are directly integrated into the implementation process (Amstutz, 1993, p. 133). Reflexive norms want to induce conformity through deeper insight into the correctness of rules (self-engagement) rather than solely through external restrictions induced by sanctions and control (external engagement). The reflection on problems is solely an external factor. Companies bring about goals resulting from this as well as the required implementation and necessary structures. Through commonly constructed company rules, involvement should occur naturally, stimulating in turn an intrinsic motivation for obeying self-imposed rules (Haueisen, 2000, p. 261).

The second crucial element in the innovative development in the field of sociopolitical action is the participation of concerned stakeholders in the process of regulation (Ladeur, 1996, p. 181; Teubner, 2000). This participation is not based on an informal coordination of behavior but is rooted in the positive implementation of organized decisions made in social sub-systems (Henry, 1983). Like their formal corporate counterparts, organizations such as Greenpeace, Amnesty International and other non-governmental organizations have the potential to communicate effectively with multinationals (Teubner, 2000). The formal integration of these organizations into international proceedings for the purpose of normalization is a constitutive element of the process of standardization. If demands made in a practical discourse can be clarified and acceptable rules of conduct can be agreed upon, then a standard can be considered as being legitimate.

Integrating the knowledge of stakeholders into company reflection – and into decision-making processes (as long as these are addressees of regulations) – represents another opportunity to trigger institutionalized dialogues of the actors. Stakeholder dialogues can be useful for a company in many respects since stakeholders can also be seen as 'knowledge holders' and be called upon as such (Ladeur, 1996). This means that even the continued participation of stakeholders as an object of standardization is an expression of the principle of reflexivity. A continuous stakeholder dialogue is about 'maintaining a plurality of options, fighting dissent, the possibility of making language (games) transparent and allowing for (positive) change through a process of dialogue and interruption' (ibid., p. 273):

Global, non-governmental standards ask for different legal control compared to general rules of business or global codices of international organizations (Teubner, 2000). Credibility plays a key role for the foundation of standards. Credibility is created with an element of trust so that actors can expect authenticity. So far, we have identified two crucial aspects that comprise core elements of reflexive modernity: reflection and integration of stakeholders. Hence the emerging conditions for the implementation of these claims needs to take into account the reflective problem identification in the relevant context initiated by the person itself (e.g. sustainable development) and the reflection on (and consideration of) measures of implementation in order to resolve identified problems. *Stakeholders must be involved* in the evolution of rules starting from problem identification to measures of implementation. The discourse with stakeholders is based on the credibility of the information given to stakeholders.

To sum up, the two principles of reflection and inclusion of stakeholders are crucial with respect to *an active ethical involvement of businesses in society* since they address important questions: What is the problem? Who am I (with regard to the problem)? And how am I related to others? We will now apply the preceding claims more specifically to the role of business in developing countries, we will focus on the social standards SA 8000 and AA 1000.[1]

SOCIAL STANDARDS: SA 8000 AND AA 1000

Social Accountability 8000

Social Accountability 8000 (SA 8000)[2] was founded in 1997 by the Initiative Council on Economic Priorities (CEP)[3]. Today the SA 8000 is under the control of Social Accountability International (SAI). The Council comprises such companies as Otto and Avon as well as a number of non-governmental organizations. The background of the organization was based on the development of a standard for the social engagement of companies that would bring about worldwide consensus. At the same time, economic reasons were playing an important role in its establishment (McIntosh, 1998; Zadek, 1998; Waxenberger, 2000; McIntosh et al., 2003). Thus, there is a call for the SA 8000 to avert consumer boycotts or claims for compensation. A large number of different stakeholders have been involved in the formation of SA 8000 norms. Further development of SA 8000 is planned as an open, dialogue-oriented exchange of opinion.

The subject of SA 8000 consists mainly of working conditions and rights for co-workers. The standard of the International Labour Organization (ILO) aligns itself with the SA 8000, but resorts mainly to UN conventions for matters of human rights. The goal of the norm (SA 8000) is twofold. Its first goal is to 'develop, maintain, and enforce policies and procedures in order to manage those issues which it can control or influence'. Its second goal is to 'demonstrate to interested parties that, policies, procedures and practices are in conformity with the requirements of this standard' (I of SA 8000). In section IV, the SA 8000 has several requirements for social rules of evaluation. They concern child labor, forced labor, health and safety, freedom of association and collective bargaining, discrimination, disciplinary practices, working hours, remuneration and management system. These rules are imperative and define the *standard of content.* Therefore, the problems that need to be addressed are quasi premeditated. There is no extra calling for identifying problems and reflecting on them.

Under the section 'management systems' of SA 8000 we find a description of the implementation of the rules of social evaluation. First, top management has to define a policy obliged to obey all requirements of the SA 8000 as well as all national and other applicable laws. Further, the norm stipulates that sustainable improvement has to be effectively documented, shared and put into application. Taken a step further, the company has to make sure that all requirements set by the norm are understood and implemented on all different levels of the organization. In addition, sufficiency, commensurability and the continuous effectiveness of the company's procedures and accomplishments in respect to this norm are put under scrutiny. For this reason, a reflection on the implementation of measurements is possible, but indeed it is not formally regulated as, for instance, in AA 1000 (see below). There are no guidelines for how reflection should take place. In the final phase a report informs all participants on a regular basis about dates and other information concerning the company's activities. Again, there are no concrete rules to abide by in terms of method and publication style.

In line with SA 8000 Certification the company is obliged to obey SA 8000 regulations and to apply for certification with an accredited authorization auditor (preparation phase). After the implementation phase a first assessment can be done. The certifier will contact local authorities and NGOs to obtain information about the company (certification phase). If the examination leads to a positive result, the company will be rewarded with an SA 8000 Certificate, which is valid for three years. Every six months an inspection through the certification center will take place in what is the surveillance period. After a period of at least three years, the company has to apply for an extension (Gilbert, 2001, pp. 136-138; 2003).

SA 8000 does not allow independent problem identification. The standard disposes of normative requirements that need to be respected, limiting freedom and flexibility in terms of its application. The reflection process refers only to a context-specific application of required normative standards. These requirements can be modified through the SAI. However since, it will interfere with the norm itself, it triggers a long-lasting process of voting.

General stakeholder dialogue is not part of the norm. Stakeholders can only attend when it comes to basic changes to the norm (through SAI) and in the certification process. The latter only refers to respecting the already existing norms of SA 8000. The certification system is altogether in alignment with the system of the ISO (third party audits) and can therefore be considered reliable (Gilbert, 2001, p. 128; 2003).

ACCOUNTABILITY 1000

AccountAbility 1000 (AA 1000) was created within the framework of an international consultation process of the Institute for Social and Ethical AccountAbility (ISEA).[4] The ISEA unites companies and NGOs as equal partners, as well as, to a lesser extent, management consultants and scientists. Standardization and revision processes take place within an organization comparable to SA 8000. Again, all of the stakeholders are invited to partake in the further development of the basics. ISEA is concerned with developing a worldwide network of companies and stakeholders. Workshops, scientific programs, and the Internet are means to this end.

The founder of AA 1000 is SEAAR (Social and Ethical Accounting, Auditing, and Reporting), which compiles, controls and publishes ethically relevant facts and their results in organizations. The main goal of AA 1000 is so-called 'stakeholder engagement'. The engagement of stakeholders enables AA 1000 to establish building confidence and giving legitimacy as prerequisites for a good reputation. To this end, there are five goals:

- Aligning its systems and activities with its values;
- Learning about the impacts of its systems and activities, including stakeholder perceptions of these impacts;
- Serving as part of a framework for internal control to enable the organization to identify, evaluate and better manage the risks arising from its impacts on and relationships with its stakeholders;

- Meeting the legitimate interest of stakeholders in information about the social and ethical impact of the organization's activities and its decision-making processes;
- Building competitive advantage through the projection of a defined stance on social and ethical issues.

AA 1000 works on two levels. On the top level it deals with the principles of 'accountability' and 'inclusivity'. The principle of 'inclusivity' asserts that the proceeding claims and needs of the stakeholder should be taken into account on all levels. From a broader perspective, this also means that 'silent' stakeholders, i.e. future generations, should also be considered. 'Accountability' refers to the company's report in terms of its activity, omissions, risks and dependencies. Being transparent on the proceedings and activities in a company is the foundation for the dialogue of stakeholders. On the subordinate level, the AA 1000 is part of a process consisting of five elements with thirteen associated sub-processes (Table 6.1).

Table 6.1   Description of Processes of AA 1000

Primary processes	Sub-processes
Planning	– Establish commitment and governance procedures – Identify stakeholder – Define/review values
Accounting	– Identify issues – Determine process scope – Identify indicators – Collect information – Analyze information, set targets and develop improvement plan
Auditing and reporting	– Prepare report(s) – Audit reports – Communicate report(s) and obtain feedback
Embedding	– Establish and embed systems
Stakeholder engagement	– Dialogue

Reflexive elements of standards become visible in the sub-processes. The planning of the model documents the self-image of the company. In the primary 'accounting process', problems are identified and measures are implemented in order to resolve problems that have already been identified. The next step in the process deals with the fundamental reflection of the firm from a social vantage point. Part of this primary process is the compilation of a report, which provides the basis for the dialogue with stakeholder (see Figure 6.1). In March 2003, standards for an independent report model were launched. AA 1000 sets itself up by looking at the GRI - guidelines for sustainability reports. It is based on four principles: integrity, materiality, continuity and expedience. AA 1000 contains the two important aspects that can be claimed from standardization, with emphasis placed on the orientation of the stakeholders. Problem identification is explicitly required. In contrast to SA 8000, no normative guidelines are pre-defined. Instead guidelines should be the result of the internal and external dialogue with stakeholders. Moreover, reflection processes that are based on it are in reference to a "system audit". As the foundation for the dialogue of stakeholders, the report should be audited, but no certification instructions have been available thus far. AA 1000 was not intended as a certification standard but rather as an "audit and report" mechanism.

Comparison and Criticism

In this section, we compare SA 8000 and AA 1000 on the basis of the indicators that we have developed above.

Reflexivity

(1) As a largely *material norm,* SA 8000 is not very flexible. It is very much the normative elements (ILO Standards) that are crucial for determining the problem area. Concrete regimentation offers clear-cut guidance and takes the weight off the single company to carry out its own interpretations and reoccurring situational analyses. These are provided through the given through the SA 8000 norm. The disadvantage is that material norms are rather limited whereby autonomous action which would lead to an ethical solution becomes broadly restricted (Waxenberger, 2000). AA 1000 – similar to ISO 14000 or the EMAS - System in the field of environment management – is considered to be a *formal norm.*[5] For this reason AA 1000 is quite demanding in terms of the company identifying the particular problem. Formal norms are certified for high flexibility but are criticized for being substantially void (Waxenberger, 2000). This void can be filled with the

requirements of stakeholders. We shall further see that this is the reason why the presence of stakeholders is required for the creation of formal norms.

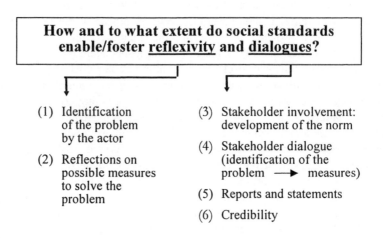

Figure 6.1   Reflexive Modernity and Social Standards

(2) With regards to the development of possible methods of resolutions, reflection processes have (analogous to problem identification) different meanings in both cases of the social standards being examined. The textual dimensions ask for different requirements, in terms of the implementation of the reflection process. While a first compliance audit serves the purpose of knowledge retrieval, the system audit serves as a perception of social and environmentally relevant action. A system audit also requires the reflection of employees. Thus, the perspective becomes much more comprehensive and sensitive to different aspects of reality (Paulesich and Reiger, 1996, p. 505). For a system audit, the question concerning organizational structures is not really the crucial issue. Rather, the question should be whether *co-workers understand and share* already existing structures and procedures and their functioning. Hence, interviewing co-workers is critical since awareness regarding one's own ideas and actions happens through dialogue. Both the exchange of and the reflection on ideas is observed from a secure distance (Senge, 1990, p. 243). SA 8000 mentions audits but they are given relatively little importance. In the case of AA 1000 things look very different. Its

reflection processes for practical solutions (those which are the key elements for learning processes) attract the most attention. AA 1000 is aligned with ISO - standards which resort to system audit. All the same, this is not a guarantee for reflection in the meaning outlined above (Müller, 2001, p. 151). Further comprehension requires more explanations and instructions for the auditor.

Dialogues

(3) For creating the respective norms, elaborate dialogue processes proceeded the creation of AA 1000 as well as the SA 8000. In both cases, diverse actors (companies, NGOs, academic institutions, political representatives, etc.) played an active role in the shaping of social standards. Both of these norms claim that they focus on important societal problems rather than being abused as an instrument for meeting economical and political ends.

(4) The integration of stakeholders is not achieved though the fact that a social standard is available. In fact, dialogue with stakeholders is of major importance when it comes to the implementation and realization of social standards through companies. If it is only the members of an organization who reflect upon an issue, they run the risk – through the force of habit – to ignore important problems pertaining to sustainability or to set wrong priorities (i.e. specific to the individual firm only). It is quite striking that stakeholder dialogues are not precisely stipulated in the SA 8000. This is not only the case in comparison with AA 1000 but also in comparison with the above mentioned environment standards. Unlike SA 8000, ISO 14000 and EMAS, the AA 1000 is characterized by stressing stakeholder dialogue. The reason is, as we have already mentioned above, that AA 1000 waives the need to have material standards but proposes instead a procedure during which solutions for social problems can be developed. This rather empty procedure relies on an interactive process since it is only through the dialogue of different interest groups within the company that possible solutions can be expressed and implemented. In the case of AA 1000, the integration of stakeholders is a part of both the problem identification phase and the feedback phase.

(5) An important aspect in supporting the interactive process of stakeholders is finding a common base for exchanging information. This creates a solid basis for audits and reports concerning the ethical involvement of the firm (the latter being an integrated part of both standards). AA 1000 gives comparatively more exhaustive explanations about this procedure, underlining the importance of critical feedback as a source for organizational learning processes. Different groups of stakeholders can, for instance, give

their opinion during the report session. Through the AA 1000, a broad reference to the Global Reporting Initiative (GRI), which provides wide-ranging coverage, can be guaranteed (see Table 6.2).

(6) We assume that both SA 8000 as well as AA 1000 contribute to making the social activities of the company more credible. In both cases we are faced with unsolicited arrangements that can be certified by any independent party. The credibility of such a certification finds critical voices in evaluations (Müller 2001, p. 262).

Table 6.2   Comparison of SA 8000 and AA 1000

Meta-criteria	Subcriteria	SA 8000	AA 1000
Reflection	Problem-identification	Given	Independent (Stakeholder)
	Reflection on the process of implementation	No explicit requirements	Explicit requirements
Stakeholders	Participation of stakeholder in constitution of norms	Comprehensive	Comprehensive
	Report	Intended but no concrete requirements	Relation to GRI
	Stakeholder dialogue (interaction)	Not intended	Intended explicitly
	Certification	Possible	Possible

In line with Paine (1994), we distinguish between two principal approaches to the implementation of management systems. The compliance approach tries to achieve compliance with rules through extrinsic incentives (reward or punishment), in contrast to the integrity approach focuses on insight, commonly developed values and standards, and the thereby attainable intrinsic motivation of its actors.[6]. According to this ideal-type classification, SA 8000 tends to correspond to a compliance approach, contrary to AA 1000 which tends to correspond to an integrity approach (Haueisen, 2000). If one is concerned about the reflection on one's own action, then it is mostly a question of interactive dialogue and not only of making practical use of norms. In the context of sustainability, it is not sufficient to simply make use of norms. It is more crucial to legitimate and justify action in the appropriate situation. Through dealing with the individual conflict-causing situation, an internal and external dialogue with stakeholders can be initiated and can lead to reasons for the adoption or refusal of certain norms (Gilbert, 2001, 2003). In this respect, the AA 1000 has demonstrably greater impact since the integration of internal and external stakeholders is considered to be crucial. Organizational learning processes also account for key components of the standard.

However, a critical comment has to be added here. First, there is a total lack of normative elements that have wide legitimacy, such as UN Human Rights. Combining commonly acknowledged norms with the formal orientation of the AA 1000 is desirable and would also help cut the cost of transactions. Companies operating in developing countries and countries with emerging markets could take advantage of this.

It should also be pointed out that the integration of suppliers and subcontractors has been neglected thus far. While SA 8000 explicitly states that a supplier has to meet the same social requirements in order to eventually receive SA 8000 certification, AA 1000 does not stipulate such a requirement. In times of increasing globalization and fragmentation of supply chains these requirements are very important. Next to qualitative criteria and criteria concerning price, social factors can also play a role in the decision-making regarding acquisition. This could reinforce the tendency to introduce social standards in developing countries and countries with emerging markets.

The result of these previous points could be recommendations for action in the development of social standards. The link between generally acceptable norms provides interesting opportunities. These norms involve a strong formal stakeholder orientation as found in AA 1000. Thus, even small and medium-scale companies in developing countries and in countries with emerging markets might be inclined to participate in social standards.

Second it is important to anchor social standards and their development in supply chains. Suppliers and consumers should be part of the reflection process. So far, AA 1000 only applies to individual businesses. Integrating social standards into the policy of suppliers as part of a norm could lead to the adoption of social norms by developing countries and countries with emerging markets. SA 8000 demonstrates a promising approach that should be seen as an option for further development. Dealing with the criticism that this only serves the purpose of establishing new social trade barriers, an integrative approach should be applied taking into consideration the situation in developing countries. Such an integrative approach could help develop a process for the implementation of social norms by comprising norms for education and the development of internal and external communication concepts.

CONCLUSION AND FURTHER PERSPECTIVE

In this chapter, we have investigated the relevance of social standards as a governance mechanism in the globalized world. In such a globalized society political regulations are less and less able to offer solutions for social problems (Sales and Beschorner, 2005). This shift concerns also business theories and business ethics theories that have been based on traditional ruling mechanisms.

Evaluating the scope of social standards (and other institutional measures) is always based, implicitly or explicitly, on an underlying social theory, i.e. on the basis of certain assumptions of how societies function. Therefore, there is a tendency to stress the autonomy of sub-social systems and, in particular, the logic inherent to the economic system. Instead of following this traditional economic perspective, we argue that social standards result from tensions and conflicts between diverse social sub-systems. Therefore, a clear categorization and definition of one single 'sphere of value' is neither possible nor desirable. Instead, we have argued that social standards represent 'social hybrids' and, as such, provide possibilities for an active ethical involvement of businesses towards achieving greater justice in the era of globalization. In other words, we avoid a neoclassical interpretation of social standards in the sense of they either 'pay off' or 'reduce costs'. Rather we suggest following Hollingsworth's idea of multiple social logics of society:

Various coordinating mechanisms provide actors with vocabularies and logics for pursuing their goals, for defining what is valued, and for shaping the norms and rules by which they abide. In short, in contrast to the logic of the neoclassical paradigm, the argument here is that economic coordinating mechanisms place severe constraints on the definition of needs, preferences and choices of economic actors. Whereas the neoclassical paradigm assumes that individuals and firms are sovereign, this article is based on the assumption that firms are influenced by the hold that institutions have on individual decision making. (Hollingsworth, 1998, p. 486).

We have specified this basic idea by relying on theories of a reflexive modernity. These feature two main characteristics: *reflexivity and stakeholder dialogue*. Based on these criteria, the most important social standards, SA 8000 and AA 1000, were examined. We acknowledge that these two standards are very different in their respective inherent logic. While SA 8000 focuses very much on material normative basic principles, the AA 1000 puts greater emphasis on a formal orientation and hence on the importance of dialogue and the organization's capacity to learn. The difference in these social standards also reflects the common categorization of business ethics into compliance and integrity approaches.

We suggest in particular two further *developments* of social standards. On the one hand, it is necessary to build upon commonly accepted standards (such as those found in SA 8000) and dialogue-oriented approaches (such as stipulated in AA 1000). On the other hand, we suggest that social standards should be rooted more firmly in supply chains. The implementation of social standards occurs in structures. Formal regulations ought not to be seen as a contradiction to social standards but rather as a compliment. It is necessary that public and private actors collaborate in order to implement social standards in the spirit of a reflexive modernization process. As this chapter has argued, standards can play an important part within this process.

NOTES

1. We narrow the scope down to SA 8000 and AA 1000, based on the fact that these are the only two standards that have been in circulation sufficiently. Other standards such as Sustainability Integrated Guidelines for Management (SIGMA) and Ethics Compliance Management Systems (ECS 2000) are still in their developmental phases).
2. See http:/www.cepaa.org/sa8000.htm.
3. CEP is a non-profit research group in New York that deals with consumer responsibility.
4. See http://www.accountability.org.uk.
5. See e.g. Waxenberger (2000). In fact, within the scope of the EMAS decree and ISO 14001, existing national laws (as well as material requirements) need to be respected.
6. See especially Paine (1994); Steinmann and Olbricht (1998).

REFERENCES

Amstutz, M. (1993), *Konzernorganisationsrecht - Ordnungsfunktion, Normstruktur, Rechtssystematik*, Zürich, Bern: Dissertation.

Beck, U. (ed.) (1991), *Politik in der Risikogesellschaft*, Frankfurt a. M.: Suhrkamp.

Beck, U. and W. Bonß (eds) (2001), *Die Modernisierung der Moderne*, Frankfurt a. M.: Suhrkamp.

Beck, U., A. Giddens, and S. Lash (eds) (1995), *Reflexive Modernization. Politics, Tradition and Aesthetics in the Modern Social Order*, Cambridge: Polity Press.

Beschorner, T. (2004a), 'Institutionen – Kultur – Wandel', FUGO – Forschungsgruppe Unternehmen und gesellschaftliche Organisation, Universität Oldenburg (eds), in *Perspektiven Einer kulturwissenschaftlichen Theorie der Unternehmung*, Marburg: Metropolis, pp. 119-153.

Beschorner, T. (2004b), 'Unternehmensethiken - Eine theoretische Einführung', in T. Beschorner and M. Schmidt (eds), *Integritäts - und Umweltmanagement in der Beratungspraxis*, München: Mering, pp. 151-178.

Beschorner, T. (2004c), 'Unternehmensethische untersuchungen aus gesellschaftlicher perspektive von der gesellschaftsorientierten unternehmenslehre zur unternehmensorientierten gesellschaftslehre', *Zeitschrift für Wirtschafts- und Unternehmensethik (zfwu)*, **5** (3), 255-276.

Beschorner, T. (2006), 'Social Responsibility of Firms', in J. Beckert and M. Zafirovski (eds), *International Encyclopedia of Economic Sociology*, New York: Routledge, pp. 618–622.

Crane, A. and D. Matten (2004), *Business Ethics. A European Perspective. Managing Corporate Citizenship and Sustainability in the Age of Globalization*, Oxford; New York, US: Oxford University Press.

Friedman, M. (1970), 'The social responsibility of business is to increase its profits', *The New York Times Magazine*, September, **13** (33), 122-126.

Giddens, A. (1997), *The Consequences of Modernity*, Palo Alto, US: Stanford University Press.

Gilbert, D. U. (2001), 'Social accountability 8000 – Ein praktikables instrument zur implementierung von unternehmensethik in international tätigen unternehmen?', *Zeitschrift für Wirtschafts- und Unternehmensethik (zfwu)*, **2** (2), 123-149.

Gilbert, D. U. (2003), 'Institutionalisierung von unternehmensethik in internationalen unternehmen: Ein ansatz zur erweiterung der zertifizierungsinitiative social accountability 8000', *Zeitschrift für Betriebswirtschaft : ZfB*, **73** (1), 5-48.

Graafland, J.J. (2002), 'Sourcing ethics in the textile sector: the case of C&A Business Ethics', *A European Review*, **11** (3), 282-294.

Haueisen, G. K. (2000), 'Regelkonformität als Organisatorisches Steuerungsproblem: ritische Überlegungen zur Förderung der Extrinsischen und Intrinsischen Handlungsmotivation', A. Clermont (eds), *Personalführung und Organisation*, München: Mering, pp. 249-268.

Henry, S. (1983), *Private Justice*, London, UK: Routledge and Kegan Paul.

Hollingsworth, J. Rogers (1998), 'New perspectives on the spatial dimensions of economic coordination: tensions between globalization and social systems of production', *Review of International Political Economy*, **5** (3), 82-507.

Homann, K. and Blome-Drees, F. (1992), *Wirtschafts- und Unternehmensethik*, Göttingen: Springer.

Jones, T. M. (1980), 'Corporate social responsibility revisited, redifined', *California Management Review*, **22** (3), 59-67.

Ladeur, K.-H. (1996), 'Öffentlichkeitsbeteiligung an Entscheidungsverfahren und die Prozedurale Rationalität des Umweltrechts', A. Rossnagel and U. Neuser (eds), *Reformperspektiven im Umweltrecht*, Baden-Baden: Nomos, pp. 171-192.

McIntosh, M., R. Thomas, D. Leipziger and G. Coleman (2003), *Living Corporate Citizenship: Strategic Routes to Socially Repsonsible Business*, London, UK: FT Prentice Hall.

Müller, M. (2001), *Normierte Umweltmanagmentsystem und Deren Weiterentwicklung im Rahmen Einer Nachhaltigen Entwicklung Unter Besonderer Berücksichtigung der Öko-Audit-Verordnung und der ISO 14001*, Berlin: Duncfker & Humblot.

Norman, W. and C. MacDonald (2004), 'Getting to the bottom of "triple bottom line"', *Business Ethics Quarterly*, **14** (2), 243-262.

Orts, E. W. (1995), 'Reflexive environmental law', *Northwestern University Law Review*, **89** (4), 1227-1340.

Paine, L. S. (1994), 'Managing for organizational integrity', *Harvard Business Review*, **72** (2), 106-117.

Paulesich, R. and H. Reiger (1996), 'Verwissenschaftlichung des prüfungssystems von managementleistungen zur verbesserung der umweltbeziehungen von unternehmen', *ZfU*, Heft **4**, 489-520.

Pearson, R. and G. Seyfang (2001), 'New' hope or false dawn? Voluntary codes of conducts, labour regulation and social policy in a globalizing world', *Global Social Policy*, **1** (1), 49-78.

Preuss, L. (2001), 'In dirty chains? Purchasing and greener manufacturing', *Journal of Business Ethics*, **34** (3/4), 345-359.

Sales, A. and T. Beschorner (2005), 'Societal Transformation and Business Ethics. The Expansion of the Private Sector and its Consequences', in N. Stehr, C. Henning and B. Weiler (eds), *The Moralization of Market*, New Brunswick, New J, US: Transaction Books.

Senge, P. (1990), *The Fifth Discipline. The Art and Practice of the Learning Organization*, New York, US: Doubleday.

Steinmann, H. and T. Olbricht (1998), 'Ethik-Management: Integrierte Steuerung Ethischer und Ökonomischer Prozesse', in H. Steinmann and G. R. Wagner (eds), *Umwelt und Wirtschaftsethik*, Stuttgart: Kohlhammer, pp. 172-199.

Teubner, G. (1989), *Recht als Autopoetisches System*, Frankfurt: Suhrkamp.

Teubner, G. (2000), 'Privatregimes: Neo-Spontanes Recht und Duale Sozialverfassung in der Weltgesellschaft?', in D. Simon and M. Weiss (eds), *Zur Autonomie des Individuums*, Baden-Baden: Nomos, pp. 437-453.

Teubner, G. and H. Willke (1984), 'Kontext und autonomie: Gesellschaftliche selbststeuerung durch reflexives recht', *EUI Working Paper #93*, Florence, Italy: European University Institute.

Waxenberger, B. (2000), 'Bewertung der unternehmensintegrität II. Schritte zu einem system prinzipiengeleiteten managements', *Working Paper 87*, St. Gallen, Switzerland: Institut für Wirtschaftsethik der Universität.

Weber, Max (1915/1988), 'Zwischenbetrachtung: Theorie der Stufen und Richtungen religiöser Weltablehnung', in *Gesammelte Aufsätze zur Religionssoziologie I*, Tübingen: Mohr, pp. 536-573.

Wolf, R. (1996), 'Der ökologische Rechtsstaat als Prozedurales Programm', in A. Rossnagel and U. Neusser (eds), *Reformperspektiven im Umweltrecht*, Baden-Baden: Nomos, pp. 57-95.
Zadek, S. (1998), 'Making value count: Contemporary experience in social and ethical accounting', auditing and reporting', *Association of Chartered and Certifield Accountants Research Report 57*, London, UK: Institute of Social and Ethics AccountAbility.

7. Managing for Compliance and Integrity in Practice

Andreas Rasche and Daniel E. Esser[*]

INTRODUCTION

Achieving credibility and trust vis-à-vis stakeholders is one of the key organizational challenges of the present day. Adherence to an existing legal framework is often insufficient to ensure legitimacy, because existing loopholes in laws and regulations render any regulatory framework imperfect and reasoning beyond the text of the law or regulation is required to adapt generally applicable provisions to specific contexts. This gap can be at least partially filled by a stronger consideration of ethical issues in practice. In the context of organizational leadership, 'ethics management' is the term introduced here to delineate management that ensures the sustainability of the 'moral basis of the free market economy itself' (Steinmann and Olbrich, 1998: 65).

This need for ethics management poses the question of 'how to'. In the literature, we find two approaches that are commonly mentioned when the question arises of how to align the activities of ethics management in organizations: *compliance and integrity* (Paine, 1994; Becker, 1998; Trevino et al., 1999; Robbins, 2002; Jacobs, 2004; Crane and Matten, 2004:170-171). Compliance as a purely legalistic perspective is concerned exclusively with preventing criminal misconduct by meeting the demands of existing laws and regulations. These are externally given and thus not self-imposed. By contrast, the integrity approach bases an organization's ethics management

[*] The arguments expressed in this chapter do not necessarily represent the views or positions of any organization and should therefore, in accordance with the usual disclaimer, only be attributed to the two authors. Dirk Ulrich Gilbert (University of Erlangen-Nürnberg, Germany), Michael Behnam (Suffolk University, Boston, USA), and Martin Messner (HEC, Paris, France) provided much appreciated reviews of earlier version of this chapter.

on the espoused values and commitments of all employees. The proactive nature of integrity fosters an inclusion of moral questions into daily organizational decisions.

While there is much discussion about the general nature of both approaches, most arguments are rather difficult to translate into organizational practice, i.e., the nitty gritty of everyday operations. The debate provides little insight on how corporations can implement a tool designed to guide ethical behavior – whether compliance to external regulations or to internal codes. The theoretical recognition and practical application of compliance and integrity thus fall apart. As a parallel development, there has been increasing recognition and proliferation of so-called *accountability standards* (e.g., SA 8000, AA 1000, the Global Reporting Initiative or the United Nations Global Compact) in recent years, which qualify as tools for turning ethics into practice (Goodell 1999; Leipziger, 2001, 2003; McIntosh, 2003). Unfortunately, these standards are often presented in an unstructured manner, which leads to confusion about the possibilities and restrictions of their use (Nadvi and Wältring, 2001). As a result, there is uncertainty about the extent of support that accountability standards can provide for shaping either a compliance or integrity approach towards ethics. The same applies to the inversion of the argument: because no framework exists to date to assess the impact of these tools on either compliance or integrity, the tools cannot be extended in a meaningful way.

The research question posed against this background is the following: What sort of guidance can organizational leaders expect from accountability standards if, based on internal deliberations or external pressure, they decide to be engaged in (or are forced to be engaged in) ethics management? The objectives of this chapter are therefore threefold. First, we provide a brief discussion of compliance and integrity as approaches for managing ethics in organizations. Second, we develop a framework that allows an assessment of the interrelation between both approaches and existing accountability standards. This framework is supposed to show to what extent such standards can help manage for compliance and/or integrity. Third, we apply this framework to one specific tool – SA 8000 – to clarify the usefulness of this initiative to support and fit a compliance and/or integrity strategy. By doing so, we discover suitable ways to extend the initiative in either direction. In addition, a discussion of the relationship between accountability standards and strategies for ethics management also addresses the question of whether we should discuss compliance and integrity in a mutually exclusive (i.e., either/or) or mutually enhancing (i.e., both/and) way. Within this chapter we define 'ethical practice' as the situated and socially accomplished flow of activities that are in some way consequential with regard to the legitimization of an organization's activities. A firm's ethics management, which we analyze through the idealized conceptions of compliance and integrity, can influence this practice. Our question, then, is to what extent accountability standards can have an impact on the *management* of this practice.

We will proceed by introducing compliance and integrity and providing a short review of both approaches. In the following section, we briefly outline accountability standards as tools to 'manage' ethical practice in organizations. Based on these remarks, we develop a model for analyzing the relation between accountability standards and compliance/integrity by arguing that most standards possess 'option-excluding' (compliance) as well as 'discourse-opening' (integrity) moments. In the fourth section, we analyze SA 8000 as an exemplary accountability standard and examine its appropriateness for both compliance-and integrity-based ethics management. The conclusion suggests potential foci of future research.

COMPLIANCE AND INTEGRITY AS STRATEGIES FOR ETHICS MANAGEMENT

Compliance: 'Follow the Rules!'

A compliance strategy is founded on conformity with externally imposed norms. Such third party regulation can refer to either the law itself or to stakeholder-specific claims. Hence, the basic principle of the concept is to comply with certain demands on a *re*active basis. Generally speaking, there are two levels of compliance. The boundaries of individual action may either be defined internally by management (e.g., through a code of conduct) or derive from external requirements imposed on the organization by the legal environment. In the United States, for instance, the Federal Sentencing Guidelines (FSG) compiled by the United States Sentencing Commission (USSC) have played a pioneering role in creating a legal framework for sentencing organizations. Companies try to ensure the proper execution of the law by controlling and monitoring employee behavior as well as by sanctioning unlawful actions (Paine, 1994, p. 109). This orientation calls for strict standards with which to comply as well as for obedience to authority (Trevino et al., 1999, p. 132). The moral responsibility is put in the hands of the individual who is perceived to be the final moral authority and decision-maker (Andrews, 1989, p. 100).

Through the development and implementation of a compliance standard, management demonstrates a zero-tolerance policy towards the violation of principles. As a consequence, it is not primarily the organization itself that is supposed to stay out of trouble. On the contrary, most compliance programs are designed to protect top management from blame – both internal and external – and legal consequences (Trevino et al., 1999, p. 139). The ethical program required to achieve this objective is therefore based on strict monitoring mechanisms. Every compliance approach is useless as long as the members of an organization do not stick to the rules. It is, therefore, the task of top management and internal auditors to guarantee the adherence to existing principles.

At the operative level, compliance is usually enforced through sanctioning and training (McKendall et al., 2002). Internal as well as external audits evaluate employees' awareness by controlling adherence to the respective norms (Eliason, 1999). Disciplinary measures can be another powerful tool to ensure that employees really 'live' the standard rather than paying lip service to it. Compliance-based training methods, as one possible way of enforcement, have to raise general awareness for the desired norms. They exclude options for individual actions by imparting narrowly defined standards and fostering a student-teacher-type education. A compliance-based ethics strategy demands that employees learn about regulations that concern their area of work. Since there is no 'one-size-fits-all' approach towards compliance management, it is obvious that education has to be customized to the individual organization and sometimes even broken down further within it, as ethical problems differ substantially from department to department. In addition to training and sanctioning mechanisms, compliance can also be enforced through adequate communication. Practices commonly mentioned for communicating a set of regulations include the measurement of legal performance and an institutionalization of compliance - responsibilities at certain points in the organization (e.g., in the legal department, the ethics office, or the board). Indeed, a well-organized incentive system is often an underestimated aspect for communicating a compliance program to employees (Flannery et al., 1996, p. 58). Finally, the visibility of norms has to be ensured, reminding people of what is expected from them without reverting immediately to hierarchical distance.

While compliance enables 'straight talk' about how to behave ethically, there are clearly many drawbacks to this kind of understanding of ethics management. First, because compliance-based tools hamper ethical reflection and foster the irrevocability of decisions, they are only able to support 'single-loop', or adaptive, learning processes (Senge, 1990). Compliance acts as a correcting authority for the actions of employees but does not support the process of questioning underlying assumptions and goals of both individual and collective *behavior*. Second, a compliance strategy fails to encourage reflection on *norms*. People are deprived of the right to clarify intersubjectively what they perceive to be right. From the viewpoint of ethics, this is a serious drawback – the corporation does not lend itself to a discussion of ethical guidelines. The process of defining norms is not an internal, discursive endeavor, but is instead carried out by management, external consultants, or law setters. Paine (1994, p. 111) problematizes this approach by pointing out that '[t]he law does not generally seek to inspire human excellence or distinction'. Compliance cannot achieve inspiration because the approach focuses on prescriptions and does not rise to the level of communicating values and demanding moral self-governance. Even the U.S. Central Intelligence Agency (CIA) had to recognize that a legal compliance program erodes commitment and hampers motivation (Pekel, 2002). After all, a compliance strategy often brings organizations down to an absolute moral minimum, a common denominator that fails to address the individual ethical aspirations of staff members. The question is, can integrity do any better?

Integrity: Corporate Ethics from the Perspective of Organizational Culture

The guiding principle of integrity shifts the modus of ethical governance. Whereas compliance assumes third party control, integrity supposes an orientation based on value oriented self-commitment and self-governance. This requires moral autonomy of employees as well as the recognition of the supra-organizational character of corporate responsiveness, whose implications reach beyond the realm of employees and managers and include a variety of 'outside' stakeholders. Integrity implies that self-imposed *values* become the guiding principles of ethical behavior. The development of organizational values is, therefore, at the heart of any integrity-based strategy (Eliason, 1999). Of course, the process of developing joint values needs to be communicative in nature (Ulrich, 1998). Deeply rooted within these values is the assumption that there is a primacy of ethical thinking over an exclusively economic perspective based on pure profit maximization.

The objective of integrity can thus be characterized as directed towards enabling responsible conduct (Paine, 1994, p. 111). Responsibility in this context calls for responsiveness because integrity assumes that decisions are not only made for affected people, but that the latter are already included in the norm-definition process. Hence, integrity implies not simply imposing a set of norms on employees but instead, developing these norms collectively with affected stakeholders.

We argue that integrity needs to be understood as culturally conscious ethics management (Trevino and Nelson, 1999) in that it accepts reflection on the idiosyncratic characteristics of specific organizations. Indeed, the most important aspect in this context is to let management 'walk its talk', i.e., demonstrate that values that have been developed discursively and in the context of the individual organization are taken seriously. In this case, ethical leadership ensures consistency between organizational values and actions. A strong integrity culture can contribute to overall legitimacy by fostering freedom of expression and requiring critical reflection from employees. This opens organizations for discourse and enables a consistent development of values. Contrary to compliance, integrity is based on procedural norms acting as a framework to take various context-specific stakeholder claims into account. The need for such open norms, to be interpreted and applied to a specific context, becomes even more obvious if we consider that no predefined norm can perfectly regulate all possible contexts in advance (Derrida, 1992). Procedural integrity-based norms are therefore dynamic, acknowledging the need to be modified by employees in order to fit specific circumstances. Certainly, such an approach towards ethics demands more than the unquestioned acceptance of a code of conduct. For this reason, integrity depends on enacted values, and not on strictly defined external norms.

When moving on to the operational level, we inevitably face the question of whether values can be enforced. Unlike compliance norms, organizational values cannot simply be passed through the organization by means of sanctioning and monitoring mechanisms. Although the literature remains notably silent with respect to discussing activities that can support integrity in organizations, we believe that some actions can be taken. In integrity-driven environments, ethics training should not be about educating employees on specific contents of a code of conduct but about fostering their sensitivity towards moral consequences of their daily activities. Situation-specific dilemma trainings and thought-experiments can be employed to set the arena. The communication of values requires change agents that have to be acknowledged by all workers and stakeholders. Cultural change agents like incentive systems or coaching and mentoring programs can help initiate a conducive environment. Trevino and Nelson (1999, p. 222) also highlight the power of organizational heroes, rituals, and stories to shape an ethical culture. As Trevino et al. (1999, p. 131) argue that integrity starts with bottom line employees seizing opportunities to speak up and report misconduct without fear of retribution.

With integrity-based management being deeper, broader and more demanding than mere compliance (Paine, 1994, p. 111), it is precisely this holistic nature that causes problems. Since corporate culture is a rather 'fuzzy' phenomenon, statements about its management often tend to be of a rather general nature. Another obstacle is engrained in the discourse-oriented character of the strategy. This view demands an inclusion of all relevant stakeholders in the norm justification process. Unfortunately, organizations have far too many stakeholders to be able to consult them in a direct manner, given both time and resource constraints. In addition, classification frameworks available in stakeholder theory (Clarkson, 1995; Mitchell et al., 1997; Agle et al. 1999; Phillips, 2003), although theoretically well developed, leave a lot of room for interpretation when it comes to drawing boundaries between who, in practice, can still be considered a stakeholder and who falls off the brink. The depth of the integrity approach is therefore both opportunity and predicament. In many cases, organizations are left without practical advice on how to initiate a cultural change process strong enough to alter the structure of the organization (Owen and Swift, 2001, p. 4). Such disorientation can lead to a hands-off approach that fails to provide employees with an anchor for their process of reasoning. As a result, 'moral free-riders' take advantage of existing interpretations. Considering the problems of compliance and integrity, it seems clear that neither approach on its own can entirely ensure ethical behavior (Eliason, 1999).

Our review of compliance and integrity as approaches for ethics management reveals that most managers find it hard to translate these conceptions into concrete activities. How can compliance and integrity be achieved in practice? What can be done to consider both approaches in the everyday activities that people in organizations perform? In the following, we suggest to consider accountability standards as tools that influence the management of ethical practice in organizations.

MANAGING FOR COMPLIANCE AND INTEGRITY – THE ROLE OF ACCOUNTABILITY STANDARDS

The Proliferation of Accountability Standards

Our discussion of compliance and integrity reveals a significant problem: although both strategies are discussed frequently in the literature, rarely do we find any practical advice on how to implement them. Simply subcontracting the development of a code of conduct to an external agent or demanding culturally conscious management leaves managers in a gray area with regard to concrete terms of reference or the scope of reflection, respectively. For compliance, the challenge emanates from having to verify compliance externally using pre-given norms without just acquiring an 'off-the-shelf' package from a consulting firm. While managers increasingly look for independent verification of their compliance systems, this does not necessarily indicate that they are questioning their underlying convictions and objectives (Trevino et al., 1999, p. 147). In integrity-driven environments, managers find it difficult knowing how to start unfolding stakeholder dialogues (Rasche and Esser, 2006). Most organizations lack experience in facilitating discourses with employees and other stakeholders (Belal, 2002). Put differently, people in charge of ethics management have difficulties translating the fuzzy construct of integrity into specific actions.

We posit that the problems regarding implementation of compliance and integrity can explain at least partly the recent popularity and widespread use of accountability standards like SA 8000 or AA 1000. Such standards represent predefined norms for organizational behavior using a specific set of issues (e.g., social or environmental) whereby their adoption leads to a prescribed level of ethical performance (Smith, 2002, p. 21; also Rasche and Esser, 2006, p. 253). Typically, third party institutions ensure adherence to these norms, which enhances the credibility of the standard. Leipziger (2003) identifies 32 initiatives in her latest book, thus demonstrating that accountability standards have become an important tool for managing ethical issues within and between corporations. While we agree that such standards will continue playing an important role in ethics management because they possess certain advantages (e.g., enhanced supply chain management, protection of reputation, improved trust by stakeholders), confusion remains over the ability of these initiatives to support compliance and integrity. Does a standard foster compliance or integrity, or maybe both strategies? How can managers assess the potential of a standard for supporting the ethics strategy they pursue? Based on our remarks in the previous section, we are now going to address these questions by developing a framework that allows managers to appraise the specific role of standards in the context of compliance and integrity.

'Quasi-Regulation' – Between Option-Excluding and Discourse-Opening Moments

We propose the identification of 'option-excluding' and 'discourse-opening' moments *within* accountability standards as the key process to make an assessment of these tools both possible and practicable. Option-excluding moments ensure that employees do not take an unmoral and illegal opportunities into consideration, thus supporting a compliance orientation. By excluding possible actions, option-excluding moments prescribe what needs to be done, but also close the organization for further reflection. This is not limited to what one should *not* do, as a prescription of action, i.e., what employees should do, equally sanctions alternative paths of non-compliance. By referring to option-excluding moments, management demonstrates that certain goals are not to be achieved at any price but only under consideration of particular predefined norms. By contrast, discourse-opening moments ensure that employees and other stakeholders can participate in the norm-definition process. Such moments provide a discursive infrastructure that enables responsible conduct. While option-excluding moments tell employees what is *not* possible or allowed, discourse-opening moments foster the evolution of shared values by demanding feedback and encouraging proactive behavior from staff (Ulrich et al., 1998, p. 138). Discourse-opening moments are supposed to support an open, non-sanctioned discourse about ethical decisions and the more general role of the organization in society. Ideally, the discursive clarification of conflicting norms becomes part of the organization's everyday reality and thus corporate culture (Paine, 1994).

Based on Leipziger's (2003) and McIntosh et al.'s (2003) reviews of existing standards, we find that most tools are 'quasi-regulative' – they support compliance *and* integrity at the same time. Quasi-regulation shapes awareness for the complementary nature of compliance and integrity elements in standards. The Global Compact, for instance, which is one of the most widely used accountability standards, prescribes ten principles that organizations have to follow in order to show compliance. These principles exclude options for employees and management alike. However, the initiative also requires organizations to participate in its learning network and to foster dialogue with stakeholders (Kell and Levin, 2002; McIntosh et al., 2003, p. 182; Williams, 2004; Kell, 2005). These discourse-opening moments demonstrate that the Global Compact also supports an integrity strategy aimed at exchanges both *between* and *within* organizations.

Our framework for assessing the impact of accountability standards on compliance and integrity management fulfills two functions (Figure 7.1). First, it allows us to *assess* what existing initiatives regarding their impact on compliance and integrity. The framework demonstrates to which extent a standard supports either strategy for ethics management. Second, the framework can be used to *extend* standards to meet the demands of compliance and integrity even better. By doing so, an analysis of option-excluding and discourse-opening moments is a valuable exercise to appreciate the contribution of existing initiatives and to advance their conceptualization in a meaningful direction.

This framework can also be applied to other tools in ethics management (e.g., codes of conduct or ethics hotlines) as these are characterized by a similar mix of option-excluding and discourse-opening moments. A code of conduct, for instance, prescribes certain norms and thus excludes options for further actions. At the same time, a code can also be developed together with affected stakeholders to be tested and adjusted over time and thus opens organizations for discourse (Lozano, 2001). In the next section, we will apply our framework to SA 8000 as a case in point, because (a) the initiative belongs to the currently most widely used ones (881 production facilities in 47 counties use its guidelines as of June 2006), and (b) SA 8000 represents a variety of other standards since it provides a system to verify ethical performance, via independent audits, that has acquired international recognition (Thaler-Carter, 1999; Leipziger, 2003).

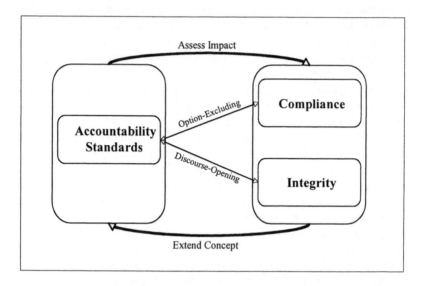

Figure 7.1   *Framework for Assessing the Relation Between*
                 Accountability Standards and Compliance/Integrity

QUASI-REGULATION BY SOCIAL ACCOUNTABILITY 8000

Social Accountability 8000 – Basic Conception and Implementation Procedure

SA 8000 can be characterized as 'a global, verifiable standard for managing auditing and certifying compliance with workplace issues' (Leipziger, 2001, p. 1). By focusing exclusively on social issues, the standard addresses a specific field of application within the triple-bottom-line approach (Elkington, 2002). The normative framework of the initiative includes selected fundamental ILO principles, the UN Universal Declaration of

Human Rights, and the UN Convention on the Rights of the Child (Gilbert and Rasche, in press). Based on these regulations, the SA 8000 guidelines propose procedures to achieve social accountability and to set reliable international standards in areas such as child labor, collective bargaining, fair wages, working hours, and anti-discrimination. Social Accountability International (SAI), an NGO located in New York City, administers the standard. Whereas SAI together with a multi-stakeholder advisory board, is responsible for creating guidelines that act as specific requirements for certification, auditing bodies accredited by SAI, conduct the required audits.

The process works as follows. A corporate organization seeking SA 8000 certification hires an auditing company. The certificate is awarded only for a specific production facility and not for an entire multinational corporation or a complete supply chain. Since many multinational corporations do not own their production facilities, which are increasingly located in developing countries, but rather establish flexible supplier relations (Mamic, 2005), SAI has set up a Corporate Involvement Program (CIP) to which large multinationals can sign up and then demand certification from their suppliers. An issue widely discussed in this context is the nature and amount of costs related to the accreditation process, which vary with the size of the production facility. The types of costs relate to the charges for the audit itself, the opportunity cost of management time (e.g., for preparing the audit), the expenses of taking corrective measures, as well as the costs for continuous monitoring (Leipziger, 2001, p. 7; Thaler-Carter, 1999).

SA 8000 may be analyzed at two interrelated levels of analysis (Gilbert and Rasche, in press). At the *macro-level*, we find a universally valid norm catalogue, which is being revised by SAI on a regular basis. By contrast, at the *micro-level*, norms are put into action in a specific production facility. Indeed, SAI acknowledges that its 'universal' norms cannot be valid regardless of space and it allows for 'local modifications' with regard to geographic location and the current political and economic situation of the respective country. Although SA 8000 is supposedly valid globally and it can be applied by companies in different industries, the guidelines can nonetheless be adjusted to fit the cultural heritage, sector, and size of the production facility seeking certification. Leipziger (2001, p. 107) identifies a variety of regional issues that affect implementation. For instance, religious norms in some Muslim countries demand that men and women work separately. Segregated factories do not violate SA 8000 in these countries, as long as all other conditions (i.e., fair pay and secure working conditions) are met. Another issue that often calls for adaptation is the sector a production facility works for. Conditions in firms producing for the export market often vary dramatically from those producing for the local market (ibid., p. 108). This said, neither SAI nor currently operating auditing bodies have provided more detailed information on the possible extent and precise handling of local modification up to this point.

Implementation at the micro-level is guided by practices known through the ISO 9000 and ISO 14000 series for quality control and environmental management and follows the well-known Plan-Do-Check-Act model (Deming, 2000). During the 'planning stage', managers are asked to review carefully the SA 8000 guidance document and conduct a self-assessment that is supposed to generate a list of problems. During the 'do' - phase, workers are supposed to elect an SA 8000 representative. Management is supposed to develop a contextualized internal manual that introduces the guidelines to employees. At this point, all suppliers should be notified about SA 8000, and consultation with external parties begins. The 'check'-phase must only be initiated once internal monitoring indicates that the production facility is audit-ready. Less expensive and less time-consuming pre-audits are often used to check whether a facility has achieved the status required. Afterwards, the main audit is carried out and the certificate awarded for a period of three years. Auditors are forced to consult with and learn from all interested parties, such as employees, NGOs, or other civil society groups. Moreover, auditing bodies are asked to implement systems (in cooperation with the certified facility) that allow interested parties to report cases of non-compliance. The last phase, 'act', reflects SA 8000's concern for continuous improvement: to prevent the audit from taking a snapshot, certified facilities undergo monitoring exercises on a semi-annual basis. Unannounced surveillance visits can occur any time (DeRuisseau, 2002, p. 228). Feedback is incorporated from multiple sources such as employees, local NGOs, or labor unions.

SA 8000 is in the process of becoming a widespread tool for ethics management in the international context (Göbbels and Jonker, 2003) since it is the first global standard for workplace conditions that is verifiable. Nevertheless, the question of whether or not the initiative supports compliance and/or integrity remains unanswered. In order to offer a structured analysis, we first assess SA 8000's impact on compliance and integrity by identifying option-excluding and discourse-opening moments that help managers to better evaluate the standard to then discuss measures to extend the initiative to include additional option-excluding and discourse-opening moments.

The Impact of Social Accountability 8000 on Compliance and Integrity

Designing an organization's ethics management based on SA 8000 opens it up for a discursive clarification of conflicts because employees become actively engaged in launching and sustaining the resulting management system. While this enables SA 8000 to fulfill the guiding idea of integrity, the codified nature and visibility of the norms act as a stimulus for compliance. Options for individual actions are excluded by demanding clear job descriptions and plain hierarchy. We therefore characterize SA 8000 as a 'quasi-regulative' tool for ethics management and argue that in order to assess its potential one needs to consider both its option-excluding and discourse-opening moments.

With regard to the option-excluding nature, the norms for assessing workplace conditions are not determined in a Habermasian communicative rational manner, but instead predefined by SAI, and it is senior management that translates the guidelines into contextualized norms. Indeed, the SA 8000 guidance document states: 'Top management shall define the company's policy for social accountability and labor conditions' (SAI, 2001, p. 7). In practice, even if worker representation is ensured in the design of codes, individual workers have no say in the process of development of the regulations, because they just receive a copy of the policy *ex-post*. Although SA 8000 demands non-management personnel to determine a representative to facilitate communication with senior management (SAI, 2001, p. 7), it remains questionable whether or not such a form of integration can deeply embed values into the daily activities of employees as required by the integrity approach. In a similar vein, the Institute of Social and Ethical AccountAbility (ISEA) (1999a, p. 18) concludes that SA 8000 'does not include stakeholder engagement as a core part of the accounting process'.

Another option-excluding moment of the standard comes to the fore when considering that SA 8000 requires certified production facilities to demand compliance with the standard from suppliers and sub-suppliers. The guidance document urges, 'The company shall establish and maintain appropriate procedures to evaluate and select suppliers/subcontractors (and, where appropriate, sub-suppliers) based on their ability to meet the requirements of this standard' (SAI, 2001, p. 7). Suppliers are only notified about the launch of SA 8000 and asked to comply with the externally imposed guidelines. However, they are not consulted for their opinion or even asked to assess their actual ability to meet the guidelines. Not surprisingly then, Gilbert (2001, pp. 141-142) argues that such a behavior comes close to a forced self-commitment of the supplier and, therefore, misses the voluntary and dialogical nature of the integrity approach.

Yet another option-excluding moment can be identified when considering the role of enforcement via monitoring and sanctioning systems. Although we agree with Leipziger (2001, p. 70) that monitoring of activities and clear definition of roles, responsibility, and authority are necessary to ensure that the requirements of the standard are understood and implemented, we remain skeptical whether such a top-down approach alone can guarantee compliance. Given that on its web page SAI advertises the standard to managers by arguing that SA 8000 enables a corporation to 'walk its talk', this requires more than budget breakdown charts and clearly defined lines of authority and reporting. This argument also holds for the assessment of training practices. Employees are supposed to own a copy of the manual with the key provisions of the standard. However, more than a general awareness of norms cannot be expected from such measures. As Trevino and Nelson (1999, p. 264) argue, training needs to be designed to suit the group of individuals being trained to enable people to understand and evaluate the values of the organization (also Crane and Matten, 2004, p. 147). Although Leipziger (2001, p. 76) claims that '[t]he SA 8000 Manual, with all of the policies of the company, can serve as a text for training', there is a need for critical reflection about the practical relevance of this type of training. Understanding training in terms of the provision of manuals only bears the risk that workers are left without sufficient guidance about the consequences of their day-to-day behavior.

Even though many aspects of SA 8000 seem to point in the direction of compliance, there are indeed some discourse-opening moments enabling managers to foster an integrity strategy. First, the standard has been developed (and remains subject to continuous improvement) through consensus-based stakeholder dialogue. Even though this macro-level stakeholder involvement does not directly affect integrity-based ethics management in a corporation (micro-level), it nonetheless enables management to justify the decision for SA 8000 against the background of integrity. This is discourse-opening in the sense that a firm that implements SA 8000 and/or participates in the Corporate Involvement Program is requested to contribute to the communicative process that establishes and improves the SA 8000 norm catalogue. Moving to the bottom line, we also acknowledge that SA 8000 demands managers actively seek feedback from employees. Although employees are not included directly in setting up the management system (e.g., by discussing the usefulness of certain norms), the standard asks for active participation of workers in *advancing* a company's social accountability policy. In practice, placing suggestion boxes in the workplace or asking employees to mail in their suggestions anonymously implements this discourse-opening moment. Some corporations (e.g., Chang Shin Vietnam Co.) have also installed an open-door policy that allows workers to voice their concerns (Leipziger, 2001, p. 75). Thus, there is evidence that SA 8000 also fosters integrity by demanding workers not just reproduce the guidelines but also to give feedback regarding the implementation of the regulations.

Another discourse-opening moment is constituted by the possibility of modifying pre-given norms to fit the local context. Leipziger (2001, p. 96) points out that NGOs, because of their community involvement, often understand local needs better than managers. Considering that the standard allows for reasonable adjustments within the scope of the provided definitions (SAI, 2001, pp. 4-5), a discourse with NGOs can be of much help to interpret the guidelines to make them applicable to the local context. The requirement to communicate regularly with outside parties (ibid., p. 8) can hence be understood as a discourse-opening moment. The trust that many NGOs have built up during previous community involvement has the potential to render positive effects for managing integrity since workers may share with an NGO aspects they may not express towards management. The involvement of NGOs and other grass-roots groups can thus (a) foster the development of the social accountability policy and (b) positively influence a 'lived' value-orientation within a corporation. The discussed option-excluding and discourse-opening moments of SA 8000 are summarized in Table 7.1.

Table 7.1   *Option-Excluding and Discourse-Opening Moments of SA 8000*

	Compliance: Option-Excluding Moment	Integrity: Discourse-Opening Moment
General Definition	Exclude actions by prescribing what needs to be done Closes the organization for reflection	Ensure that employees and other stakeholders can participate in the norm-definition Process
Exemplary Application to SA 8000	Top management defines the social accountability policy	Overall SA 8000 framework was developed discursively
	Suppliers and sub-suppliers are forced to comply	Employees are asked to give feedback once SA 8000 is implemented
	SA 8000 is implemented in a top-down manner	Local modification requires feedback (e.g. from NGOs)

From our discussion of option-excluding and discourse-opening moments, we conclude that SA 8000 can be characterized as a 'quasi - regulative' tool. This characterization of the standard is useful because it demonstrates that SA 8000 combines many advantages of a 'straight-forward' compliance-orientation with a communicative and value-based understanding of integrity. At the same time, it must not be interpreted as only discussing those aspects of SA 8000 that are advantageous since a manager who uses SA 8000 as a tool for ethics management also faces a variety of problems. Since our framework for assessing the interrelation between compliance/integrity and accountability standards also allows for a discussion of how to extend SA 8000, we summarize possible problems with SA 8000 below and provide suggestions for a meaningful extension of the tool.

Extending Social Accountability 8000

We argue that both option-excluding and discourse-opening aspects of SA 8000 can indeed be extended. Certainly, an extension does not necessarily mean pushing compliance towards integrity and *vice versa* but, instead, is meant to address the dysfunctionalities that hamper the positive impact of the tool. In the following, we focus on an extension of SA 8000 towards the inclusion of more discourse-opening moments since the 'fuzzy' nature of these moments tends to be neglected by management, whereas option-excluding moments are comparably more 'visible' and thus attract attention more easily and readily.

First, it seems expedient not to make supplier-commitment to SA 8000 rest *entirely* on external pressure. Many suppliers face considerable financial constraints, which do not allow them to pay for an audit immediately. In the end, such an approach is similar to passing on responsibility to lower entities in the supply chain. As a result, suppliers forced to comply with the standard will try to obtain a certification as cheaply as possible. Since monitoring by auditing bodies and NGOs can never be considered complete, such an approach is likely to result in moral mediocrity. We believe that suppliers' involvement should be understood as a more sustainable and inclusive process during which the supplier and the client interact towards mutual benefit. This, for instance, could include financial assistance for the first audits but also content-related support (e.g., through consulting) with regard to the implementation of the management system.

The discussion above has indicated that employees would need to be granted more decisive influence on the norm-definition process. After all, if employees are supposed to give feedback about the standard, why not include them from the very beginning? A stronger inclusion of workers would go beyond their representation through some sort of advocate. Corporations would have to install 'loci' for dialogue from the very beginning and ensure an open and unbiased discourse. Gilbert and Rasche (in press) consider this point when arguing in favor of a discourse-theoretical extension of SA 8000. Drawing on Habermasian discourse ethics (Habermas, 1996, 2001), they show that employee engagement within SA 8000 can contribute to a more profound understanding of what a discourse actually is, which claims a discourse justifies, and under which conditions a 'just' discourse operates. Such clarifications act as prerequisites for demanding 'more dialogue' from an initiative. Concerning SA 8000, we believe that the standard has to extend its notion of stakeholder engagement to include the process of social accounting itself. A good point of departure for such an endeavor would be the integration of AA 1000's stakeholder accountability model into the SA 8000 guidelines (ISEA, 1999b). In more general terms, we believe that the entire field of social and ethical accounting (Gray, 2002; 2001) could benefit significantly from a discussion and potential inclusion of stakeholder theory (Freeman, 1984; Donaldson and Preston, 1995).

The last issue raised here concerns the nature of the audit itself. SA 8000 demands what can be called a 'compliance audit', i.e., an audit that checks whether the guidelines proposed have been implemented accordingly. While this is necessary, its limited reach overlooks the forces that motivated the occurrence of undesirable acts in the first place. We therefore recommend extending the option-excluding nature of the compliance audit towards a 'cultural audit'. Cultural audits seek to identify underlying causes of corporate misconduct by actively including and exploring the views and values of stakeholders (Castellano and Lightle, 2005). For this reason, cultural audits do not only exclude options for behavior, but also enable dialogue among affected parties. Such an altered understanding of the audit process has to begin with the auditing bodies themselves. It does not demand a 'check-the-boxes' approach, but requires an assessment of, for instance, employees' perception of leader integrity instead, thus placing greater responsibility on the shoulders of participating organizations. Besides using open-ended employee-interviews, this also implies that auditing bodies and certification companies have to develop a sense of judgment regarding the ethical climate within a corporation. Such prudence can be fostered actively by educating auditors about the company history, prior misconduct, the specific circumstances of its local environment, and its relation to (sub)-suppliers; in short: its context.

CONCLUSIONS AND OUTLOOK

In light of the title of this book, a thorough investigation of SA 8000's conception confirms that it is a usable tool for turning ethics into practice. This chapter adds to our knowledge about ethics in practice in that, it (a) shows that compliance and integrity are idealized approaches to think about how ethics can be turned into practice and (b) clarifies that accountability standards support both approaches and thus, it can be used as 'quasi-regulative' tools. This chapter has aimed at introducing and connecting two worlds. First, the world of compliance and integrity as *approaches* for managing ethical practice; second, accountability standards (i.e., SA 8000) as *tools* to organize these management efforts. Indeed, our treatment of compliance and integrity and its application to SA 8000 is supposed to encompass more than a simple dichotomy, revealing both option-excluding and discourse-opening moments and how they interact, and thus demonstrating that tools for ethics management do not follow a pure compliance *or* integrity strategy. In practice, most measures support a both/and-orientation, in which compliance and integrity are integrated meaningfully. Clearly, we do not try to advocate a normative position for or against any of the two ethics strategies, as neither compliance nor integrity alone can ensure moral conduct in corporations. Integrity is not necessarily better than compliance – both approaches are different ways of managing ethics. Hence we do not derive a normative argument for a combination of compliance and integrity from this line of reasoning since we so far have to do without an empirical substantiation of our arguments. Our key finding is therefore more conceptual in nature: if we look at the key characteristics of compliance/integrity and accountability standards as described in the literature, it is reasonable to assume that many standards support both approaches.

Our remarks on possible extensions of SA 8000 also show that some questions remain unanswered. Empirical research could, for instance, focus on the scope of stakeholder inclusion in the context of local production facilities. Although Leipziger (2001, pp. 21-40) presents a variety of short cases, we still miss extensive bottom-line reports about how auditing really takes place and which problems occur – particularly in developing countries with less leverage for local civil society institutions (for a laudable exception see DeRuisseau, 2002). If managers are supposed to make justified decisions for or against a standard, we need to offer more than just one-dimensional treatments of complex tools. To understand ethics as a practice, we need more research that actually looks at how managers identify themselves with compliance and integrity, and which also measures accountability standards that are used to implement both strategies. Finally, we would like to highlight that this framework can be applied to other accountability standards and tools for ethics management as well. For example, evolving standards like the Global Reporting Initiative (GRI) or the Global Compact may benefit from an analysis of their option-excluding and discourse-opening moments. Such analyses are timely since managers, while familiar with the content of the standards, often miss practical guidance with regard to implementation. Assessing the link between compliance and integrity as well as the effectiveness of contemporary tools catalyses the creation of much needed knowledge on implementation and helps to bridge the gap between conceptual considerations and ethical practice of which the field of business ethics has often been accused (Gray, 2001).

REFERENCES

Andrews, K. R. (1989), 'Ethics in practice', *Harvard Business Review*, **67** (5), 99-104

Agle, B. R., Mitchell, R. K. and J. A. Sonnenfeld (1999), 'Who matters to CEOs? An investigation of stakeholder attributes and salience, corporate performance, and CEO values', *Academy of Management Journal*, **42** (5), 507-525.

Belal, A. R. (2002), 'Stakeholder accountability or stakeholder management: A review of UK Firms', Social and Ethical Accounting, Auditing and Reporting (SEAAR) Practices, *Corporate Social Responsibility and Environmental Management*, **9** (1), 8-25.

Becker, T. E. (1998), 'Integrity in organizations: Beyond honesty and conscientiousness', *Academy of Management Review*, **23** (1), 154-161.

Castellano, J. F. and S. S. Lightle (2005), 'Using cultural audits to assess the tone at the top', *CPA Journal*, **75** (2), 6-11.

Clarkson, M. B. (1995), 'A stakeholder framework for analyzing and evaluating corporate social performance', *Academy of Management Review*, **20** (1), 92-117.

Crane, A. and D. Matten (2004), *Business Ethics: A European Perspective*, Oxford, UK: Oxford University Press.

Deming, W. E. (2000), *Out of the Crisis*, Cambridge, MA, US: MIT Press.

Derrida, J. (1992), 'Force of Law: The "Mystical Foundation of Authority"', in D. Cornell, M. Rosenfeld and D. G. Carlson (eds), New York, US and London, UK: Routledge, pp. 3–67.

Donaldson, T. and L. E. Preston (1995), 'The stakeholder theory of the corporation – concepts, evidence, and implications', *Academy of Management Review*, **20** (1), 65-91.

DeRuisseau, D. (2002), 'Social Auditing – An Auditors Perspective', in A. G. Scherer et al. (eds), *Globalisierung und Sozialstandards*, München/Mering: Hampp, pp. 223-233.

Eliason, M. J (1999), 'Compliance plus integrity', *The Internal Auditor*, **56** (6), 30-33.

Elkington, J. (2002), *Cannibals with Forks – The Triple Bottom Line of 21st Century Business*, Oxford, UK: Capstone.

Flannery, T. P., D. A. Hofrichter, and P. E. Platten (1996), *People, Performance and Pay – Dynamic Compensation for Changing Organizations*, New York, US: Free Press.

Freeman, R.E. (1984), *Strategic Management: A Stakeholder Approach*, Boston, US: Pitman.

Gilbert, D. U. (2003), 'Institutionalisierung von Unternehmensethik in internationalen Unternehmen – Ein Ansatz zur Erweiterung der Zertifizierungsinitiative social accountability 8000', *Zeitschrift für Betriebswirtschaftslehre*, **73** (1), 1-24.

Gilbert, D. U. and A. Rasche (in press), 'The ethics of SA 8000 – Towards a discourse – Theoretical extension', accepted for publication in *Business Ethics Quarterly*.

Göbbels, M. and J. Jonker (2003), 'AA1000 and SA8000 compared: A systematic comparison of contemporary accountability standards', *Managerial Accounting Journal*, **18** (1), 54-58.

Goodell, E. (1999), *Standards of Corporate Social Responsibility*, San Francisco, CA, US: Social Venture Network.

Gray, R. (2001), 'Thirty years of social accounting, reporting, and auditing: what (if anything) have we learnt?', *Business Ethics: A European Review*, **10** (1), 9-15.

Gray, R. (2002), 'The social accounting project and Accounting Organizations and Society – Privileging engagement, imaginings, new accountings and pragmatism over critique?', *Accounting, Organizations and Society*, **27** (7), 687-708.

Habermas, J. (1996), *Postmetaphysical Thinking: Philosophical Essays*, Cambridge, MA, US: MIT Press.

Habermas, J. (2001), *Moral Consciousness and Communicative Action*, Cambridge, MA, US: MIT Press.

ISEA – Institute of Social and Ethical Accountability: (1999a), *AccountAbility 1000 – Introduction to the Standard*, London, UK: ISEA.

Jacobs, D. C. (2004), 'A pragmatist approach to integrity in business ethics', *Journal of Management Inquiry*, **13** (3), 215-223.

Kell, G. (2005), 'The global compact – Selected experiences and reflections', *Journal of Business Ethics*, **59** (1/2), 69-79.

Kell, G. and D. Levin (2002), 'The evolution of the global compact network: An historic experiment in learning and action', working draft for the *Academy of Management Annual Conference 'Building Effective Networks'*, August 11-14, 2002, Denver (Colorado).

Leipziger, D. (2001), *SA8000 – The definite Guide to the New Social Standard*, London, UK et al.: FT Prentice Hall.

Leipziger, D. (2003), *The Corporate Responsibility Code Book*, Sheffield, UK: Greenleaf.

Lozano, J. F. (2001), 'Proposal for a model for the elaboration of ethical codes based on discourse ethics', *Business Ethics: A European Review*, **10** (2), 157-162.

Mamic, I. (2005), 'Managing global supply chains– The sports footwear, apparel, and retail sectors', *Journal of Business Ethics*, **59** (1), 81-100.

McKendall, M., B. DeMarr and C. Jones-Rikkers (2002), 'Ethical compliance programs and corporate illegality: Testing the assumptions of the corporate sentencing guidelines', *Journal of Business Ethics*, **37** (4), 367- 384.

McIntosh, M., R. Thomas, D. Leipziger and G. Coleman (2003), *Living Corporate Citizenship – Strategic Routes to Socially Responsible Business*, London, UK: FT Prentice Hall.

Mitchell, R.K., B. R. Agle and D. J. Wood (1997), 'Toward a theory of stakeholder identification and salience: Defining the principles of who and what really counts', *Academy of Management Review*, **22** (4), 853-886.

Nadvi, K. and F. Wältring (2001), 'Making sense of global standards', joint discussion paper of the Institute for Development Studies at the University of Sussex (UK) and the Institute for Development and Peace at the University of Duisburg (Germany), Duisburg.

Owen, D. L. and T. A. Swift (2001), 'Social accounting, reporting and auditing: Beyond the rhetoric?', *Business Ethics: A European Review*, **10** (1), 4-8.

Paine, L. S. (1994), 'Managing for organizational integrity', *Harvard Business Review*, **72** (2), 106-117.

Pekel, K. (2002), 'The need for improvement – Integrity, ethics, and the CIA., http://bss.sfsu.edu/fischer/ IR%20360/Readings/Ethics.htm, Accessed 8th July, 2002.

Phillips, R. (2003), *Stakeholder Theory and Organizational Ethics*, San Francisco, US: Berrett-Koehler.

Rasche, A. and D. E. Esser (2006), 'From stakeholder management to stakeholder accountability – Applying Habermasian discourse ethics to accountability research', *Journal of Business Ethics*, **65** (3), 251-267.

Robbins, J. M. (2002), 'Integrity', *Mortgage Banking*, **62** (7), 17-18.

SAI – Social Accountability International (2001), *Social Accountability 8000 Guidance Document*, New York, US: SAI.

Senge, P. M. (1990), *The Fifth Discipline – The Art and Practice of the Learning Organization*, London, UK et al.: Random House.

Smith, D. (2002), *Demonstrating Corporate Values – Which Standard for Your Company?*, London, UK: Institute of Business Ethics.

Steinmann, H. and T. Olbrich (1998), 'Business Ethics in U.S.- Corporations – Results from an interview series', P. Ulrich and J. Wieland (eds), *Unternehmensethik in der Praxis – Impulse aus den USA, Deutschland und der Schweiz*, Bern, Switzerland/Stuttgart, Germany/Wien, Austria: Haupt, pp. 63-89.

Thaler-Carter, R. E. (1999), 'Social Accountability 8000 - A social guide for companies or another layer of bureaucracy', *Human Resource Magazine*, **44** (6), 106-111.

Trevino, L. K. and K. A. Nelson (1999), *Managing Business Ethics – Straight Talk About How to Do it Right*, (2nd edition), New York, US: John Wiley.

Trevino, L. K., G. R. Weaver, D. G. Gibson and L. B. Toffler (1999), 'Managing ethics and legal compliance – What works and what hurts', *California Management Review*, **41** (2), 131-151.

Ulrich, P. (1998), 'Integrative economic ethics – Towards a conception of socio-economic rationality', *Berichte des Instituts für Wirtschaftsethik der Universität St. Gallen*, **82**, St. Gallen.

Ulrich, P., Y. Lunau and T. Weber (1998), 'Ethikmassnahmen in der Unternehmenspraxis - Zum Stand der Wahrnehmung und Institutionalisierung von Unternehmensethik in deutschen und schweizerischen Firmen: Ergebnisse einer Befragung', in P. Ulrich and J. Wieland (eds), *Unternehmensethik in der Praxis – Impulse aus den USA*, Deutschland und der Schweiz, Bern/Stuttgart/Wien: Haupt, pp. 121-193.

Williams, O. F. (2004), 'The UN global compact – The challenge and the promise', *Business Ethics Quarterly*, **14** (4), 755-774.

8. Meeting Responsibilities 'On the Stage' and Claiming Rights 'Behind the Scenes': The Re-Casting of Companies[*]

Sue Llewellyn

INTRODUCTION

The debate on the ethical behaviour of companies has been driven by the corporate social responsibility agenda. This chapter contends that behind the corporate social responsibility 'stage' there is something else going on. While this 'something else' is not yet fully visible, but when pressed 'behind the scenes', companies are claiming (or being granted) additional rights in relation to their new social responsibilities – they are being 're-cast'. The purpose of this chapter is to raise awareness of this re-casting through exploring the interrelationships between what's 'on the stage' and what's 'behind the scenes': corporate responsibilities and corporate rights. We see responsibilities and rights as mutually intertwined (Hohfeld, 1923; Kramer, 1998; Edwards, 2000). The corporate social responsibility movement has argued for 're-casting' – in the sense of pressing responsibilities upon companies whenever rights are impugned. But the other side of the coin is that rights are implied where responsibilities are asserted. Therefore, there is a *prima facie* case for assuming that companies will respond to a 're-casting requirement' to 'be more responsible' by claiming additional rights.

Discourses on responsibilities and rights used only to make reference to governments and individuals – not companies. Business was dissociated from non-business; companies were accountable only for economic performance.

*The author is grateful for the helpful comments of Markus Milne, Reg Matthews, Matthew Haigh, John Hasseldine and Bob Berry in developing this work

The work of Habermas (1976, 1987) has been influential in structuring our understanding of this dissociation between non-business and business or, in Habermasian terms, between the 'lifeworld' and the 'systemworld'. Morality and ethics were embedded in peoples' 'lifeworld' and were not expected to be much in evidence in the 'systemworld' of big business, where money and power drove peoples' behaviour. Only democratically elected governments and expert individuals were held to be sufficiently responsible to have a mandate to address the ethical complexities of profound social and political problems. Consequently, only they had the rights that enabled them to make discretionary decisions over these issues. The expectation was that governments would use their rights to regulate the systemworld of business. But as the power and 'reach' of companies increased exponentially throughout the 20th century, globalization cast nation states in a parlous position vis-à-vis control over companies' activities. Browne (2001) argues that the very idea of state sovereignty now has an 'antique ring'. Monbiot (2000) asserts that the state is now 'captive' to the power of corporations.

As corporations pursued profits, activist groups, particularly in the West, became prominent in publicizing the wider impact of their conduct. They exposed human rights violations and adverse impacts on the natural environment. Activists and NGOs have also drawn public attention to the powerlessness of governments to curtail the undesirable downside of companies' legal profit making. Indeed, as Higgins (2003) points out, exploitation of human rights and environmental abuses are especially prevalent where governments are acting in concert with multinationals, as in the case of inward investment in countries where governments are reliant on foreign investment to exploit their countries' natural resources. Consequently, even where activist groups seek to amend a country's laws in attempts to strengthen regulatory frameworks, they may now target corporations rather than governments (Spar and La Mure, 2003). Impressed by this activist-inspired agenda, the public began to worry more about the impact of companies. People now want companies to become more than merely legally and economically accountable; they want firms to be guided by ethical principles and to behave morally. In short, we wish companies to become responsible – to be accountable for more than their traditional obligations to make profits, pay taxes, create jobs and obey laws – we want corporations to become actively responsible moral agents[1]. But if we re-cast companies in this way, are we assigning to them new roles without fully anticipating their likely responses? Specifically, if companies take on the burden of greater responsibilities will they demand more rights?

This chapter reflects on some of the consequences of our new responsibility/rights agenda for companies through exploring the equation between responsibilities and rights both analytically and empirically in the context of three case studies: first, Nike and the rights to free speech; second, the granting to companies of property rights vis-à-vis carbon commerce; and third, the right that companies are pressing under the North America Free Trade agreement (NAFTA) to sue governments over laws that harm them financially.

Before looking at these cases in detail, this chapter sets a context by exploring on contemporary view of companies and, then draws on this perspective to connect with the agenda set by the corporate social responsibility movement.

THE POWER, INFLUENCE AND CHARACTER OF COMPANIES

We depend on organizations (governmental, non-governmental and private sector) to achieve human purposes (Lindkvist and Llewellyn, 2003). The conclusion that private sector companies are the most powerful and influential of all our organizations now seems inescapable. This assumption permeates literature aimed at the 'educated layperson'. Three examples illustrate this. First, in *The Company: A Short History of a Revolutionary Idea*, Micklethwaite and Wooldridge (2003, p.2) claim that companies are now the foundational 'building blocks' of society:

> Hegel predicted that the basic unit of modern society would be the state, Marx that it would be the commune, Lenin and Hitler that it would be the political party. Before that, a succession of saints and sages claimed the same for the parish church, the feudal manor, and the monarchy. The big contention of this small book is that they have all been proved wrong. The most important organization in the world is the company.

Second, Klein (2000, pp. 339-340), in *No Logo*, comments on the power of companies:

> Corporations... are much more than purveyors of the products we all want; they are also the most powerful political forces of our time. By now we have all heard the statistics: how corporations like Shell and Wal-Mart bask in budgets bigger than the gross domestic product of most nations; how, of the top hundred economies, fifty-one are multinationals and only forty-nine are countries .... corporations have become the ruling bodies of our era, setting the agenda of

globalization. We must confront them, in other words, because that it where the power is.

Third, in *The Corporation*, Bakan (2004, p. 5) contends: 'Today, corporations govern our lives. They determine what we eat, what we watch, where we work, and what we do. We are inescapably surrounded by their culture, iconography and ideology.'

These comments portray high-profile corporations as more than mere profit-making machines, however powerful – they speak of companies as institutions. An institution is an organization that subscribes to central values and has socially integrating myths – it is an organization, which has acquired a character (Parker, 2000, p. 43). Of all institutions, the character of corporations is arguably, now, the strongest influence on contemporary culture – as well as determining economic welfare and setting the political context within which states operate.

Consequent upon this influence, we fear our dependence on companies and we worry about their power. We believe that their constitution determines their character and that this character is driven by the 'steering' mechanisms of money and power (see Habermas, 1976, 1987). In their pursuit of money and power, Bakan (2004, p. 56-57) argues that companies are inherently irresponsible, manipulative, grandiose, a-social, superficial and lacking in either remorse or empathy; in short, he sums up the character of companies as 'psychopathic'. Moreover, we cannot inhibit psychopathic companies by controlling the individuals who own (or run) them. Habermas' work indicates that companies are not just an aggregate of individuals – corporations have a 'life of their own'. Hence, we cannot begin to change companies by focussing only on the behaviour of the individuals within them, Mander (1991, p.121) captures this:

> With corporations....the basic problems are actually structural. They are problems inherent in the forms and rules by which these entities are compelled to operate.... If someone attempted to revolt against these tenets, it would only result in the corporation throwing the person out, and replacing that person with another who would act according to the rules.

The activities of 'psychopathic' corporations are seen as driving our current problems. The impact of the profit-seeking agendas of companies on water, air and ecosystems raise environmental concerns over the sustainability of natural resources in the face of business practices. The financial orientation of companies prompts them to shift capital across national borders in search of lower labour costs; this chase is frequently seen as intensifying exploitative labour practices in developing countries. The economic rationales of companies justify the marketing of unhealthy 'fast food', unnecessary 'lifestyle' accessories and over-priced 'luxury' goods – promoting a global consumerist orientation that can erode local cultures. Generally, we are concerned that private sector companies do not care about anything but the economic 'bottom line'.

ACCOUNTABILITY, RESPONSIBILITY AND CORPORATE PERSONHOOD

If governments now lack the power to regulate fully companies and it is not possible to control corporations through influencing the individuals who own (or run) them, how can we begin to curtail the negative impacts of companies and turn them away from an exclusive focus on the economic bottom line? The corporate social responsibility movement seeks an answer in the 're-casting' of corporations. Companies are to be 're-cast' so that they not only cease to be a major cause for concern in themselves but they become better equipped to address global issues. How can this re-casting be accomplished? In probing for answers to this question, the accounting and management literature has turned to the concepts of accountability and responsibility.

Several authors have argued for new understandings of the accountability of companies; instead of a narrow and closed 'for profit to shareholders' point of reference; corporate accountability should be for more things to more people (Gray et al., 1997, 1987; Roberts, 1991; Milne, 1996). Corporate accountability should be extended from the purely economic to encompass the social and environmental impact of companies' activities. 'Externalities', should become 'corporate responsibilities'. Matters that had been viewed as the unfortunate, but as the unavoidable (at least in the short term) results of economic growth should become unacceptable. Companies should also have to account to a wider audience than their shareholders: their affairs should become more publicly transparent. The global nature of multinational corporations necessitates consideration of the impact of their activities across national boundaries and the principle of sustainable development looks to the future as well as the past. Hence, these calls for an increase in the scope of accountability also, frequently, imply a 'dual extension in space and time' (Pérez, 2003, p. 80). The responsibilities of companies and the risks associated with their conduct are now seen to be timeless global ones (Bauman, 1998, 2000; Beck, 1992, 1999, 2004). In addition, public pressure for governmental intervention in to the activities of companies has, to a greater extent, given way to the feeling that these are issues that companies themselves can, and should, address. Indeed, much activism seems to be driven by the idea that complex social and political problems can only be solved if the modus operandi of corporations changes because, as Klein (2000) argued, that is now 'where the power is'.

But, a shift from a narrow financial-legal accountability to a wider social responsibility has some significant implications for companies and societies because our understandings of the implications of 'accountability' and 'responsibility' differ. For example, Bovens (1998, p. 27) designates responsibility as an *active* form of accountability where there is a positive engagement with the world, where an agent acts to prevent unwanted consequences and where there is decision-making on the question of 'What is to be done?' In contrast, accountability, in Bovens' view, is a *passive* obligation to an external party that is limited to a post-hoc defence of actions taken; the question addressed is, 'Why did you do it?' In distinguishing responsibility from accountability, Lindkvist and Llewellyn (2003, p. 252-253) comment that the concept of the responsible agent connotes an inner morality, the consideration of the good or bad impacts of action and the exercise of discretion.

Sometimes the debate on the moral agency of companies extends to the idea of corporate personhood. Assertions that companies should be more morally responsible are thought to be more compelling if, in key respects, they are held to be equivalent to persons. So advocates of more corporate social responsibility sometimes argue their case on the basis of corporate personhood; four such advocates are considered here. First, Shearer (2002) calls for a refocusing of the traditional object of accountability; a company should not only be accountable for-itself but also to-the-other, she comments that the discourses (around subjectivity and intersubjectivity) that ground personal accountability to-the-other also locate corporate accountability to-the-other, thus she concludes that there is an equivalence between the two. Second, Schweiker (1993) argues that the accounts that economic entities offer of themselves are sufficiently similar to those of an individual to allow the conclusion that economic entities have moral agency. Third, Graham (2001, p. 22) considers that a collective entity (such as a company) is a part of a moral universe either by virtue of what it does (its agency) or through what happens to it (its participation in the world of events). He is primarily concerned with the latter, and addresses the ways in which collectivities acquire moral agency through being engaged in activities. Fourth, Bovens (1998, pp. 54-57) distinguishes three positions in philosophical arguments on corporate personhood: for, 'against' and 'in-between'. French (1979, 1984) is cited as an example of the 'for' position; he argues that companies do indeed have 'moral personhood'; his criterion for this categorization is that corporations act with intent. Bovens cites Ladd (1970) as the prime exponent of the 'against' camp. Ladd considers that it is logically wrong for companies to be seen as persons, arguing that companies do not (indeed, should not) possess moral agency, as their objectives are purely rational and economic. However, Bovens notes that several writers are somewhere 'in-between' these two extremes; they argue that some, but not all, moral categories are appropriate to organizations (see Donaldson, 1982; DeGeorge, 1983; Flores and Johnson, 1983; Thompson, 1987; Fisse and Braithwaite, 1993; and Wells, 1993). Bovens (1998, p. 57) counts himself amongst these 'in-between' authors, he believes both that responsibility is a moral category applicable to companies and that an organization does not have complete moral personhood, so he concludes that companies have moral personhood with regard to their responsibilities.

Aside from business ethics, the debate on the corporation as a person has been conducted mainly within the disciplinary boundaries of law. The law in most countries introduced charters of incorporation to create organizations as 'corporate bodies'; this status implies that if companies act illegally they can be called to account in the same way as persons (Wells, 1993, for a discussion of Anglo-American law on incorporation). On the other hand, there have been moves to abolish the notion of 'corporate personhood' for companies from the law. Kelly (2001, pp. 166-167) describes how in the US both Mayer, in a *Hastings Law Journal* article, and Ralph Estes, head of the activist group Stakeholder Alliance, have drafted amendments to deny that corporations can ever be considered as persons. But, although challenged, the current position at law remains that companies can be considered as persons.

In sum, if we now expect companies to be socially responsible (rather than merely financially and legally accountable) the literature on the topic points to them as possessing an inner morality. The corollary of this literature is to expect companies to consider the good and bad consequences of their decisions and to rely on their judgement and discretion over the question of 'what is to be done?' These expectations point to a debate on the rights of companies in relation to these increased responsibilities. Any presumption of corporate personhood confirms that such a discussion is necessary because people have rights; hence there is a strong case to consider the rights of corporate persons. But how can these expectations be squared with our view of companies as essentially a-moral or, even, psychopathic in character? The next section takes a closer look at rights as a theoretical issue and explores the past and present rights of companies.

THE RIGHTS OF COMPANIES

Historically, the rights of companies have been quite circumscribed: to carry out commercial and financial activities (and to own assets in respect of those activities); to enter into contracts; to employ (and dismiss) staff; and to go to court to seek redress. If the responsibilities of companies are increased why might one anticipate that their rights may increase in concert?

First, there are conceptual arguments. The mutual entailment between rights and responsibilities is recognized in philosophical discussions on ethics. One influential expression of this is Hohfeld's (1923) correlativity thesis. This has been interpreted recently to imply that a right is created through the imposition of a duty or responsibility (see the discussion in Kramer, 1998). For example, Edwards (2000) equates rights with responsibilities in his discussion of non-governmental organizations. He argues that only by demonstrating that they are willing to act responsibly can NGOs convince their critics that they are deserving of the right to intervene on behalf of others.

Second, there are pragmatic issues over costs. Where duties are imposed, these responsibilities tend to both restrict activities and entail costs (Steiner, 1994, p. 55). Assuming greater responsibilities will place a financial burden on companies; it may be expected, therefore, that they will claim rights in relation to these responsibilities – in so far as additional rights allow them to either lower their costs or increase their revenues.

Third, there are the consequences of meeting 'corporate responsibilities'. These consequences may, in themselves, push companies into assuming rights as they exercise judgement and discretion in complex political situations. Litvin (2003, p.xiii) draws attention to this problem:

> there may be inherent limits to the capacity of large multinationals to manage social and political issues in developing countries effectively, a problem that applies as much to their explicit attempts to behave ethically (as with the current fashion for 'corporate social responsibility') as to their efforts to protect their assets from local political attack. For the social situations they face on the ground are often too complex involving as they do ingrained suspicions of foreign firms, unavoidable ethical and political dilemmas, and ever shifting local power structures.

Tackling these complexities may actually be beyond the competences of the companies facing them. However if they do try to resolve such ethical dilemmas, companies may be propelled into making difficult political judgements, which we have tended to think of as the rightful preserve of expert natural persons or elected national governments. We may find that companies have to assume the right to make complex political judgments to fulfil the 'corporate social responsibilities' that we have thrust upon them.

Where companies have claimed additional rights they have often invoked 'corporate personhood'. For example, in the US, companies have claimed rights under the Fourteenth Amendment, which prohibits states from appropriating property without due process, under the Fifth Amendment double jeopardy clause, under Fourth Amendment protection against search and seizure and under the First Amendment to invalidate the banning of advertising by tobacco companies (Kelly, 2001, p. 163-164).

If companies continue to press for greater 'personhood' rights, in relation to their responsibilities, what may this imply? The rights of persons, as proclaimed in the Universal Declaration of Human Rights 1948 (see, www.unhchr.ch), are set out under 30 articles and include rights to: life, liberty and security; freedom of movement; property ownership; legal redress; asylum; freedom of thought, conscience and religion; freedom of opinion and expression; work; a standard of living adequate to health and well-being; education; cultural pursuits; and freedom from slavery, torture and inhuman or degrading treatment or punishment. The Declaration ends by relating these rights to responsibilities through locating an individual with rights within a community towards which s/he has duties.

As companies do not have physical bodies, many of the rights accorded to persons do not apply (clauses on rights to a decent standard of living and freedom from torture, for example). Without a body, a company has no natural life span; potentially, it could live forever, physicality does not present any limits to its existence. There is, however, a constraint on the survival of any company its profitability. We allow private sector companies to 'die' if they don't achieve the bottom line.

Of the human rights listed above, three apply to companies and are relevant to their profitability: freedom of movement; property ownership; and freedom of expression. Globalization has been driven, in part, by the increasing freedom of movement of capital. Free trade policies enable the free movement of companies, allowing them to pursue global strategies. If a company has a global strategy, it treats the world as one big market. Expansion into new markets increases opportunities for cost savings due to economies of scale; it also allows for greater market share, which will augment revenues. An extension of the property rights of companies opens up trading in new areas; domains that had previously been untouchable, so far as markets are concerned, can become commodified. New types of goods or services to trade create additional opportunities for commercial exploitation and profit making. Freedom of expression would allow companies to say what they like in terms of promoting their products and defending their reputation. This freedom would enable companies to protect their brands and enhance their revenues. The next section looks at three empirical cases where these rights have been either claimed or granted: first, Nike claims the right to free speech; second, new property rights to trade in atmospheric pollution emissions are granted to companies; and, third, a free trade agreement confers the right to sue national governments where national law impacts negatively on companies' profitability.

CASE ONE: SHOULD NIKE HAVE THE RIGHT TO FREE SPEECH?

Background

By the late 1990s Nike had been heavily criticized by many NGOs for running sweatshop factories across Asia. The allegations were that Nike continually shifted production to locations where wage rates were lowest. In such factories, sexual and racial abuse were often tolerated as a routine part of the normal working practices. These allegations were widely published in the media and on the internet; Nike's dominant brand position ('Just Do It') facilitated a high profile activist campaign focussed on a 'Just Stop It' rallying call (see www. NikeWatch.org). Nike responded by issuing rebuttals that asserted, amongst other things, that 'the company paid, on average, double the minimum wages as defined in countries where its products are produced and that its workers are protected from physical and sexual abuse' (April 7, 2003, www.corpwatch.org/bulletins). In 1998 such statements prompted the activist Marc Kasky to sue Nike, under a Californian state law that prohibited 'false advertising'. Kasky argued that Nike knew that its rebuttal statements were untrue.

Nike's Right to Free Speech

The Californian court's ruling in the *Kasky v. Nike* case hinged on the distinction between 'commercial speech' (that could be accused of constituting 'false advertising) and 'political speech'. Nike argued that its statements should be considered as 'non-commercial speech' or 'political speech' as they encompass matters of public concern. In effect, Nike was defining 'political speech' to include any company pronouncements that touched on social issues such as working conditions. Commentators pointed out the ramifications of Nike's broad ranging definition of 'political speech'. For example Adam Kanzer, Director of Shareholder Advocacy for Domini

Social Investments, said, 'Nike's definition of political speech – any commercial speech that also touches upon matters of public concern – is alarmingly broad, potentially affecting nearly every aspect of a corporation's business from treatment of stock options to compliance with environmental regulations' (April 7, 2003, www.corpwatch.org/bulletins).

The Californian State Court found that Nike's statements could be protected as non-commercial speech. However, the Californian Supreme Court ruled against this; they judged that Nike's statements were 'Commercial speech for the purposes of applying state laws barring false and misleading commercial messages'. Nike appealed to the US Supreme Court. However, the US Supreme Court, after hearing oral arguments, failed to take on the complex constitutional issues involved. In June 2003 they dismissed the case and referred it back to the Californian Supreme Court. In September 2003 the parties to *Kasby v. Nike* settled out of court. Nike agreed to make a payment of $1.5 million to a Fair Labor Association.

Nike was looking for its statements in the Kasky case to be considered as 'political speech' because proclamations under this rubric enjoy the protection of the US First Amendment, guaranteeing free speech to all US citizens. Therefore, underlying Nike's assertions about 'political speech' was a fundamental claim that Nike could be considered a person.

The question of Nike's new role as a corporate person generated strong emotions and several commentators voiced regret that the US Supreme Court had failed to rule on this 're-casting' (see September 12, 2003, www.sanjose.bizjournals.com). The Northern California American Civil Liberties Union filed an amicus brief supporting Nike. They stated, 'The purpose of our brief was to assure that the question of the truthfulness of Nike's assertions was judged by the same set of rules that would apply were someone to question the truthfulness of the assertions of its critics' (June 11, 2003, www.corpwatch.org/bulletins). In contrast, ReclaimDemocracy.org was opposed passionately to any proposal that resulted in the equating of Nike with a person. They argued 'the notion that corporations entities unmentioned in our constitution should enjoy protections created for living human beings is a concept deserving burial deep in the same dark closet as the legal precedents of slavery and "separate but equal"' (June 11, 2003, www.corpwatch.org/bulletins). The National Voting Rights Institute joined with ReclaimDemocracy.org in a further statement, which clearly linked Nike as a re-cast corporate person with corporate rights. They commented:

> The claim that corporations possess a right to intentionally deceive the public has no basis in the US constitution. Incorporation is a privilege granted by the people's representatives in state governments, and corporations must remain subordinate to our democratic institutions. The discredited judicial creations of 'corporate

personhood' and corporate 'political rights' should be unequivocally rejected by the court' (June 11, 2003, www.corpwatch.org/bulletins).

The question of Nike's corporate personhood is a matter of some political complexity. The idea that Nike's statements should always be viewed as 'commercial speech' does not necessarily advance the cause of Nike's critics. One downside, from Nike's critics' point of view, is that a ruling that all debate with activists comes under the remit of 'commercial speech' is likely to be used by companies as an excuse not to engage in public exchanges. Companies will argue that their position is unfair as their statements are subject to more stringent rules on 'truthfulness' than those of their critics.

Re-Casting Nike as a Corporate Person...?

In the corporate social responsibility movement wanted to recast Nike by trying to force it to be a 'more responsible corporate entity'. Nike responded to this proposed recasting by demanding an even bigger and more powerful role, that of a 'corporate person' with the corresponding right to free speech.

CASE 2: SHOULD COMPANIES HAVE PROPERTY RIGHTS THAT ALLOW THEM TO ENGAGE IN 'CARBON COMMERCE'?

Background

Global warming has been declared to be the world's biggest problem; Sir David King (chief scientific advisor to the UK government) stated, 'Climate change is a far greater threat to the world than international terrorism' (see news.bbc.co.uk, 9 January 2004, Global Warming 'Biggest Threat'). Greenhouse gases (principally, CO_2) prevent energy escaping from the earth's surface and atmosphere; it is argued that the effects of CO_2 emissions are causing climate change. The consequences of these climate changes precipitate effects such as flooding, risk to human life and damage to property. The Earth Institute warns, 'Risk analysis reports over half of the World's population exposed to one or more major natural hazards' (www.earthinstitute.columbia.edu/library/videos.htm).

International agreements, such as the 1997 Kyoto Treaty, have been mooted to mobilize all nation states to commit to reducing greenhouse gas emissions. The Kyoto Protocol (see, www.kyotoprotocol.com) requires all

industrialized nations to reduce greenhouse gases to around 5.2 per cent below their 1990 levels over the next decade. Initial discussions decided that to come into force the Protocol must to be ratified by at least 55 countries and participating countries must be responsible for at least 55 per cent of the world's carbon emissions. After Russia ratified, these conditions were finally reached, some eight years after the Treaty was put together. The Kyoto Protocol entered into force on February 16 2005 (see, www.en.wikipedia.org/wiki/Kyoto_protocol). The US. is the world's biggest emitter of greenhouse gases, both in absolute terms and per head; it was responsible for 36 per cent of emissions in 1997 – this has now risen another 19 per cent (see, www.bbc.co.uk, Climate Change: The Big Emitters, 4 July, 2005). America is a signatory to the Treaty but this signature remains symbolic, as the US has failed to ratify. George W. Bush justified, 'America's unwillingness to embrace a flawed treaty' on the grounds of the potential harm to the US economy, some scepticism about the scientific grounds for alleged CO_2 impact on climate change and objections to some of the present country exemptions
(www.en.wikipedia.org/wiki/Kyoto_protocol#Position_of_the_UnitedStates).

Property Rights to the Atmosphere through 'Carbon Commerce'?

Companies are big polluters. *The Guardian* (16 May, 2006) reported:

> Five companies in Britain produce more carbon dioxide pollution together than all the motorists in UK roads combined … a league table … identifies EON UK, the electricity generator that owns Powergen, as Britain's biggest corporate emitter of greenhouse gasses. It produced 26.4m tonnes of carbon dioxide last year-slightly more than Croatia did.

To incentivize companies to work towards reductions in greenhouse gas emissions, they are allowed to trade in rights to pollute the environment (see, www.bbc.co.uk, 'EU agrees pollution market', 9 December 2002). The environmental lobby are concerned by the idea of property rights to the atmosphere, they asserted 'Greenhouse gasses can now be traded online by companies … who want to buy their way out of trouble without cleaning up their act' (www.bbc.co.uk, 'Pollution trading goes online', 20 November 2000).

In the pollution market companies will be able to buy and sell emission rights within the fifteen nation EU bloc, in which, six industries are involved: energy; steel; cement; glass; brick making; and paper and cardboard. Any company that anticipates exceeding its pollution target will be able to buy emission rights from any other company that looks as if it will come in under its allowance. Margaret Beckett, UK Secretary for Environment, Food and Rural Affairs, defended the pollution market in the following terms, 'The allocation of emission allowances has been set at a challenging but achievable level, which will encourage industry to invest in emission abatement and take advantage of the opportunities that trading has to offer' (www.bbc.co.uk, 'Emission cuts to lift energy bill', 19 January 2004).

In 2000, trading went online and CO2e.com was launched. CO2e.com describes itself as a 'global hub for carbon commerce' (www.CO2e.com) and describes its operations as follows 'CO2e incorporates both a marketplace and a full suite of online carbon commerce support including: a web-based broker assisted marketplace for the trading of emission reduction' (see, www.co2e.com/common/faq.asp?intPageElementID=30175&intCategoryID= 29). Buying and selling marketable or tradable rights to pollute is expected to become one of the world's fastest growing commodity markets. A spokeman for PricewaterhouseCoopers, who have assisted in developing eCO2.com, attempted to alleviate the concerns of environmentalists over the pollution market by insisting that, 'CO2e.com will not just be an online marketplace, but also an information resource educating companies about their environmental responsibilities' (www.bbc.co.uk, 'Pollution trading goes online', 20 November 2000).

Several commentators warned that companies saw 'Kyoto' more as a trading opportunity than an environmental agreement (see, www.bbc.co.uk, 'Kyoto treaty in the balance', 29 September, 2003). This early warning seems to have been borne out, as by 16 May 2006 *The Guardian* had reported, 'companies failing to hit a [emissions] target ... must buy permits to pollute from rivals that have successfully cut emissions. Critics said the first phase of the trading scheme has made global warming worse by giving European companies more permits than needed.'

Re-Casting Companies Through Granting Them Trading Rights in New Domains

As argued earlier, traditionally the rights of companies have been quite circumscribed as befitting their limited responsibilities. When governments ask companies to take on additional responsibilities, they re-cast them by granting them new rights, and in this case, trading rights in a previously 'sacrosanct' area, the atmosphere.

CASE 3: SHOULD COMPANIES HAVE THE RIGHT TO SUE UNDER FREE TRADE AGREEMENTS OVER NATIONAL LAWS THAT HARM THEM FINANCIALLY?

Background

The Cato Institute in the US poses the case for free trade in terms of 'human liberties'; its website states, 'The case for free trade goes beyond economic efficiency. The freedom to trade is a basic human liberty, and its exercise across political borders unites people in peaceful cooperation and mutual prosperity' (www.freetrade.org/about.html). One manifestation of the freedom to trade is the existence of world trade blocs. In 1994 the North America Free Trade Association (NAFTA) was implemented; uniting US, Canada and Mexico in the world's largest free trade zone, it created a market of 400 million people with $6.5 trillion worth of goods and services traded annually (www.news.bbc.co.uk/1/hi/business/1250181.stm). In 2001 President George W. Bush sought to expand this agreement under *Fast Track*[2] to include 31 more Latin American countries by 2005 under the Free Trade Area of the Americas (FTAA). This proposed extension served to highlight further a previously little known section of NAFTA that was becoming controversial, although it has not yet been implemented (www.freerepublic.com/focus/news/703456/posts).

Companies' Rights to Sue Under 'Chapter 11'

Organizations such as *Corpwatch* had been publicizing a particular provision in NAFTA: Chapter 11 (www.corpwatch.org). This section of the free trade agreement had been set up to protect investors if foreign governments attempted to seize their assets; essentially, Chapter 11 was targeted at Mexico, which had nationalized its foreign oil refineries in 1938 (www.are.berkeley.edu/courses/EEP131/Nafta_Chapter11.pdf).   Moyers (2002) has produced an exposé on Chapter 11, in which he states:

> One provision was too obscure to stir up controversy. It was called Chapter Eleven, and was supposedly written to protect investors from having their property seized by foreign governments. But since NAFTA was ratified, corporations have used Chapter Eleven to challenge the powers of government to protect its citizens, to undermine environmental and health laws, even to attack our system of justice.' (http://www.corpwatch.org/article.php?id=1372).

Critics of Chapter 11 argued that this provision was giving companies' rights to sue governments if national laws adversely impacted on their profitability. Public Citizen (2004) declared, 'NAFTA allows corporations to sue the national government of a NAFTA country in secret arbitration tribunals if they feel that a regulation or government decision affects their investment in conflict with these new NAFTA rights. If the corporation wins, the taxpayers of the 'losing' NAFTA nation must foot the bill' (www.citizen.org/trade/nafta/CH_11/). Any lawsuit under Chapter 11 is termed an 'investor-to-state' case and is litigated by a three person arbitration panel established by a special body formed by the World Bank and the United Nations; hearings are closed to the public. At least twelve lawsuits have been filed by companies under Chapter 11; and seven of these have arisen with respect to environmental laws (www.ems.org/chapter11/sub2_chapter11.html). Methanex, a Canadian Company, brought one such case.

The Rights of Methanex to Challenge US Environmental Law

Methanex is the world's biggest producer of an ingredient in methyl tertiary butyl ether (MTBE), an additive that, whilst reducing air pollution by causing gasoline to burn more cleanly, also causes cancer. In 1999 gasoline with MTBE was banned, under Californian law, after the pollution of lakes, public water systems and groundwater sites had been detected. Shortly after the ban had been introduced Methanex invoked Chapter 11 to demand either the lifting of the ban or $970 million in damages (see www.freepublic.com/focus/news/703456/posts). In August 2002 a NAFTA arbitration panel rejected all but one of the defences raised against Methanex's claim. The final issue required a 'fresh pleading' in November 2002. In August 2005, NAFTA ruled against Methanex (see, www.methanex.com/newsroom/mxnaftabackground.html).

Rights and Responsibilities in Relation to Free Trade

In this case, at first sight, it appears that companies are exploiting a loophole in NAFTA to obtain an extension in their rights without any corresponding increase in their responsibilities. However, the right to sue for damages across national boundaries is also being advocated by activist groups speaking on behalf of foreign communities. Foreign investors' right to sue when national law impacts negatively on their profits (Chapter 11) mirrors the Corporate Responsibilities Bill (sponsored by CORE[3]) that recognizes a 'foreign direct liability' for communities abroad to seek damages in the UK for human rights or environmental abuses by UK companies. The idea of 'foreign direct liability' is being mobilized by companies as an extension of their rights and by activist groups to push for an extension to the responsibilities of companies.

Re-casting Companies in Relation to Free Trade

The practice of free trade has always been a central motif in our ideas about the rights of companies but even 'free trade' has, traditionally, bowed to national law. The actions of groups like CORE are, albeit inadvertently, lending ammunition to companies to demand that they are re-cast in more powerful roles vis-à-vis free trade. If they are responsible for a direct foreign liability with respect to communities abroad this strengthens their case for rights to 'compensation' when foreign national law impacts on their profitability.

DISCUSSION: CORPORATE RESPONSIBILITIES AND CORPORATE RIGHTS

This chapter has argued that while the discourse on corporate responsibility continues, there has been another movement, not fully articulated, but pressed 'behind the scenes' – companies are claiming (or being granted) additional rights in respect of these responsibilities. The purpose of this chapter has been to raise awareness of the interrelationships between these two domains: corporate responsibilities and corporate rights.

One touch-point for both responsibilities and rights is the idea of corporate personhood. The idea of the corporation as a person has been both promoted and reviled. The academic literature has promoted 'corporate personhood' as a construct that underpins arguments for the extension of corporate responsibility (see the earlier arguments of Schweiker, 1993; Bovens, 1998; and Shearer, 2002). But where companies have mobilised 'corporate personhood' to press their claims for additional rights, generally the notion has been vehemently rejected (Kelly, 2001 and see, also, the 'Nike' case above).

An examination of the three cases discussed above reveal various dimensions of the responsibility-rights equation. First, in the Nike case, pressures on the company to assume greater responsibility with respect to working conditions in its overseas factories resulted in the company claiming the right to free speech with respect to its pronouncements about those conditions. Second, in the push to make corporations more responsible in their policies on emissions of greenhouse gases, companies have been granted additional tradable rights – rights to trade in atmospheric pollution. Third, under the banner of free trade, companies have seized the right to sue national governments over regulations that impact negatively on their profits.

In the first two instances there are clear indications that a direct equation between responsibilities and rights is operating – either, as in the 'Nike' case rights are being claimed when responsibilities are pressed or, in the 'Kyoto' case, rights are being granted to secure compliance with greater responsibilities. The 'Chapter 11' case can be seen as an indirect example or as a general trend to equate the rights and responsibilities of companies in relation to foreign direct liability.

Can arguments for corporate responsibility be advanced without any corresponding extensions of the rights of companies? Activist campaigns frequently damage the reputation of companies; if corporations fear that their share price may drop, consequent upon adverse publicity, they may take on increased responsibilities without any corresponding claims for extra rights. Spar and La Mure (2003) argue that the risk of financial harm can cause firms to accede to the demands of activist groups over additional responsibilities and that three issues are key to an assessment of the threat posed: transaction costs, brand impact and competitive position. Crudely, where companies gauge that the reputation of a high profile brand is threatened, competitive position is undermined and the costs of capitulation are fairly low, they will accede to activist demands. Conversely, higher transaction costs – with respect to compliance with activist's demands – along with a profile that is less vulnerable to the reputational risks associated a high brand position, are likely to result in companies resisting the imposition of their 'corporate responsibilities'. This analysis leads to the conclusion that companies will respond differentially to the corporate social responsibility agenda (Spar and La Mure, 2003). For example, natural resource businesses with high capital costs but no well-known brand to protect may simply ignore activist pressures for change.

However, if shareholders all became more 'socially responsible' and 'shareholder activism' reigned then the differential response of companies to 'social responsibilities' would be evened out. Companies would be more equal in their responsiveness to the corporate social responsibility agenda. Such a situation would not mean that companies did not enter into cost-benefit calculations before deciding whether or not to accede to demands for increased responsibilities but it would imply that these calculations were not as decisive. So, in such a situation, companies may not look to claiming additional rights that either increased their revenues (or lowered their costs) to meet expenditures associated with the imposition of increased responsibilities. However, the scenario of across-the-board 'shareholder activism' does not look very probable in the near future. Also, in any case, we are likely to see companies seeking to extend their rights in order to make the complex political and social decisions inherent in 'corporate social responsibilities'. And if the essential character of companies is a-moral then one would anticipate that corporations would always seek to exploit any move to impose more responsibilities with claims for additional rights.

CONCLUDING COMMENTS

Many firms already hint that they should be considered as 'corporate persons' or 'citizens'. The Novartis Group Companies, for example, state that it, 'is committed to serving as a responsible corporate citizen' (see, www.us.novartis.com/corporate_citizenship/index.shtml). The case studies demonstrate that companies are now claiming (or being granted) some of the same rights as citizens (for example, free speech, additional property rights and greater freedom in relation to trade). The consequences of extending the rights of companies are profound, particularly where they are being expected to solve complex social and political problems – as this extension blurs the 'line' between the economic and political realms. Market democracies separate the economic and political spheres; this separation acts as a safeguard against the accretion of power (Keegan, 1992, p. 31). If companies assume more of a political role – through acquiring additional rights – this 'safeguard' starts to break down. One consequence of this breakdown is the re-casting of companies – as political agents – through being involved in social and political events. As argued earlier, companies, as collectivities, will have assumed the right to make political decisions through being 'responsibly' engaged in political events (Bovens, 1998; Graham, 2001). But this re-casting will result in the character of companies beginning to dominate both the economic and the political realms. The 'corporate social responsibility' movement – in assuming that the responsibilities of companies can be pressed 'on the CSR stage' without corporations seeking any corresponding extension in their rights 'behind the CSR scenes' – can be charged with a certain naivety.

NOTES

1. The activist publication 'What's wrong with McDonalds? – Everything they didn't want you to know' laid the following responsibilities at the door of McDonalds: starvation in the

developing world; destruction of rainforests; promotion of unhealthy food; targeting children with manipulative marketing; inhumane treatment and killing of animals; and exploitative working conditions for employees. London Greenpeace, who produced the leaflet, called for a change to the whole system of multinational corporations – a social revolution (see, www.mcspotlight.org.).

2. Fast Track is a term that designates a procedure under which Congress would delegate constitutional authority over international trade to the President for a period of six years.

3. CORE is a group of NGOs, charities, faith-based groups and trade unions that have combined to form the Corporate Responsibility Coalition (CORE). CORE is pressing for a common set of enforceable rules on corporate responsibility. Standards are being demanded in three areas: mandatory reporting against a set of social, environmental and economic performance indicators; a 'duty of care' for company directors for both society and the environment in addition to financial responsibilities to shareholders; and a recognition of 'foreign direct liability' to allow communities abroad to seek damages in the UK for human rights or environmental abuses by UK companies. On 30 January 2004 the Corporate Responsibility Bill relating to new company law to enact these rules was 'talked out' by the Minister of Trade and Industry
(see www.foe.co.uk/campaigns/corporates/core/about/bill.html). Now CORE is concentrating on influencing the forthcoming UK Company Law Reform Bill.

REFERENCES

Bakan, J. (2004), *The Corporation: The Pathological Pursuit of Profit and Power*, London, UK: Constable.

Bauman, Z. (1998), *Globalization: The Human Consequences*, New York, US: Columbia University Press.

Bauman, Z. (2000), *Liquid Modernity*, Cambridge, UK: Polity Press.

Beck, U. (1992), *The Risk Society: Towards a New Modernity*, London, UK: Sage.

Beck, U. (1999), *The World Risk Society*, Cambridge, UK: Polity Press.

Beck, U. (2004), *A Critical Introduction to the Risk Society*, UK: Pluto Press.

Bovens, M. (1998), *The Quest for Responsibility*, Cambridge, UK: Cambridge University Press.

Browne, J. (2001), 'Governance and Responsibility. The Relationship Between Companies and NGOs: A Progress Report', *Judge Institute*, 29 March 2001, www.ragm.com/archpub/ragm/032901judge_institute.html, January 2001.

DeGeorge, R. T. (1983), 'Can Corporations Have Moral Responsibility?', in T. I. Beauchamp and N. E. Bowie (eds), *Ethical Theory and Business*, London, UK: Prentice Hall, pp. 57-67.

Donaldson, T. (1982), *Corporations and Morality*, Englewood Cliffs, NJ, US: Prentice Hall.

Edwards, M (2000), *NGO Rights and Responsibilities: A New Deal for Global Governance*, London, UK: The Foreign Policy Centre.

Fisse, B. and J. Braithwaite (1993), *Corporations, Crime and Accountability*, Cambridge, UK: Cambridge University Press.

Flores, A. and D. G. Johnson (1983), 'Collective responsibility and professional roles', *Ethics*, **93**, 537-545.

French, P.A. (1979), 'The corporation as a moral person', *American Philosophical Review*, *16*, 207-215.

French, P. A. (1984), *Collective and Corporate Responsibility*, New York, US: Columbia University Press.

Graham, K. (2001), 'The moral significance of collective entities', *Inquiry*, **44**, 21-42.

Gray, R. H., D. L. Owen, and K. T. Maunders (1987), *Corporate Social Reporting: Accounting and Accountability*, Hemel Hempstead, UK: Prentice Hall.

Gray, R., C. Dey, D. Owen, R. Evans and S. Zadek (1997), 'Struggling with the praxis of social accounting: Stakeholders, accountability, audits and procedures', *Accounting, Auditing & Accountability Journal*, **10** (3), 325-364.

The Guardian (2006), 'New figures reveal scale of industry's impact on climate', 16th May.

Habermas, J. (1976), *Legitimation Crisis*, London, UK: Heinemann.

Habermas, J. (1987), *The Theory of Communicative Action: The Critique of Functionalist Reason: Vol 2*, Cambridge, UK: Polity Press.

Higgins, E. R. E. (2003), 'Global strategies – Contradictions and consequences', *Corporate Governance: International Journal of Business in Society*, **3** (3), 52-66.

Hohfeld, H. (1923), 'Some Fundamental Legal Conceptions as Applied in Judicial Reasoning', in W. Cook (eds), *Fundamental Legal Conceptions as Applied in Judicial Reasoning*, New Haven, US: Yale University Press, pp. 23-64.

Keegan, W. (1992), *The Spectre of Capitalism: The Future of the World Economy after the Fall of Communism*, London, UK: Radius.

Kelly, M. (2001), *The Divine Right of Capital*, San Francisco, US: Berrett-Koehler.

Klein, N. (2000), *No Logo*, London, UK: Flamingo.

Kramer, M. H. (1998), 'Rights Without Trimmings', in M. Kramer, N. E. Simmonds and H. Steiner (eds), *A Debate Over Rights*, Oxford, UK: Oxford University Press, pp. 7-111.

Ladd, J. (1970), 'Morality and the ideal of rationality in formal organizations', *The Monist*, **54**, 488-516.

Lindkvist, L. and S. Llewellyn (2003), 'Accountability, responsibility and organization', *Scandinavian Journal of Management*, **19** (2), 251-273.

Litvin, D. (2003), *Empires of Profit: Commerce, Conquest and Corporate Responsibility*, London, UK: Texere.

Mander, J. (1991), *In the Absence of the Sacred: The Failure of Technology & the Survival of the Indian Nations*, San Francisco, US: Sierra Club Books.

Micklethwaite, J. and A. Wooldridge (2003), *The Company: A Short History of a Revolutionary Idea*, London, UK: Weidenfeld & Nicolson.

Milne, M. J. (1996), 'On sustainability, the environment and management accounting', *Management Accounting Research*, **7** (1), 135-161.

Monbiot, G. (2000), *Captive State*, London, UK: Macmillan.

Moyers, B. (2002), 'Trading democracy', January, http://www.corpwatch.org/article.php?id=1372

Parker, M. (2000), *Organizational Culture and Identity*, London, UK: Sage.

Pérez, R. (2003), 'About "global responsibility" in management', *Corporate Governance: International Journal of Business in Society*, **3** (3), 78-89.

Roberts, J. (1991), 'The possibilities of accountability', *Accounting, Organizations and Society*, **16** (4), 355-370.

Schweiker, W. (1993), 'Accounting for ourselves: Accounting practice and the discourse of ethics', *Accounting, Organizations and Society*, **18** (2/3), 231-252.

Shearer, T. (2002), 'Ethics and accountability: From the for-itself to the for-the-other', *Accounting, Organizations and Society*, **27** (6), 541-574.

Spar, D. L. and L. T. La Mure (2003), 'The power of activism: Assessing the impact of NGOs on global business', *California Management Review*, **45** (3), 78-101.

Steiner, H. (1994), *An Essay on Rights,* London, UK: Blackwell.

Thompson, D. F. (1987), *Political Ethics and Public Office,* Cambridge, MA, US: Cambridge University Press.

Wells, C. (1993), *Corporations and Criminal Responsibilities*, Oxford, UK: Oxford University Press.

Major Websites

www.bbc.co.uk
www.CO2e.com
www.citizen.org/trade/nafta/CH_11/
www.essentialaction.org
www.kyotoprotocol.com
www.sanjose.bizjournals.com
www.unhchr.ch
www.us.novartis.com

PART THREE

PERFORMING ETHICS

9. Integrity: Talking the Walk Instead of Walking the Talk

Wim Vandekerckhove

1. INTRODUCTION

In today's discourse on organizations, integrity is a very popular concept. Integrity is present in many codes of conduct and mission statements. As Solomon points out:

> part of the demand for 'integrity' ... has to do ... with the expectation that [employees] will (on the basis of past experience and accumulated confidence) resist and perhaps straighten out structural distortions in the organization (Solomon, 1993, pp. 81-82).

The expectation is that people with integrity will resist opportunism. Another reason for the popularity of integrity has to do with its connotation of self-regulation. Paine (1994) distinguishes two kinds of strategies to implement organizational policies: compliance strategies and integrity strategies. The ethic of compliance strategies is to observe and obey rules and orders. These strategies are based on an anthropological model that describes humans as isolated creatures whose behavior is guided by material self-interest. Integrity strategies, on the other hand, imply an ethic of self-regulation based on chosen standards. Their anthropological model assumes that humans are social creatures, not guided merely by material self-interest, but also by values, ideals, friendship, and peers. Also, De George (1993) argues that integrity implies self-imposed norms. Because of these reasons integrity is a term that is accepted and used more easily by companies than is the term 'morality'. Morality bears the connotation of an external imposition of rigid norms about what is right and wrong, what is good and bad. Integrity, on the other hand, connotes with at least partly self-chosen and hence more flexible standards of behavior. Still, these norms must nevertheless be ethically justifiable, and they must be 'proper, and integral to the self-imposed process of forming a whole with a set of positive values' (De George, 1993, pp. 6-7). De George, just like Paine, describes the subject of integrity as autonomous, acting willingly, but also as acting according to certain values.

However, the concept of integrity – despite its frequent usage – remains somewhat unspecified. The question 'what does integrity mean?' very often gets answered with vague adages such as 'practice what you preach' or 'walk the talk'. Etymologically, integrity draws on the Latin *integritas* – wholeness, and *integer* – untouched, what has not taken a turn yet, still in abeyance. The latter adds to the concept of integrity the moral connotations of objectivity, impartiality, incorruptness in a modern sense of the word. The former meaning – wholeness – is opposed to an older meaning of corrupt as fragmented. Late capitalism has left us with fragmented identities, but this does not mean we regard ourselves as corrupt. But we do seem to be convinced that it takes people of integrity to fight corruption and people of integrity are regarded as being able to resist opportunism.

This chapter attempts to specify the concept of integrity by paying particular attention to the demands for flexibility that organizations nowadays face. More precisely, the question that guides this chapter is: What type of integrity can organizations, faced with the demand for flexibility, expect and demand from their employees and what organizational processes are needed to foster such an integrity? The chapter attempts to answer these questions by first taking a short look at how integrity relates to autonomy and values (section 2). It shows that defining integrity as the consistency of autonomous decision-making and values is unsatisfactory in an organizational context. There is a second kind of consistency that needs to be addressed, namely that between personal and social values. Section 3 gives some insight into one of the key concepts of today's organizational context that must be constitutive of the conceptualization of integrity, namely flexibility. In section 4, I examine four potential delineations of integrity as 'wholeness'. Each of those candidates is situated at a different level: the functional level, the temporal level, the spatial level, and the interactive level. The question driving the examination is to what extent a particular conceptualization of integrity adequately comprises both senses of consistency pointed out in section 2, and remains tenable in an organizational context that is characterized by flexibility. I argue that the delineation of integrity as 'wholeness' at the interpersonal level appears most fruitful in this regard. Section 5 examines to what extent this delineation aligns with a third way between the objectivist/subjectivist divide on integrity, as set forth in section 2. Finally section 6 concludes this chapter with a discussion of the organizational processes that are implicated by the consistent conceptualization of integrity.

2. INTEGRITY, AUTONOMY AND VALUES

Robert Meyers (1999) has studied quite extensively the relation between integrity, autonomy and values. Underlying Meyers' work is an ambiguity concerning the relation between values and individuals. On the one hand, individuals develop personal values through subsequent choices they make. On the other hand, because individuals are part of communities, communal or social values cannot be disregarded. Furthermore, an individual might recognize some values as values that others hold but to which she does not want to subscribe (for example values held by other communities). Meyers describes individual autonomy as the ideal of individual behavior. It is achieved to the extent that one's actions are governed by one's own choices. Personal integrity too is an ideal, requiring people to be true to 'all values that apply to them' (Meyers, 1999, p. 73). Meyers uses this phrasing to emphasize the possible disparity between those values developed as a result of past choices – which Meyers calls the relative values individuals happen to have – and the social values of one's community – values one did not chose. Personal integrity requires that persons pay allegiance in their actions both to relative values they happen to have and to whatever values 'should happen to be' (Meyers, 1999, p. 143). Meyers argues that individual autonomy cannot be seen independently from personal integrity. First of all, they are not independent, for governing your actions by your choices achieves little if those choices themselves are not true to your values. Second they should not be independent, because they allow people to develop individual autonomy – to govern their own actions by their own choices. It is personal integrity, which then requires them to take proper account of those choices. In other words, individual autonomy leads people to value things independently of their commitment to the overall good. Therefore, promoting the overall good implies an equal importance of both individual autonomy and personal integrity. In that sense, individual autonomy and personal integrity are correlative aspects of a more comprehensive ideal of individual behavior which Meyers calls 'self-governance'. A self-governed person is then:

> not someone who simply performs actions that will reflect her values and commitments as fully and accurately as the circumstances allow; she is someone who also tries to make the circumstances ones in which her values and commitments can be reflected as fully and accurately as possible (Meyers, 1999, p. 144).

Written law and unwritten conventions, to a large extent shaping the possibilities of action, will be of concern to such a person, but a self-governed person will also enter negotiations to set and live by rules from which each one of them would benefit.

Similarly Solomon contrasts a person with integrity in an organizational setting with 'the opportunist' and 'the chameleon' (Solomon, 1993, pp. 168-174). Neither of them is dishonest or hypocrite, nor do they involve inconsistency. The opportunist is true to himself, a self in hermitage, divided from any sense of community and in this sense the contrary of a self in the midst of others. The opportunist has no principles relating to the overall good but 'does whatever it takes'. Hence, the opportunist is an ethical hermit merely using others as his instruments. The chameleon's drive is to 'fit in and do whatever seems to please other people'. Solomon describes the organizational chameleon as 'the typical corporate "yes-man"'. The chameleon's values and actions are consistent with whatever values happen to be in vogue. However, within an organizational setting, this is a fragile consistency, as it depends on the uniformity of other people. Exactly this uniformity is tenuous in today's organization, characterized by the perceptions of flexibility, decentralization, uncertainty and hence contradictory demands and principles. Thus, the opportunist lacks integrity because he is true to a self that is cut loose from its social situation. And the chameleon lacks integrity because he lacks an independent voice that goes beyond the mere adoption of the prevailing social values.

Both Meyers and Solomon insist on a definition of integrity as 'true to self' that is part of a community. Both refer to integrity as a consistency between personal and social values. And both also refer to integrity as entailing autonomy – expressed in the consistency of actions and values. This latter sense of consistency is what is heard in popular adages, defining integrity as 'walking the talk' or 'practice what you preach'. However, that other sense of consistency – between personal and social values – seems just as important to the concept of integrity within an organizational setting.

This leads to the philosophical question of how values and actions need to relate to each other in order to speak of integrity. In an objectivist view, integrity is speaking and acting in accordance with values that are morally justified on an objectivist basis, for example the promotion of long-term survival and well-being of individuals as rational beings (Becker, 1998). The subjectivist view reduces the notion of integrity to that of personal integrity, which only requires a consistency of commitments in speaking and acting (McFall, 1987). What is the position of Meyers' notion of self-governance and Solomon's communitarian view on integrity within the objectivist/subjectivist debate? Meyers' work is an explicit attempt to tackle the ambiguity inherent in the relation between individuals and values. He puts forward the notion of self-governance to balance the ideals of individual autonomy and personal integrity. Hence, he fits in neither of the two camps.

Instead, the notion of self-governance entails a civic aspect. The self-governed person does not merely act according to her own values but also tries to make the circumstances ones in which her values are reflected, which means that these values are acceptable to the community and are defendable as social values. This reflects the Aristotelian inspiration in Meyers' work, namely that one cannot be virtuous outside of society. Commitment to the polis – and addressing the polis – is an absolute necessity for human existence. The same is true for Solomon's position. He also takes a neo-Aristotelian approach. One must be true to the self, but the self is always part of a community. Hence, Solomon's approach does not fit into the objectivist camp because Solomon does not take an atomistic view on morality. And he does not fit into the subjectivist camp because the self is only self to the extent that it is part of and therefore interacts with others in a community. So clearly, both Meyers and Solomon take up a third position within the debate on what kind of values integrity entails. This third position does not assume an atomistic view on morality nor does human interaction pose a problem for it. As will become clear further on, this third position is very important for a conceptualization of integrity that is tenable in organizations. The following sections will further clarify the assumptions of this third position.

3. FLEXIBILITY – A KEY CONCEPT FOR TODAY'S ORGANIZATION

The goal of this chapter is to develop a conceptualization of integrity that is applicable to individuals within an organizational context that is characterized by flexibility. Flexibility seems to be a core concept not just in today's discourse on and within organizations, but also with regard to those other crucial issues including efficiency discourses in which new regulations are lobbied against with the argument that this would reduce organizational flexibility and hence the competitiveness of business.

According to Sennett (1998), the concept of flexibility originally designated the capability of a tree or a branch to bend with the wind without breaking. With regard to organizations, then, a flexible organization is an organization that has a specific structure, which allows it to adjust to foreseen and unforeseen but inevitable changes in an organization's environment. Indeed, regarding flexibility as a necessary characteristic of organizations requires the assumption of uncertainty and inevitability with regard to the conditions of the complex environments in which organizations operate. Within organizational discourse, complexity refers to the myriad of factors relevant to planning and to the numerous information units to be processed in order to make a decision. This has urged organizations to shift their perspective from a central point of decision making to decentralized decision making (Castells, 1996; Guéhenno, 1999) and to shift the focus of control from product to process (cf. audit standards and quality standards such as ISO or EFQM).

Hence notions of uncertainty, complexity and flexibility implicitly criticize the notion of compliance as inadequate. It has become common sense that it is impossible to set out rules which fully cover desirable behavior. A rule-based approach is seen as inadequate, first, because the necessity to decentralize decision-making entails the increase of the discretionary authority of more people in the organization and, second, under those conditions, one simply cannot foresee what the desirable behavior will be in terms of concrete actions and decisions. Still, any organization needs to assure coordinated activities towards organizational goals. Hence, for organizations it has to be predictable that the numerous autonomously made decisions within the organization will result in coordinated action towards organizational goals. In this context, the demand for integrity is symptomatic for the perception of the inability to control through structure and rules.

4. INTEGRITY AS WHOLENESS, BUT OF WHAT?

Above I have argued that the etymological root of integrity refers to the notion of wholeness and that this notion seems at odds with our current view of identity as fragmented. This has implications for how we can understand integrity as 'wholeness' with regard to individuals in organizations. Four levels of analysis seem relevant to be examined in this respect. These levels relate to how individuals act in and on behalf of organization. They are the functional, the temporal, the spatial and the interactive level. In what follows, I will argue that the first three levels are highly problematic in an organizational context in which making sense of organizing and organizations takes place through the concepts of flexibility. The fourth level, which is the interactive level, allows conceptualizing integrity in a way that is more promising in this respect.

At the functional level, integrity designates a wholeness of personality throughout the different roles that an individual assumes. It is based on the psychological foundation of a well-integrated personality, referring to a stable identity when being a mother, a friend, a worker, a customer, etc. However, it is unclear just what that identity might be. Etzioni writes that '[people] can, and do, use these multi-memberships (as well as limited, but not trivial, ability to choose one's work and residential communities) to protect themselves from excessive pressure by any one community' (Etzioni, 1998, p. xiv). But then, who or what is the 'self' they are protecting? Is it the mother at work, or the customer as a friend? The worker might be a volunteer at one place but an employee in another, and within the same organization, a single employee might have both subordinates and bosses. All these denote several role-patterns and manifest themselves in different contexts. From an organizational perspective, it is not always desirable or efficient to have the mother at work or the friend as a customer. As an individual, we are part of many communities, and carry out different roles with different values in each of them. Hence, the way in which the notion of a well-integrated personality makes sense is as a successful balancing of all our role prescriptions so that the consistency of action and values in each of our roles does not imply a fragmentation of that consistency in any of the other roles. Still, it remains unconvincing in terms of integrity. Let us consider the hypothetical situation of a consistency between actions and values within each role pattern. The consistency of personal/social would then be the possibility of a coexistence of all our consistencies of action/values, meaning the unproblematic coexistence of the mother, the friend, the customer, the employee, the supplier, the colleague, etc. Issues such as work/life balance, favoritism, and nepotism show that organizations struggle with multiple roles and fragmented identities. By requiring employees to be 'stand by' – even during holidays – or to change their working hours every week, flexibility tries to establish the individual's organizational function as her most important role, to which all other roles are subordinate – family time, friendships, social and cultural activities, etc. At the same time, especially with regard to the issue of work/life balance, organizations present themselves as flexible to the advantage of the employee, allowing them to come in to work somewhere between 7 and 11 am or offering child care to parents when they need to work overtime. But this, too, tries to make the prioritization of the organizational function possible. This prioritization is something else then a wholeness of the different roles we assume. Thus, the delineation of integrity as wholeness at the functional level is problematic because the assumption is that multiple roles and fragmented identities can be overcome and 'resolved'.

At the temporal level, integrity refers to a wholeness or consistency of action/value and of personal/social over a time period. This means that not only are there to be those consistencies, they are also to be kept constant. I am today who I was yesterday and that is who I will be tomorrow. Integrity at this level implies a problem with changing our minds, our convictions or our values. The concept of flexibility designates at a temporal level the perceptions of constant change, new opportunities, new challenges, and unpredictability. Dealing with new situations surely implies approaching the newness of the situation with already acquired value appraisals. Yet dealing with those new situations will just as well entail questioning the appropriateness and maintainability of those value appraisals, and might very well alter them. Moreover, temporal integrity seems to hold an internal contradiction in the required consistency between the personal and the social. Even if I were not to change my personal value appraisal, all or some of the relevant others might change theirs. They might do so in such a way that causes a shift in the social value appraisal. Hence, if I am to maintain consistency between the personal and the social, an evolution in social values requires me both to question my personal value appraisal and the social value appraisal. And, such a questioning implies a possibility of change. Thus, although a certain degree of predictability is sought for in the organizational demand for integrity, flexibility and the personal/social consistency itself also demand a continuous questioning of the personal and the social.

The third level at which integrity as wholeness could be conceptualized is the spatial level. Globalization partly refers to the recognition of the existence of geographically spread multiple sets of rules and norms regarding organizing, production, labor, and marketing. The flexible organization incorporates the existence of those different sets into its strategic planning. This is most blatantly the case in transnational organizations. But indirectly it also holds true for small and medium-sized enterprises (SMEs), and for self-employed people that are affected by the global supply and demand chain. Hence, integrity at the spatial level can be described as the wholeness of organizational practices across communal boundaries. An organizational practice entails behavior of individuals in function of organizational goals and this behavior is always carried out within relations. Both aspects of an organizational practice – behavior and relations – pose a problem for integrity in today's organizational context, if it is to be understood at the spatial level. Crossing communal borders implies that the same behavior will not be maintainable, for the simple reason that different regions have different norms and regulation about behavior. Also, the kind of organizational activity differs according to its geographical presence. Designing a product, producing the product, marketing the product for consumption, all these different activities are performed in different regions of the world, just as the place of decision making regarding that spread is also located in specific areas. The ability of corporations to use these options to their advantage – for example to maximize shareholder value – is what makes them flexible at a spatial level. The point is however that these different organizational activities require different relations. For example, workers require different representation mechanisms in different countries. In this sense, the same relational frame for organizational practices across communal boundaries is not desirable.

Thus, the notion of integrity at the spatial level, as a wholeness of organizational practices across boundaries, seems to implode, because the same behavior across communal boundaries is not acceptable and neither are the same relations across these boundaries desirable. Nevertheless, multinational corporations have mission statements and value statements with global validity. Often, mission statements differentiate between stakeholders and hence between different kind of relations, but they do not differentiate between communities and between communal values. Corporations expect and demand that their employees – their representatives in different regions and communities across the world – uphold the corporate values, indeed, act with integrity as wholeness at the spatial level. I have already examined integrity at the functional, the temporal and the spatial level, but all three levels proved to be problematic with regard to an acceptable conceptualization of integrity for today's flexible organization. As I will show in the next section integrity at the interactive level is able to provide integrity a meaning that is capable of embracing flexibility. What 'wholeness' does integrity address at this level? And what are its different dimensions? First, there is the perception of a situation. Individuals make sense of what is happening. Second, there is acting upon that perception with a particular intention. And third, there is the social dimension of a situation – I share a situation with others. These others might be the subject of my acting or my acting might intend to make something clear to them or I might want to hide my acting, etc. The point is that there is an infinite number of ways to act, but there are always others who also perceive a situation, act upon that and share a situation with others.

How is there to be a wholeness of those dimensions? Stephen Carter (1997) has defined integrity as the wholeness of three steps: (1) discerning what is right and what is wrong, (2) acting on that discernment, and (3) openly stating the connection between acting and discernment. Carter's three steps correspond to what I have called the three dimensions of acting. It is in perceiving a situation that we will make sense of – and give meaning to – an experience. This implies a discernment of the perceived situation on a continuum between good and bad. Carter's second step, acting on that discernment, ensures the wholeness of the perception and action dimensions. And his third step involves what I have called the social dimension of a situation: we share a situation with others. Exceptional in Carter's definition of integrity is precisely his third step, the explicit recognition of the other as a necessary aspect of integrity. And this is why Carter's definition is so important for a conceptualization of integrity as wholeness at the interactive level. Human interaction is an important aspect of individuals in an organizational context. Action within or by members of an organization might involve human interaction, but not necessarily (for example entering data into a computer). But Carter's third step – speaking about one's action based on one's discernment – ensures that action has an interactive aspect. It is the extent to which one speaks to others about one's actions and discernments, that one is showing integrity. Hence, the crux of the conceptualization of integrity as a wholeness at the interactive level is speaking to others about what one is doing and why. Hence, integrity includes an attitude towards the other, namely the willingness to discuss, explain, justify and negotiate what to do and why and how to do it. It is the presence of this attitude that makes someone a person of integrity.

If we recognize the legitimacy of others questioning our actions and our behavior, integrity as a wholeness on the interactive level implies that in order to behave with integrity, we need to respond to this questioning. This is the case for the mother when she punishes her son for his bad behavior. It is the case for the politician who, faced with changed circumstances, has to recall some of her promises. It is also the case for the spokesperson of a company who needs to answer community concerns a over possible noise hazard from a new planned production plant. And it is also the case for the lorry driver in a multinational company who needs to justify why he is paying bribes to transport goods in Nigeria, or for the shop floor assistant who refuses to treat a client. Indeed, this conceptualization of integrity seems suitable for all kinds of situations, as Carter (1997) argues. My concern here, however, is with regard to individuals in an organizational context. An important distinction between the various domains of life to which this interactive conceptualization of integrity is applicable, lies in who the others are to whom we must speak about our discernments and actions in order to behave with integrity.

5. TO WHOM MUST WE SPEAK?

One way to approach the question of who the relevant others are would be to say that since integrity denotes a consistency of discerning a situation, acting in that situation and speaking about this discernment and acting, the relevant others are those with whom we share a situation. While this hardly narrows it down, it does give us an idea about the philosophical background of speaking and responding to others as a decisive element of integrity. For Emmanuel Lévinas (1961), ethics is the first philosophy and starts in the encounter with the other. The philosophy of Lévinas is a philosophy of radical difference. The nature of the self requires a response that lies beyond it; the idea of self implies that of not-self, of the Other (see also Rhodes and Westwood's chapter in this volume). It is the face of the other which we cannot deny and which forces us to respond. It is the other who holds us responsible, or, it is in the face of the other that we must be able to respond – hence response-ability or responsibility. What's more, the other is irreducible. The other is the Other. That is to say, there is a complete Otherness in the other, incomparable with the self. Because the Other is radically different and cannot be reduced to the self or the 'same', Lévinas calls it infinite. And so is our responsibility towards the other. It is an infinite responsibility. And we have the duty of responsibility for each and everyone.

What is the implication of Lévinas' viewpoint for our attempt to clarify the relevant others as all those we share a situation with? From the point of Weberian sociology, everyone who renders meaning to a situation is to be considered as sharing that situation. Hence, anyone that comes up to me and questions my behavior is sharing a situation with me and therefore I need to respond to her and speak about my discernment and action. Integrity implies the duty to explain and justify. But what about Lévinas' infinite duty? How must we interpret that for the integrity of individuals in an organizational context? The duty to respond is infinite in the sense that speaking and responding is a *fait accompli*. It is not something we can do first and then go on with doing other things. Rather, it is an open-ended duty.

Anyone who questions our actions is a relevant Other for an interactive conceptualization of integrity. However, this can only be a part of the answer. So far I have now only treated responding, the speaking in reaction of a questioning. But integrity also includes a proactive speaking. Those relevant others cannot be the same as the relevant others of the responding, simply because I cannot know who I am sharing a situation with until someone asks me for a response.

The relevant others of our speaking are those with whom we make up a community. In our case, this is the workplace community, our team members, colleagues, and management. The relationships between these individuals are constitutive of that community. And therefore, speaking about our discernment and action to those with whom we form a community reemphasizes not only that community but also us as being part of it. If I did not speak with those others, I would not recognize my relationships within that particular community. Of course, if the organization I work for is a big company, with hundreds or thousands of employees in plants across the world, I will have to rely on organizational processes to make my speaking accessible for all relevant others. I will come back to that in the final section of the chapter. For now, it is important that to emphasize who the relevant others are: the organizational members I form a community with and everyone who questions my actions.

I have put forward the interactive conceptualization of integrity as the most fruitful way to think about integrity – a wholeness of discernment, action and speech – especially in an organizational context. This is because it makes sense in organizations characterized by the need for flexibility and because it also fits well with the two reasons I mentioned for the popularity of the concept of integrity: to act according to self-imposed norms, but justified towards others. This contains the two consistencies of action/value and personal/social. In justifying the norms, reference is made to values. The justification process links the personal to the social value appraisal.

The other reason I gave for the popularity of integrity was symptomatic for the perception of the inability to control through structure. Integrity at the interactive level leaves enough flexibility for value reflection and changes in value appraisal to cope with new and complex situations, whilst it also allows a certain control in its third situational dimension, namely communicating about the link between action and value. It is through that communication process that control can be exercised. This communication process must be seen as a learning process, in which distances between personal and social value appraisals are diminished. Hence, control of decentralized decision-making and of actions within increased discretionary power is achieved through the assurance that one has to communicate about how one manifests the consistency between action and values, and the consistency between personal and social value appraisal. Hence, at the interactive level, 'talking the walk' is more relevant to integrity than 'walking the talk'.

At the end of section 2, I mentioned the debate between the objectivist and the subjectivist view on integrity. There, I wrote that Meyers and Solomon gave us a clue about a possible third position. The conceptualization of integrity that I have put forward develops this third position further. The delineation of integrity as wholeness at the interactive level establishes its moral justification precisely within human interaction. This conceptual delineation of integrity is based on Carter's wholeness of three steps: discernment, action and speaking openly about the connection between acting and discernment. The wholeness is only attained by speaking about how a situation is perceived and how one acts upon that perception. Hence, the moral justification of acting upon discernment takes place by speaking openly about it and by putting ourselves as moral agents under the scrutiny of others. Acting with integrity is interacting in the sense that by speaking openly about our discernment and our action in a given situation, we invite others to reflect on the extent to which our discernments and actions divert or are in contradiction with collectively held values.

Thus, the delineation of integrity as wholeness at the interactive level represents an intersubjectivist view on integrity. Compared to the objectivist and the subjectivist views, the intersubjectivist view emphasizes human interaction – speaking openly – as a necessary condition for acting with integrity. Hence, a first conclusion is that the delineation of integrity as a wholeness at the interactive level denotes an attitude towards the social, with implications for the personal.

Another salient aspect of the intersubjectivist view on integrity is it is a far more dynamic one. The intersubjective view seeks to establish a consistency of personal and social values through speaking openly about discernment and action. Hence, wholeness here is not something that has to be preserved, but rather something that has to be attained. It is by individuals speaking openly and thereby putting their moral agency under scrutiny of others that collective (social) values will be examined on their applicability to new situations, resulting in a collective reinterpretation of these social values and an adjustment of personal values. This collective examination, reinterpretation and adjustment form an ongoing process. Wholeness, in this sense, is something that is collectively constructed time and time again. A second conclusion therefore is that the delineation of integrity as a wholeness at the interactive level entails a notion of wholeness that is always provisional.

6. TALKING THE WALK – IMPLICATIONS FOR ORGANIZATIONAL PROCESSES

Integrity as wholeness at the interactive level implies an organizational duty. More precisely, the organization, which demands integrity from its members, has the duty to ensure that it is reasonable for individuals to speak openly about discernment of actions. In his book on corporate integrity, Marvin Brown (2005) has developed a relational approach to integrity at a corporate level. Brown takes a neo-Aristotelian approach that emphasizes the importance of relationships for the flourishing of individuals. Brown's relational integrity is strongly related to the type of communication patterns within organizations. Corporate integrity is achieved to the extent to which communications within the organization are open to difference and disagreement. With Pearce (1989), Brown calls such communication patterns *cosmopolitan*, because they are reflexive in nature – one can communicate about the communication – and allow us seeing others as having stories that are possibly different to ours. To make this idea of cosmopolitan communication clearer, Brown draws on the dialogical process of Martin Buber's *Ich und Du* (1983). Buber distinguishing two types of relations: I-Thou and I-It. With this distinction, Buber reminds us of the work of Lévinas (Verlinden, 2006). In the I-It relation, the other is not seen as an independent person with a different story, but rather as an object. The other is thereby reduced to the 'same': the other becomes an object that serves one's own interests. In the I-Thou relationship, in contrast, which is described by Buber as a direct relation of immediacy, individuals enter into this relation as Others with different stories. The I-Thou relationship allows for an encounter in which the other does not appear as an It. For Buber, this real encounter or dialogue is characterized by an openness or readiness towards others. In his work on corporate integrity, Brown (2005, p. 101) explains that corporations can foster such an I-Thou dialogue and a cosmopolitan communication culture that is open to differences and disagreements by providing conditions of security:

> The need for security would imply that both employee and employer could trust each other to be honest, forthright, and collaborative. Also, both would participate, assuming that their relationship was not only defined by work roles and responsibilities, but also by civic standards of non-tyranny, equality and publicity. ... If conversations followed these guidelines, they would exhibit relational wholeness and therefore promote corporate integrity.

Although Brown's reference to civic standards such as non-tyranny, equality and publicity seems to link his approach to the discourse ethics of Karl Otto Apel (1973) and Jürgen Habermas (1981), it is important to note that discourse ethics is to be distinguished from dialogue ethics. The latter is based on a neo-Aristotelian approach emphasizing human flourishing within communities and draws on feminist ethics such as that of Carol Gilligan (1982) or Nell Noddings (1984) and on the work of Lévinas and Buber. It attempts to reconcile fragmented identities, multiple roles and difference with ethics and moral justification. Discourse ethics, on the other hand, is based on a Kantian approach and seeks to pin down the norms which we need to adhere to in an argumentation. These norms include that the only authority lies in rationality of the participants (not in their status), that every rational being can participate and that any argument can be made as long as it is rational. The preoccupation of discourse ethics is to provide a procedural foundation for rules that claim universality. In contrast to dialogue ethics, discourse ethics leaves little room for irrational reasons and motives such as friendship, emotion, fear and perplexity stemming from multi-memberships.

The conceptualization of integrity as developed in this chapter allows organizations to ensure predictability through compliance understood as provisional rules that are contested, discussed, adapted and accepted 'as we go'. The implication for organizational processes is that an acceptance and even praise of dissent would be fostered. In a changing and uncertain environment, justifications of organizational actions have to emanate from interpersonal reflection and resetting of standards of behavior. A conceptualization of integrity that fits today's organizational context makes that clear. Far more than demanding that one 'walks the talk', integrity demands that one 'talks the walk' in order to foster interpersonal reflection and attunement.

An example for fostering such a narrative can be found in whistleblowing. Integrity at the interactive level implies whistleblowing as important practice (Vandekerckhove, 2006). If an employee discerns a situation as wrongdoing, the employee should come forward by communicating that perceived wrongdoing. In fact, in the case of whistleblowing, two dimensions of integrity coincide: the acting based on the discernment and the speaking about that discernment. Integrity at the interactive level stands or falls with the individual employee speaking openly about personal discernment and action. The organizational precondition for this attitude to be shown is that it is safe or even encouraged to speak openly. Likewise, preparedness to adjust personal values to examined and reinterpreted collective values requires an acceptance of being scrutinized by others. Therefore, the main task for managing the ongoing organizational process of fostering personal integrity is to make sure that speaking openly about discernment and action – talking the walk – is safe. One way of doing so is the creation of narrative platforms, in which 'dangerous truths' (Simmons, 1999) can be told as stories, leaving the storyteller free from risk of retaliation. Storytelling is a safe method for speaking openly because it emphasizes that what is being told are facts-as-experiences rather than facts-as-information (Gabriel, 2000). A platform for narratives could encourage discussion and examination of collective values (Langenberg, 2004). Ultimately this could enhance our capability to 'talk the walk'.

REFERENCES

Becker, T. E. (1998), 'Integrity in organizations: Beyond honesty and conscientiousness', *Academy of Management Review*, **23** (1), 154-161.

Brown, M. (2005), *Corporate Integrity: Rethinking Organizational Ethics and Leadership*, Cambridge: Cambridge University Press.

Buber, M. (1983), *Ich und Du*, Heidelberg: Schneider.

Carter, S. L. (1997), *Integrity*, New York, US: Harper Perennial.

Castells, M. (1996), *The Information Age, Economy, Society and Culture, Vol I: The Rise of The Network Society*, Oxford, UK: Blackwell.

De George, R. T. (1993), *Competing with Integrity in International Business*, New York, US and Oxford, UK: Oxford University Press.

Etzioni, A. (1998) (ed.), *The Essential Communitarian Reader*, Oxford, UK: Rowman & Littlefield.

Gabriel, Y. (2000), *Storytelling in Organizations: Facts, Fictions, and Fantasies*. Oxford, UK: Oxford University Press.

Gilligan, C. (1982), *In a Different Voice: Psychological Theory and Women's Development*, Cambridge, MA, US: Harvard University Press.

Guéhenno, J. M. (1999), *L'avenir de la liberté*, Paris, France: Flammarion.

Habermas, J. (1981), *Theorie des kommunikativen Handelns*, Frankfurt a.M.: Suhrkamp.

Langenberg, S. (2004), 'Parresiastic stakeholders: A different approach to ethical institutions', *Journal of Business Ethics*, **53** (1-2), 39-50.

Lévinas, E. (1961), *Totalité et infini. Essai sur l'extériorité*, The Hague: Martinus Nijhoff.

McFall, L. (1987), 'Integrity', *Ethics*, **98** (1), 5-20.

Meyers, R. H. (1999), *Self-Governance and Cooperation*, New York, US and Oxford, UK: Oxford University Press.

Noddings, N. (1984), *Caring, a Feminine Approach to Ethics & Moral Education*, Berkeley, US: University of California Press.

Paine, L. S. (1994), 'Managing for organizational integrity', *Harvard Business Review*, **72** (2), 106-117.

Pearce, W. B. (1989), *Communication and the Human Condition*, Carbondale and Edwardville, US: Southern Illinois University Press.

Sennett, R. (1998), *The Corrosion of Character*, New York, US: Norton.

Simmons, A. (1999), *A Safe Place for Dangerous Truths*, New York, US: Amacom.

Solomon, R. C. (1993), *Business and Excellence: Cooperation and Integrity in Business*, New York, US and Oxford, UK: Oxford University Press.

Vandekerckhove, W. (2006), *Whistleblowing and Organizational Social Responsibility*, Aldershot, UK: Ashgate.

Verlinden, A. (2006), 'Immigration, refugeehood and the nation-state – An ethical perspective. Plea for a dialogical approach towards worldwide migration', paper presented at the 10th Biennal Conference, IASFM, Toronto, CA.

10. Practical Wisdom: Integrating Ethics and Effectiveness in Organizations

Matt Statler and Karin Oppegaard

If the future is plagued with conflict and turmoil, this instability does not simply reside out there somewhere; it resides, and has its origin, *in ourselves*. (Sternberg, 2001, p. 237)

Each micro-decision – each micro-change in interpretive propensities that results from reflection – moves us infinitesimally towards a different moral world. (Walker, 2000, p. 144).

INTRODUCTION: ETHICS V. EFFECTIVENESS: ADDRESSING THE ANTINOMY

In a recent article, Margolis and Walsh (2003) discuss the tension between ethics and effectiveness in organizations, addressing what they call the antinomy between a firm's economic efficiency and its efforts to respond to social misery. Their discussion explicitly critiques the century-old belief, initiated (according to some, unintentionally) by Adam Smith and more recently represented by Milton Friedman (1970), that an organization's sole social responsibility is wealth creation. Margolis and Walsh's study contains a detailed analysis of current organizational research efforts to establish statistically significant relationships between firms' corporate social performance (CSP) and corporate financial performance (CFP). They show how such studies yield mixed results, including negative, positive, and absence of correlations. More importantly, they show that this stream of research tends toward a limited focus on measurable performance indicators, carrying with it the following assumptions:

1. That there is a measurable relationship between ethics and efficiency, i.e., ethical performance can be measured using indicators similar to those used to assess financial performance;
2. That the relationship between ethics and efficiency is of an instrumental nature, i.e., 'ethics pays', serving as an instrumental means to the end of financial performance;
3. That in cases where ethics does not 'pay', then ethical behaviors are by definition costly, diminishing the organization's effectiveness, and thus illegitimate from a strategic or governance perspective.

Margolis and Walsh note how research based on these assumptions that seeks to establish a link between financial and social outcomes ultimately nourishes a view of corporate social responsibility (CSR) that is limited to making the 'business case' for ethics and responsibility. They note how these assumptions lead researchers to rely on empirical data when in reality the problem is situated on the level of *values* that remain difficult if not impossible to measure. Margolis and Walsh conclude that people in organizations struggle particularly when they cannot reconcile normative principles of responsibility with the principles of profit and efficiency that nominally drive the firm (e.g., when no profit can be predicted to derived from a given social initiative). Following this line of argument, the 'antinomy' separating ethical normativity from instrumental effectiveness arises when people in organizations work from assumptions and use methods that preclude their possible integration. In the interest of moving beyond these assumptions and methods, the authors call for the development of theory which addresses the question: 'how might the role, purpose and function of the firm be specified so as to acknowledge a range of inconsistencies and concerns, and still facilitate action?' (Margolis and Walsh, 2003, p. 284).

In this chapter, we respond to this call and attempt to move beyond the view that ethics and performance are related either instrumentally or oppositionally. We do this by addressing ethics and effectiveness in terms of their possible integration. We do not, however, take up the question at the level of the firm,[1] but rather at the level of the individual decision-making actor. In line with Wood (1991), we emphasize the importance of individual managerial discretion with respect to the ethical actions associated with CSR. As such, we believe that ethics and effectiveness cannot be integrated in organizational practice unless individual decision-makers are able to deal with the above-mentioned tensions and inconsistencies in practice. And yet as we will see below, the existing theories of individual ethical decision-making within moral psychology and business ethics appear inadequate for describing how these tensions might be resolved. Our goal in this paper is therefore to elaborate a theory of individual ethical decision-making that focuses on 'practical wisdom' (following Aristotle, 1962; cf. Jones, 2005) as a description of how these tensions can be balanced.

We begin with a review of traditional models of ethical decision-making, focusing on their limitations with respect to the inconsistencies and concerns identified by Margolis and Walsh (2003). We then present the concept of practical wisdom, and draw on philosophical, psychological, and organizational theory to argue that practical wisdom refers to the virtuous habit of integrating ethical responsibility and effectiveness *in practice*. We develop this idea further by constructing an interpretative framework that describes three different modes of decision-making practice in terms of the extent to which they integrate ethics and effectiveness. We close by considering the implications of this framework for future research focusing on wise decision making practices in organizations.

ON THE LIMITATIONS OF TRADITIONAL MODELS OF INDIVIDUAL ETHICAL DECISION-MAKING

In order to address issues of individual ethical decision-making in organizations, researchers have developed various models that attempt to link given individual-level variables with normatively desirable outcomes (for a review of such models, see Jones, 1991). These models typically provide iterative descriptions of the formation of moral intent and behavior, wherein different contextual or individual moderators play a role, depending on the theoretical perspective taken (e.g. Ferrell and Gresham, 1985; Hunt and Vitell, 1986; Rest, 1986; Trevino, 1986; Dubinsky and Loken, 1989; Jones, 1991). For example, the most widely used model, that of Rest (1986), describes moral decision-making as characterized by the following four sequential steps: based on *moral awareness*, the actor exercises *moral judgment*, establishes *moral intent*, and finally proceeds to display *moral behavior*.

Despite the usefulness of such models in exploring the antecedents to ethical behavior, their underlying assumptions have been subject to various critiques. For example, within moral psychology, the tendency to focus almost exclusively on cognitive and rational processes has been called into question. In the past decades, there has been growing interest in emotional as well as identity-based elements of moral decision-making, and these literatures emphasize the importance of extra-rational processes in the formation of moral intent and behavior (see for example Blasi, 1984; Colby and Damon, 1992; Schweder and Haidt, 1993; Eisenberg 1996, 2002). In addition, it has been argued that rational models leave little room for understanding how factors such as subjective norms and values contribute to the emergence of behavior (Dubinsky and Loken, 1989). As argued by Punzo (1996), this paradigm of research, inspired by Kantian thought, limits our understanding of ethical behavior insofar as it construes the self as a disembodied observer of its own moral actions.

Furthermore, a key challenge in moral psychology has been to understand how espoused values are translated into enacted values. In effect, research actually demonstrating this link is sparse, and although correlations between moral intent and moral behavior have been found, they tend to be moderate (typically ranging from 0.30 to 0.40 – cf. Blasi, 1980; Thoma and Rest, 1986; Bay and Greenberg, 2001). Researchers have tried to strengthen this link empirically by including various contextual and/or individual moderating factors that influence the passage from moral judgment to behavior (e.g. Hunt and Vitell, 1986; Trevino, 1986). However, others (Solomon, 1992, 2004; Campbell and Christopher, 1996; Tsoukas and Cummings, 1997; Clegg and Ross-Smith, 2003), argue that the problem is not situated at the level of a lack of alignment between intended behavior and enacted behavior. They suggest that an obstacle to ethical behavior is the tendency to separate the domain of the prudential (or subjective, context-dependent, contingent) elements of a given problem from the moral considerations (understood in terms of rational, abstract principles). In other terms, problems arise when people view morality as limited to disembodied, universal, and situation-transcendent imperatives that govern their daily life. The cited authors critique excessively formulaic or rule-based descriptions of ethical behavior and emphasize the importance of *context* in defining relevant considerations in a moral decision, as well as the key role of one's practical experience in forming habits of moral behavior. Such implicit and habit-based patterns of thought and behavior are proposed to be key to understanding the enactment of ethics.

We suggest that one of the major disadvantages of the formulaic models of decision-making is the underlying assumption that ethical behavior can be *codified*. In organizations, this belief has resulted in the establishment and implementation of various extrinsically defined norms of behavior, such as corporate 'codes of ethics', mission statements and the like. This is the predominant way firms' decision-makers attempt to eliminate situational contingencies and create inventories of acceptable and unacceptable behavior (Harrington, 1991). However, as stated by Maclagan (1990, p. 17),

Codes cannot replace individuals' own capacity for moral judgment and integrity. These are *personal* qualities which contribute to managers' performance, and are acquired through process of moral learning and development including the cultivation of interpersonal skills and understanding through experience.

These authors suggest that in decisions where human and environmental well-being are an issue, abstract codification of 'correct' behavior – in terms of universalist and extrinsically-defined notions of value – is of limited usefulness.

In this light, the antinomy that appears within economic and organizational theory (where normativity appears in contradiction to effectiveness) reappears within ethical theory, where the subjective, context-specific domain of the prudential appears in contradiction to the objective, rational sphere of moral principles. But in both cases, the antinomies depend on a definition of oppositional terms, where objectivity and rationality are associated with one term, and subjectivity and irrationality with the other. It is however interesting to reflect that while both streams of theory privilege rationality, ethical theory associates it with the universal moral principles that economic theory deems irrational, at least with respect to the nominally rational goal of profit maximization. In turn, while economic theory finds profit maximization to be fully rational, within ethical theory the instrumental goal of making money, or shareholder value maximization, can appear subjectively self-serving at best.

It is not our purpose to resolve these debates, but instead to approach them from a different point of entry. We turn now to the Aristotelian tradition of virtue ethics to see whether it might helps us deal with the uncodifiability (McDowell, 1979; Maclagan, 1990; Duska, 1993; Abizadeh, 2002) and context-dependence (Hartman, 1998; Flyvbjerg, 2001; Abizadeh, 2002) of ethical issues. Our hope is that this alternative notion of ethical decision-making will provide a new perspective on the antinomy identified by Margolis and Walsh (2003).

PRACTICAL WISDOM: A COMPELLING ALTERNATIVE FRAMEWORK

Proponents of more practice-based, subjective, and contingent understandings of behavior in social contexts argue that abstract reason can never grasp all the details of a given concrete situation sufficiently to codify behavior *ex ante* (Flyvbjerg, 2001; Abizadeh, 2002). As argued by Maclagan (1990), managers are frequently confronted with dilemmas that cannot be resolved by appeal to rule-based guidelines such as codes of ethics. In other words, no universal rule or principle can possibly cover every particular contingency that may arise in the future because practical matters are: (1) mutable; (2) ambiguous; and, (3) ungeneralizable (Tsoukas and Cummings, 1997). In this sense, in reference to the guiding antinomy that seems to separate responsible and effective behaviors in organizations, 'we cannot remove the deliberating agent from ethics and politics, reducing *politike* to passive application of universal principles to particular circumstances. Judgment is needed' (Abizadeh, 2002, p. 270). Or, as emphasized by Maclagan (1990), 'there is a clear distinction between *conformity with ethical codes* and the exercise of *personal moral judgment*' (1990, p. 18). As described by Devereux (1986, quoted in Abizadeh, 2002):

> [I]n the case of practical knowledge ... it is the universals that are indeterminate and imprecise while the judgments about particular acts in particular circumstances are precise and determinate. If there is a discrepancy between the particular judgment of the practically wise person and a universal rule which applies to the situation, the defect is on the side of the universal: it is the particular judgment that is authorative (Devereux, 1986, pp. 497-498).

In an effort to understand the practical knowledge that is required to make judgments and take action in the face of mutable, ambiguous and ungeneralizable circumstances, philosophers, psychologists and organizational theorists have turned to Aristotelian moral theory and the concept of practical wisdom.

In Aristotle's *Nicomachean Ethics*, the scientific knowledge (in Greek, *episteme*) of necessary laws and principles in the natural world is distinguished from practical wisdom (in Greek, *phronesis*), which refers to 'the virtuous habit of making decisions and taking actions that serve the common good' (Statler and Roos, forthcoming).[2] This characterization of ethical decision-making involves not the rationally instrumental production of previously-identified, normatively positive outcomes, but instead a performative enactment of the common good (Gadamer, 2002 [1960]; cf. also Statler et al., 2006, and Statler and Roos, 2006). We can explain more clearly how this performative enactment takes place by focusing on two characteristics that distinguish practical wisdom from the models of ethical decision-making identified above: (1) its embodied, tacit dimensions, and (2) the normative value of balance as an end in itself.

Aristotle's emphasis on the processes of habituation required for the development of practical wisdom provide an initial indication of the importance of its extra-rational aspects, but this line of thinking has been further developed by psychologists and organizational scholars. Sternberg (1998) for example has built the 'balance theory of wisdom' on the notion of tacit knowledge (Polanyi, 1976), which refers to a form of human understanding that is not reflected on explicitly as such, but rather learned over time through an engagement in embodied practice. While the dominant assumption is that such forms of knowledge are inferior to knowledge that can be represented in cognitive abstraction, it can be argued that wisdom develops only when such abstractions are ingrained in habit. For example, Baltes and colleagues working on the issues of aging and lifelong learning at the Max Planck Institute in Berlin, have argued that wisdom is developed through a shift, over time and in the course of lived experience, from declarative (factual) to procedural knowledge (Baltes and Staudinger, 2000).

The further question of whether the 'content' of wisdom emerges from the mind (i.e., through rational reflection) or from the body (i.e., through experience and habit) becomes particularly difficult to answer when we recognize that the rules and regulations, followed by managers are themselves the socially constructed result of a complex process through which particular skills have been mastered and codified as explicit knowledge. In turn, this explicit knowledge may well be internalized through habituation, as in the case of expert or virtuoso performance (Dreyfus and Dreyfus, 1986). A pragmatic analysis of this complicated set of issues suggests that, in any case, 'once such skills are well learned, they become reflexively automatic. That is, they cannot be analyzed but become themselves the unspoken and tacit ground of any action capable of improvising in unpredictable ways around and between any sense that the rules might make' (Clegg and Ross-Smith, 2003, p. 87). In this light, the embodied, tacit dimensions of practical wisdom provide a first, clear point of distinction from the traditional models of ethical decision-making outlined above.

The emphasis on embodiment and practice re-frames (and thereby sidesteps) the problem of codifiability, but it raises another question that is perhaps more difficult, precisely because it cannot, by definition, be answered *ex ante*: how is wisdom practiced? Or, in terms of organizational theory, how can the practice of wisdom be described and studied?

Similarly, following Aristotle's notion of the 'golden mean', the exercise of such embodied, tacit knowledge in ambiguous, mutable, and ungeneralizable circumstances can be characterized as a *balance*. On this point, we draw heavily on Sternberg's balance theory of wisdom, which distinguishes two different kinds of balancing processes: one of different interests, and another of different responses to the environment. Concerning the different interests that are balanced in the practice of wisdom, Sternberg writes that

Wisdom is not simply about maximizing one's own or someone else's self-interest, but about balancing of various self-interests (intrapersonal) with the interests of others (interpersonal) and of other aspects of the context in which one lives (extrapersonal) such as one's city or country or environment or even God (2001, p. 231).

And concerning the various forms of response that are balanced in the course of wise practice, Sternberg writes that

Wisdom involves a balancing ... of three possible courses of action in response to the balancing of interests: adaptation of oneself or others to existing environments, shaping of environments in order to render them more compatible with oneself or others, and selection of new environments [when a fit between self and environmental characteristics seems implausible to attain] (1998, p. 356).

We believe that Sternberg's descriptions of these two balances should not be mistaken for abstract ethical formulae that supposedly govern wise decision-making, but rather as descriptions of the *practices* through which embodied, tacit knowledge is brought to bear on the mutable circumstances for action. In this sense, the 'balance of interests' struck by individuals in organizational contexts may well be informed by stakeholder analysis (e.g., Phillips et al., 2003), but the ethical relevance of practical wisdom emerges precisely when such analyses break down in the face of conflicting and irreconcilable interests, and when the individual nevertheless makes a decision and takes action. In such circumstances, "practical knowledge is no longer conceived in quasi-algorithmic terms, as the application of generic formulae, but in terms of acting wisely, being able to close the "phronetic gap" that almost inevitably exists between a formula and its enactment" (Taylor, 1993, p. 57, quoted in Tsoukas and Cummings, 1997, p. 666).

Thus the embodied habit of striking balances such as those identified by Sternberg can be affirmed not as an instrumental means to an end, but instead as a normatively optimal end in itself, or more precisely, as a *performative enactment of the common good*. This is a subtle and yet crucial point with respect to the limitations of existing models of ethical decision-making. It is not as though a practically wise person starts with explicit, formal knowledge of what the common good is, and subsequently sets to the task of serving it through the exercise of practical intelligence. Instead, in this striking of balances, the common good is performatively enacted. Differently phrased, at the level of individual decision-making in organizations, the common good *is* the exercise of tacit knowledge *as* a balance of interests and responses to the environment.

Of course, as Ardelt (2004, p. 260) insists, 'the moment one tries to preserve wisdom (e.g., by writing it down), it loses its connection to a concrete person and transforms into intellectual (theoretical) knowledge. I propose that even the most profound 'wisdom literature' remains intellectual or theoretical knowledge until its inherent wisdom is realized by a person'. But in this light, we suggest that the antinomial terms (i.e., ethics and effectiveness) identified by Margolis and Walsh may in fact never be reconciled *in theory*. Instead, they may only be balanced *in practice*. In this sense, the practical integration of ethics and effectiveness can emerge only because 'in performing an action the end is *acting well*, that is acting with regard to the things that are good or bad for man, and *this end is part of the performance of action*' (Tsoukas and Cummings, 1997, p. 665).[3]

In sum, we suggest that practical wisdom provides an alternative concept of individual ethical decision-making and action that does not involve abstract, rationally codifiable rules or guidelines, but instead an embodied practice of dealing with the ambiguity, mutability and ungeneralizability of the human social world. This notion undercuts the traditional distinction between practice-based, context-specific 'prudential' action and 'moral' action, seen as guided by clear-cut, universal, principles (Turiel, 1983). Practical wisdom emphasizes the tacit knowledge that is developed through the course of human experience and it refers (following our reading of Sternberg, 1998 in light of Gadamer, 2002 [1960]) to the balance of different interests and responses to the environment as an ethically normative end in itself.

So then, does practical wisdom provide a way to conceptualize the 'virtuous' integration of ethics and effectiveness? In the following section, we explore this possibility and introduce a framework that differentiates three modes of individual decision-making practice in terms of the extent to which they integrate ethics and effectiveness.

TOWARD A HERMENEUTICS OF WISE PRACTICE

As established in the sections above, the concept of practical wisdom indicates that the antinomy that separates ethics from effectiveness may be reconciled as a balance that is struck not in theory but *in practice*. Indeed the point of introducing practical wisdom as an 'alternative' concept of ethical decision-making in response to the problem of uncodifiability is that it remains impossible to substantiate precisely what the 'balance' is abstractly, in theory. Instead, we now wish to focus on concrete examples of how the balance appears to be struck in the course of organizational practice. However, in order to describe and differentiate between specific practices, we first need a methodological approach that is coherent with the concept of practical wisdom itself.[4]

Following Habermas' (1971) differentiation of technical, practical and emancipatory forms of knowledge, we suggest that hermeneutics (esp. Gadamer, 2002 [1960]) provides an appropriate methodology with which to study practical wisdom in organizations (cf. also Czikszentmihalyi and Rathunde, 1990). A practice with roots in theology and philology, hermeneutics has recently been referred to within organization studies as a mode of interpretative inquiry that focuses on the collective construction of meaning. Typically applied to communication processes (Heracleous and Barrett, 2001), it has also been applied to performance (Welker, 2004), conduct (Packer, 1985), culture (Geertz, 1973), politics (Taylor, 1976), narrative processes (Czarniawska, 1997) and ethics (Ricoeur, 1981; Gadamer, 2002 [1960]). In each of these cases, hermeneutics attends to the context-specific dimensions of the phenomenon in question; aspires to intersubjective validity in which truth claims remain always subject to further interpretation and critique, and affirms the intrinsic normativity of the interpretations themselves. A hermeneutic methodology can thus serve to develop greater understanding about *phronesis* in practice.

As a phenomenon unto itself, 'practice' has been addressed by organizational theorists (cf. Orlikowski, 2002; Contu and Willmott, 2003) seeking to integrate considerations of structure and agency, and there is growing interest in strategy-as-practice (cf. Balogun et al., 2003; Hendry and Seidl, 2003; Heracleous, 2003; Johnson et al., 2003; Régner, 2003; Whittington, 2003; Jarzabkowski, 2004). Moreover, philosophers and social theorists have argued that practice cannot be understood without reference to its normative dimensions (e.g., MacIntyre, 1984; Bourdieu, 1990; Habermas, 1990; Nussbaum, 2001, Moore, 2002; etc.). In this light, we present the terms of Margolis and Walsh's antinomy – ethics and effectiveness – as structural elements of an interpretative, hermeneutic framework for understanding the extent to which individual decision-making practices in organizations are practically wise.

In Figure 10.1, ethics should be considered as one aspect of decision-making practice, specifically, that aspect which concerns 'the good' as such. At the level of the framework, the axis itself remains neutral about what may or may not be good, functioning instead as a question to be addressed in the interpretative process: 'what is good?' Effectiveness should be considered as another aspect of decision-making practice, specifically, that aspect which concerns the instrumental relationship between means and ends. Similarly, at the level of the framework, the axis remains neutral about how specific means may or may not lead to specific ends, functioning instead as a question to be addressed in the interpretative process: 'what is effective?'

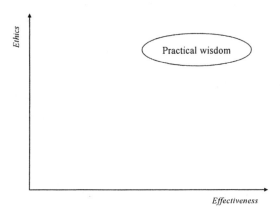

Figure 10.1 An Interpretative Framework for Understanding the Integration of Ethics and Effectiveness

The interpretative framework functions as these questions (i.e., what is good? what is effective?) are posed with respect to specific practices in concrete organizational contexts. Thus this framework can be contrasted to traditional forms of decision-making research, where the criteria of goodness and effectiveness are identified in advance, and specific behaviors are evaluated based on the extent to which they conform to these objective criteria. Instead, this framework elicits subjective criteria of goodness and effectiveness from the individual actors themselves, and in turn, enables reflection on the extent to which those actors enact the moral and performance imperatives that they espouse. In this sense, we return to the question of the discrepancy between espoused and enacted values, but without the presupposition that the values themselves should be universal, timeless and defined *ex ante.*

The framework thereby functions as a way to interpret specific practices, and to compare different practices in terms of (a) how ethics and effectiveness are defined or construed by individual actors in concrete organizational situations, and (b) the extent to which ethics and effectiveness are integrated through enactment.[5] More precisely, the framework enables an interpretation of the extent to which specific decision-making practices are practically wise.

To the extent that this framework contributes to greater understanding about the wisdom of specific individual decision-making practices, it also raises questions concerning other modes of practice. What about those practices that enact ethics but not effectiveness? Or conversely, the enactment of effectiveness, but not ethics? We propose that the two axes described above can be used to differentiate the following three modes of practice (Figure 10.2):

Practical wisdom: Individual decision-making practices that meet context-specific criteria for both ethics and effectiveness are, in accordance with the theoretical sources introduced above, practically wise. Following the analysis outlined above, such practices effectively enact the common good insofar as they strike the balance of interests, time horizons and responses to the environment.

Moral clumsiness: Individual decision-making practices that appear to enact the context-specific criteria for the ethical good without simultaneously meeting the context-specific criteria for effectiveness can be referred to as 'morally clumsy'. Hutchinson (1995, as quoted in Tsoukas and Cummings, 1997, p. 665), notes how 'it is possible to have the right values without knowing how to achieve them in practice.'[6] Morally clumsy practices may, for example, be characterized by a strong willingness to strike a balance of interests, but an inability to select the most appropriate course of action in order to achieve that balance. They may also involve a conscious and deliberate subordination of effectiveness criteria to ethical criteria – indeed, moral clumsiness may even go so far as categorically to reject efforts to meet effectiveness criteria because they are seen as intrinsically 'amoral'.

Cunning: Following Aristotle and other sources in the classical Greek tradition (cf. Detienne and Vernant, 1978), cunning (in Greek: *metis*) refers to a form of intelligence that is based in tacit knowledge (Letiche and Statler, 2005) and that seeks advantage for its own sake. Although cunning may be necessary for survival (and, by extension, for maintaining strategic advantage in an organization), Aristotle emphasizes that cunning is not sufficient for the achievement of human well-being (Statler and Roos, forthcoming). When values and normativity are important dimensions of a problem (and following the analysis of practical wisdom, these dimensions are intrinsic to all aspects of human affairs), modes of individual decision-making practice that exhibit cunning intelligence can prove deleterious.[7]

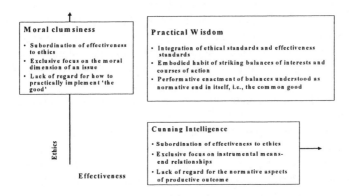

Figure 10.2   Hermeneutic Framework for Wise Decision-Making Practices

DISCUSSION AND IMPLICATIONS

The interpretative framework we have developed here should provide a way to understand how specific individual decision-making practices can be differentiated in terms of the extent to which they integrate ethics and effectiveness. As such, the framework does not enable us to state definitively and objectively that a particular practice is practically wise, or morally clumsy, or cunning. Instead, it enables the interpretation of a specific practice and the evaluation of it on comparative normative grounds – e.g., where the CEO of Monsanto is wise if one accepts his definition of ethics as 'creating genetically modified organisms (GMO) to feed the hungry'; clumsy if one contests the claim that GMOs actually will feed the hungry in the long term without bringing about ecological disaster that kills hungry and well-fed people around the world; and cunning if one analyzes the claim to socially responsible behavior as a deliberate sham to increase shareholder value.

More broadly, our choice of a hermeneutic methodology was driven by an interest to build understanding (cf. Habermas' distinction) of how certain wise practices might integrate ethics and effectiveness. The test of whether this methodology actually serves this interest will be to apply the framework to concrete organizational cases. So, for example, future research could involve interviews with individual actors in organizations, in which the individual, subjectively-determined and context-specific criteria for ethics and effectiveness are probed. These criteria could then be tracked through participant-observation of (or collaborative research methods involving) organizational practice. In turn, the researcher could present first-order findings to the individual actor for reflection and dialogue regarding the extent to which the practice did or did not integrate ethics and effectiveness as previously defined. Through this interpretative process, the wisdom of specific decision-making practices could be identified, better understood and evaluated.

This research process would not result in a universal taxonomy of behaviors, much less a codification of the rules that govern ethical behavior. Instead, it would help to substantiate a new theory of individual ethical decision-making that integrates the two elements of the antinomy presented by Margolis and Walsh (2003). In this manner, hermeneutic research could 'acknowledge a range of inconsistencies and concerns, and still facilitate action' in the organization by contributing to the individual and organizational development needs and yield findings that are directly relevant to current challenges in corporate social responsibility (Margolis and Walsh, 2003, p. 284). Such hermeneutic and participatory research may, in turn, serve as a groundwork for more traditional forms of qualitative case study research and theory development (cf. Eisenhardt, 1989). Care should however be taken to ensure that these research methods remain coherent with the phenomenon in question (i.e., do not seek to codify behavior or define universal rules).

At the level of organizational theory, we suggest that the interpretative framework contributes to the existing literature on ethical decision-making in organizations. Most importantly, it signals a need to focus on practice, including extra-rational and context-specific elements such as identity and tacit knowledge as well as specific environmental dynamics and interests. While virtue ethicists have raised these issues (e.g., Solomon, 1992, 2003, 2004; Koehn, 1995; Moberg, 2000; Jones, 2005; Moore, 2005) the broad relevance of the concept of practical wisdom for organizational theory (including CSR, strategy, leadership, etc.) has not been fully explored. In this regard, additional theoretical research might establish the tradition of virtue ethics as a meaningful alternative to the consequentialist and formalist/intentionalist notions of the moral good that are more traditionally accepted within business ethics.[8]

Finally, reflecting back on Margolis and Walsh's (2003) call for theory that redefines the role, purpose and function of the firm, we suggest that the concept of practical wisdom can not only acknowledge the contradictory performance imperatives of ethical action and firm performance, but can additionally *describe their integration at the level of decision-making practices in organizations.* We have deliberately addressed this challenge at the level of the individual rather than the firm, following Wood's (1991) claim that the ultimate moral agent in the organization is the individual decision-maker. Practical wisdom appears to provide a compelling new conceptual framework at this level of analysis. At the same time, because practice always takes place in a social milieu, our framework also implicitly addresses inter-subjective as well as structural-level variables. Thus future empirical research is necessary to understand how wise decision-making practices emerge between individuals, within groups, and at the macro-level of the organization.

In this chapter, we have not engaged the classic debate within social and organizational theory concerning whether ethics itself should be considered primarily a matter of individual choice or material determinism. Recent work on Weber has tried to re-assess the iron cage of bureaucracy (du Gay, 2000) – and in this light, we wonder indeed whether good organizations exist because wise individuals have created them, or conversely, if practical wisdom is attributed to people in fortuitous organizational situations. However difficult it may be to settle the theoretical issues at stake here, it may be even more difficult to address them empirically. Our suggestion is that future research should rely on a dynamic, process ontology (Chia, 1998; Tsoukas and Chia, 2002; Clegg et al., 2005; Statler and Roos, forthcoming) to frame the phenomenon of wise practice as it emerges.

In conclusion, Margolis and Walsh (2003) have called for a new, normative theory of the firm that enables organizational researchers better to understand better the relationship between normativity and efficiency. We have responded to this call at the level of individual ethical decision-making practices and focused on the concept of practical wisdom as a way to describe the integration of ethics and effectiveness. We have also developed an interpretative framework in the interest of producing greater understanding about practical wisdom in specific organizational contexts. While we acknowledge the provisional nature of this framework, we hope that it will contribute to the discourse focused on how social responsibility might become an integral part of organizations' strategy and operations.

NOTES

1. For an attempt at articulating notions of effectiveness and ethics at the firm level, see for example Le Menestrel (2002).

2. The distinction between *episteme* and *phronesis* is echoed in more modern times by William James' distinction between *knowledge of acquaintance* (which arises through action and experience – i.e. *phronesis*) and *knowledge about* (similar to *episteme*) (cf. Calori, 2002).

3. In order fully to appreciate how this characterization of the moral good – i.e., where the performance of the action is a normative end in itself – provides an alternative solution to the antinomy presented by Margolis and Walsh, it is necessary to clarify how it differs from the two most prominent paradigms of ethical theory, namely intentionalism and consequentialism. Intentionalism holds that the moral value of action is to be located in the actor's intention. The most prominent modern formulation of this notion is Kant's categorical imperative, which provides a simple test to determine whether an intention is moral or not – i.e., if the action can be formulated as a maxim and universalized for all rational actors without logical contradiction, then it is ethical. Within this paradigm of ethical theory, the antinomy remains salient so long as the individual decision-maker's intention to be ethical contradicts with the intention to be effective. Consequentialism, by contrast, holds that the moral value of action is located in the effects, or consequences, of action. The most prominent modern formulation of this notion is Mill's principle of utility, which suggests that moral actions should optimally produce the greatest good (i.e., utility) for the greatest number of people. Within this paradigm of ethical theory, the antinomy remains salient so long as the effectiveness of a given organizational action appears to produce only limited utility.

4. The Aristotelian tradition of virtue ethics differs significantly from both of these paradigms, primarily in terms of the extent to which the moral good can be codified in principle or in accordance with rational laws. This third paradigm of ethical theory locates the moral good in the performance of actions in accordance with virtues – where the virtues themselves do not exist as natural or rational laws, but instead emerge within communities, and remain open to interpretation by its members. Thus while the performance of ethical action remains wholly relative to circumstances, Aristotle's notion of 'the golden mean', characterized following Sternberg as a balance of interests and responses to the environment, provides a compelling ethical ideal. And while for consequentialist ethicists (e.g., following Mill), the moral good is the extrinsic goal of action, for virtue ethicists, it is the intrinsic, signature characteristic of moral action (Solomon, 1992; Nussbaum, 2001). For our purposes, , the antinomy that separates ethics and effectiveness is resolved when the balances are struck in practice, i.e., when ethics and effectiveness are performatively integrated.

5. The question whether it is possible to generate scientific knowledge about normative or ethical matters has been debated since the origins of philosophy in ancient Greece (Nussbaum, 2001). Aristotle's position on the point is that the social world is different from the natural world insofar as it does not adhere to immutable laws and thus cannot be known with any certainty – thus the need for 'phronesis'. If we accept that practical wisdom is not based on natural or logical necessity, it should not be studied using a research methodology designed to generate propositional theory or testable hypotheses. Instead, it should be studied using a research methodology that (a) acknowledges the normativity of knowledge itself, (b) accepts that the 'object' of knowledge remains historically and socially context-specific, and nevertheless (c) takes up the challenge of identifying specific forms of action as 'virtuous', presenting these claims as interpretations that remain subject (with respect to

their validity) to comparison with other interpretations developed through similar or alternative methods.

6. By highlighting points of performative contradiction (i.e., where the espoused virtue is not practiced) the framework thus directs our attention to the role of integrity in the formation of character (MacIntyre, 1984; Walker 2002; etc.).

7. Similarly, Raven (1977, 1984, quoted in Maclagan, 1990), 'distinguished persons' values from the competencies needed to realize these.'

8. Cunning behavior may also be characterized by an instrumentalization of ethics: the latter is considered to the degree that it will provide effective in promoting a given goal. In organizations, this goal is predominantly understood in terms of profit maximization. In economic models of managerial behavior (such as the principal-agent model of the firm), managers are frequently described as using resources and power, but also normative rhetoric (i.e. 'ethics') instrumentally in order to pursue self-interest. In other terms, the cunning person might argue in favor of leaving ethics aside from decision-making, by using a formalist justification. This justification would emphasize the separation of the subjective, personal, and situation-specific from the moral, framing it in abstract, universalist terms, that can be approached only by stripping an issue from its context.

9. As this document goes to press, we anticipate Dennis Moberg's upcoming keynote lecture at the 2006 annual meeting of the Society of Business Ethics, entitled 'Practical Wisdom and Business Ethics' may help change this situation. The abstract indicates that 'practical wisdom is defined and a model is presented that describes its antecedent conditions, enabling factors, and behavioral manifestations'. Moberg plans to draw on 'a number of clips from the classic film, *The Wizard of Oz*'.

REFERENCES

Abizadeh, A. (2002), 'The passions of the wise: *Phronêsis*, rhetoric, and Aristotle's passionate practical deliberation', *The Review of Metaphysics*, **56**, 267-296.

Ardelt, M. (2004), 'Wisdom as expert knowledge system: A critical review of a contemporary operationalization of an ancient concept', *Human Development, 47*, 257-285.

Aristotle (1962), *Nicomachean Ethics*, Indianapolis, US: Bobbs-Merrill.

Balogun, J., A. S. Huff and P. Johnson (2003), 'Three responses to the methodological challenges of studying strategizing', *Journal of Management Studies*, **40** (1), 197-224.

Baltes, P. B. and U. M. Staudinger (2000), 'Wisdom: A metaheuristic (pragmatic) to orchestrate mind and virtue toward excellence', *American Psychologist*, **55** (1), 122-136.

Bay, D. D. and R. R. Greenberg (2001), 'The relationship of the DIT and behavior: A replication', *Issues in Accounting Education*, **16**, 367-380.

Blasi, A. (1980), 'Bridging moral cognition and moral action: A critical review of the literature', *Psychological Bulletin*, **88**, 1-45.

Blasi, A. (1984), 'Moral Identity: Its Role in Moral Function', in W.M. Kurtines and J. L. Gewirtz (eds), *Morality, Moral Behavior, and Moral Development*, New York, US: Wiley, pp. 128-139.

Bourdieu, P. (1990), *The Logic of Practice*, Stanford, CA, US: Stanford University Press.

Calori, R. (2002), 'Essai: Real time/real space research: Connecting action and reflection in organization studies', *Organization Studies*, **23** (6), 877-883.

Campbell, R. L. and J. C. Christopher (1996), 'Moral development theory: A critique of its Kantian presuppositions', *Developmental Review*, **16**, 1-47.

Chia, R. (1998), 'Essay: Thirty years on: From organizational structures to the organization of thought', *Organization Studies*, **18** (4), 685-708.

Clegg, S. R. and A. Ross-Smith (2003), 'Revising the boundaries: Management education and learning in a postpositivist world', *Academy of Management Learning and Education*, **2** (1), 85-98.

Clegg, S. R., M. Kornberger and C. Rhodes (2005), 'Learning/becoming/organizing', *Organization*, **12** (2), 147-167.

Colby, A. and W. Damon (1992), *Some do Care: Contemporary Lives of Moral Commitment*, New York, US: Free Press.

Contu, A. and H. Willmott (2003), 'Reembedding situtedness: The importance of power relations in learning theory', *Organization Science*, **14** (3), 283-296.

Csikszentmihalyi, M. and K. Rathunde (1990), 'The Psychology of Wisdom: An Evolutionary Interpretation', in R. Sternberg (eds), *Wisdom, Its Nature, Origins and Development*, Cambridge, UK: Cambridge University Press, pp. 25-51.

Czarniawska, B. (1997), *Narrating the Organization: Dramas of Institutional Identity*, Chicago, US: University of Chicago Press.

Detienne, M. and J. P. Vernant (1974), *Cunning Intelligence in Greek Culture & Society*, Chicago, US: University of Chicago Press.

Devereux, D. (1986), 'Particular and universal in Aristotle's conception of practical knowledge', *Review of Metaphysics*, **39**, 483-504.

Dreyfus, H. and S. Dreyfus (1986), *Mind Over Machine: The Power of Human Intuition and Expertise in the Era of the Computer*, New York, US: Free Press.

Dubinsky, A. J. and B. Loken (1989), 'Analyzing ethical decision-making in marketing', *Journal of Business Research*, **19** (2), 83-107.

Duska, R. F. (1993), 'Aristotle: A pre-modern post-modern? Implications for business ethics, *Business Ethics Quarterly*, **3** (3), 227-249.

du Gay, P. (2000), *In Praise of Bureaucracy: Weber, Organization, Ethics*, London, UK: Sage.

Eisenberg, N. (1996), 'Caught in a narrow Kantian perception of prosocial development: Reactions to Campbell and Christopher's critique of moral development theory', *Developmental Review*, **16**, 48-68.

Eisenberg, N. (2002), 'Empathy related emotional responses, altruism, and their socialization', in R. J. Davidson and A. Harrington (eds), *Visions of Compassion: Western Scientists and Tibetan Buddhists Examine Human Nature*, London, UK: Oxford University Press.

Eisenhardt, K. M. (1989), 'Building theories from case study research', *Academy of Management Review*, **14** (4), 532-550.

Ferrell, O. G. and L. G. Gresham (1985), 'A contingency framework for understanding ethical decision making in marketing', *Journal of Marketing*, **49** (3), 87-96.

Flyvbjerg, B. (2001), *Making Social Science Matter: Why Social Inquiry Fails and How it can Succeed Again*, Cambridge, UK: Cambridge University Press.

Friedman, M. (1970), 'The social responsibility of business is to increase its profits, *New York Times Magazine*, Sept. 13, 32-33.

Gadamer, H. G. (2002) [1960], *Truth and Method*, New York, US: Continuum.

Geertz, C. (1973), *The Interpretation of Cultures*, New York, US: Basic Books.

Habermas, J. (1971), *Knowledge and Human Interest*, Boston: Beacon Press.

Habermas, J. (1990), *Moral Consciousness and Communicative Action*, Cambridge, MA, US: MIT Press.

Harrington, S. J. (1991), 'What corporate America is teaching about ethics', *Academy of Management Executive*, **5** (1), 1-31.

Hartman, E. M. (1998), 'The role of character in business ethics', *Business Ethics Quarterly*, **8** (3), 547-559.

Hendry, J. and D. Seidl (2003), 'The structure and significance of strategic episodes: Social systems theory and the routine practices of strategic change', *Journal of Management Studies*, **40** (1), 175-196.

Heracleous, L. (2003), *Strategy and Organization: Realizing Strategic Management.* Cambridge, UK: Cambridge University Press.

Heracleous, L. and M. Barrett (2001), 'Organizational change as discourse: Communicative actions and deep structures in the context of IT Implementation', *Academy of Management Journal*, **44** (4), 755-778.

Hunt, S. D. and S. Vitell (1986), 'A general theory of marketing ethics', *Journal of Macromarketing*, **6** (1), 5-16.

Hutchinson, D. S. (1995), 'Ethics', in J. Barnes (ed.), *The Cambridge Companion to Aristotle*, Cambridge, UK: Cambridge University Press, pp. 195-223.

Jarzabkowski, P. (2004), 'Strategy as practice: Recursiveness, adaptation and practices-in-use', *Organization Studies*, **25** (4), 529-560.

Johnson, G., L. Melin and R. Whittington (2003), 'Guest editors' introduction. Micro strategy and strategizing: Towards an activity based view', *Journal of Management Studies*, **40** (1), 3-22.

Jones, C. (2005), 'Wisdom paradigms for the enhancement of ethical and profitable business practices', *Journal of Business Ethics*, **57** (4), 363-375.

Jones, T. M. (1991), 'Ethical Decision Making by Individuals in Organizations: An Issue-Contingent Model', *Academy of Management Review*, **16** (2), 366-395.

Koehn, D. (1995), 'A role for virtue ethics in the analysis of business practice', *Business Ethics Quarterly*, **5** (3), 533-539.

Le Menestrel, M. (2002), 'Economic rationality and ethical behavior: Ethical business between venality and sacrifice', *Business Ethics: A European Review*, **11** (2), 157-166.

Letiche, H and M. Statler (2005), 'Evoking Metis: Questioning the logics of change, responsiveness, meaning and action in organizations', *Culture and Organization*, **11** (1), 1-16.

MacIntyre, A. (1984), *After Virtue: A Study in Moral Theory*, Notre Dame, France: University of Notre Dame Press.

Maclagan, P. (1990), 'Moral behaviour in organizations: The contribution of management education and development', *British Journal of Management*, **1**, 17-26.

Margolis, J. D. and J. P. Walsh (2003), 'Misery loves companies: Rethinking social initiatives by business', *Administrative Science Quarterly*, **48**, 268-305.

McDowell, J. (1979), 'Virtue and Reason', *The Monist*, **62**, 331-50.

Moberg, D. J. (2000), 'Role models and moral exemplars: How do employees acquire virtues by observing others?', *Business Ethics Quarterly,* **10** (3), 675-697.

Moore, G. (2002), 'On the implications of the practice-institution distinction: MacIntyre and the application of modern virtue ethics to business', *Business Ethics Quarterly*, **12** (1), 19-32.

Moore, G. (2005), 'Humanizing business: A modern virtue ethics approach', *Business Ethics Quarterly*, **15** (2), 237-255.

Nussbaum, M. 2001, *The Fragility of Goodness: Luck and Ethics in Greek Tragedy and Philosophy* (Updated Edition), New York: Cambridge University Press.

Orlikowski, W. (2002), 'Knowing in Practice: Enacting a Collective Capability in Distributed Organizing', *Organization Science*, **13**, 249-273.

Packer, M. (1985), 'Hermeneutic inquiry in the study of human conduct', *American Psychologist*, **40**, 1081-1093.

Phillips, R., R. E. Freeman and A. C. Wicks (2003), 'What stakeholder theory is not', *Business Ethics Quarterly*, **13**, 479-502.

Polanyi, M. (1976), 'Tacit Knowledge', in M. Marx and F. Goodson (eds), *Theories in Contemporary Psychology*, New York, US: Macmillan, pp. 330-344.

Punzo, Vincent A. (1996), 'After Kohlberg: Virtue ethics and the recovery of the moral self', *Philosophical Psychology*, **9** (1), 7-24.

Raven, J. (1977), *Education, Values and Society*, London, UK: H.K. Lewis & Co. Ltd.

Raven, J. (1984), *Competence in Modern Society*, London, UK: H.K. Lewis & Co. Ltd.

Régner, P. (2003), 'Strategy creation in the periphery: Inductive versus deductive strategy making', *Journal of Management Studies*, **40** (1), 57-82.

Rest, J. R. (1986), *Moral Development: Advances in Research and Theory*, New York, US: Praeger.

Ricoeur, P. (1981), *Hermeneutics and the Human Sciences*, Cambridge, UK: Cambridge University Press.

Schweder, R. A. and J. Haidt (1993), 'The future of moral psychology: Truth, intuition, and the pluralist way', *Psychological Science*, **4** (6), 360-365.

Solomon, R. (1992), 'Corporate roles, personal virtues: An Aristotalian approach to business ethics', *Business Ethics Quarterly*, **2**, 317-339.

Solomon, R. (2003), 'Victims of circumstances? A defense of virtue ethics in business', *Business Ethics Quarterly*, **13**, 43-63.

Solomon, R. (2004), 'Aristotle, ethics, and business organizations', *Organization Studies*, **25** (6), 1021-1043.

Statler, M. and J. Roos (2006), 'Reframing strategic preparedness: An essay on practical wisdom', *International Journal of Management Concepts and Philosophy*, **2** (2), 99-117.

Statler, M. and J. Roos (forthcoming), 'Dear Prudence: An essay on practical wisdom in strategy-making', *Social Epistemology*.

Statler, M., J. Roos and B. Victor (2006), 'Illustrating the need for practical wisdom', *International Journal of Management Concepts and Philosophy*, **2** (1), 1-30.

Sternberg, R. J. (1998), 'A balance theory of wisdom', *Review of General Psychology*, **2** (4), 347-365.

Sternberg, R. J. (2001), 'Why schools should teach for wisdom: The balance theory of wisdom in educational settings', *Educational Psychologist*, **36** (4), 227-245.

Taylor, C. (1976), 'Hermeneutics and Politics', in P. Connerton (eds), *Critical Sociology, Selected Readings*, London, UK: Penguin Books, pp. 153-193.

Taylor, C. (1993), 'To Follow a Rule...', in C. Calhoun, E. LiPumaand and M. Postone (eds), *Bourdieu, Critical Perspectives*, Cambridge, UK: Polity Press, pp. 45-60.

Thoma, S. J. and J. R. Rest (1986), 'Moral Judgment, Behavior, Decision Making, and Attitudes', in J. R. Rest (eds), *Moral Development: Advances in research and theory,* New York, US: Praeger, pp.133-175.

Trevino, L. K. (1986), 'Ethical decision making in organizations: A person-situation interactionist model', *Academy of Management Review,* **11**, 601-617.

Tsoukas, H. and S. Cummings (1997), 'Marginalization and recovery: The emergence of Aristotelian themes in organization studies', *Organization Studies,* **18** (4), 655-683.

Tsoukas, H. and R. Chia (2002), 'On organizational becoming: Rethinking organizational change', *Organization Science,* **13** (5), 567-599.

Turiel, E. (1983), *The Development of Social Knowledge: Morality and Convention,* Cambridge, UK: Cambridge University Press.

Walker, J. B. (2000), 'Choosing biases, using power and practicing resistance: Moral development in a world without certainty', *Human Development,* **43**, 135-156.

Welker, L. (2004), 'Extending the bounds of interpretive inquiry: Toward a performance approach to organizational studies', *Atlantic Journal of Communication,* **12** (1), 46-57.

Whittington, R. (2003), 'The work of strategizing and organizing: For a practice perspective', *Strategic Organization,* **1** (1), 117-125.

Wood, D. J. (1991), 'Corporate social performance revisited', *Academy of Management Review,* **16**, 691-718.

11. The Constitution of Ethics: Discourse, Practice and Conflict in a Health-Care Center[*]

Silke Seemann, Stephan Laske and Martin Kornberger

INTRODUCTION

Ethics are an ascendant topic in current organization practice and thinking (see special issues of *Academy of Management Executive* **18** (2), 2004 and *Critical Perspectives on Accounting* **15** (6-7), 2004; Wicks and Freeman, 1998, Clegg et al., 2006). In particular, Donaldson (2003) has recently argued that there is a need for theories that provide an understanding of ethics and reflect upon the possibilities of ethically sound management practice. In the past, researchers have taken a principally normative stance towards ethical *content*, defined as a set of values that *should* govern corporate conduct (Gatewood and Carroll, 1991; Brass et al., 1998; Soule, 2002), while more empirically oriented researchers have tried to establish a positive relation between ethical *context* and organizational performance (Paine, 1994; Raiborn and Payne, 1996; Joyner and Payne, 2002; Francis and Armstrong, 2003). Margolis and Walsh (2003), in a seminal contribution, take the *tension* between organizational practices and ethical values as their analytical starting point, a point of departure from which we take our cue (see also Statler and Oppegaard in this volume). Doing so, we report findings from an ethnographic action research project into one of Europe's leading health-care

*This chapter is a result of a larger inquiry into the nature of business ethics and was funded by the Austrian Science Fund (FWF) as 'Ethics in Organizations; Project Number P16531-G04'. Also, thanks (in alphabetical order) to Chris Carter, Stewart Clegg, Martin Messner, and Carl Rhodes who have contributed through ongoing discussions about ethics as practice to the development of this chapter.

centers located at the heart of the Austrian Alps. As our case study will show, in the absence of a written code of conduct the organization developed two different sets of ethical value systems. We will argue that different practices and discourses from the two main organizational units – the hospitality and the medical-therapeutical unit – constituted these different ethics. We will examine the differences between them by focusing on the different ethical relations that the units developed towards the organization's customers. The objective of this chapter is to explore how ethics is played out in organizational practice. Theoretically we will focus on ethics and how it is enacted, but not necessarily articulated, in organizational discourse and embedded in organizational practice. Our ethnographic account provides evidence that ethics is less explicitly but more implicitly embedded in the organizational context. In fact, rather than seeing ethics as written codes of conduct, ethics as can be seen as response to internal and external environmental challenges and a way of making sense of them. Furthermore, our account will explore some of the contradictions and tension that are inherently linked to ethics. As our case shows, ethics is not a clear-cut value system that defines 'good' and 'bad'. Rather, ethics is constantly negotiated and constructed as organizational members argue for and over resources and responsibilities. In this perspective, ethics is a means of organizing and necessarily linked to the exercise of power.

In doing so the chapter advances our understanding of ethics in the following ways: First, it represents an empirical case study that analyses how ethics is discursively constructed and enacted in an organization. Second, it scrutinizes theoretical contributions to the field and shows to that extent, theoretical arguments are reflected in organizational practice. Third, the chapter provides interesting implications for management practice and delineates areas for future research. Fourth, it contains helpful advice for the development of ethical discourse in organization.

THE THEORETICAL CONTEXT: FROM ETHICS AS RULES TO ETHICS AS PRACTICE

Most commonly ethics are situated as set of organizational rules expressed in a code of ethics. Whereas rules form an integral part of organizational ethics, the different interpretations, meanings and uses of these rules is critical (see also Babeau in this volume). In organization theory, Gouldner (1954) analyzed 'indulgency patterns' in organizations that described the difference between interpretation of rules by the book and their actual interpretation in practice. Put simply the meaning of rules varies with the context of their enactment. As the philosopher Wittgenstein (1968) argued, rules don't do anything by themselves but need to be interpreted and enacted situationally. It is rule *use*, not rule *existence*, which determines ethical conduct (Andrews, 1989; Paine, 1994). Furthermore, rules can act as ceremonial façades that are in contrast with the reality of day-to-day organizational life (Meyer and Rowan, 1977). From this perspective rules are an expression of an organization's attempt to rationalize its own version of rationality (Flyvberg, 2003) and to maintain an image as a rational and hence legitimate actor. Brunsson (1994) has argued that public sector organizations institutionally maintain and capitalize on the gaps between talk, action and decision. This tension between what ought to happen and what actually happens constitutes what he has described as organized hypocrisy. In this chapter we suggest that such a practice perspective on ethics results in an analytically interesting understanding of ethics. Philosophically informed by several writers such as Foucault (1977) and Bourdieu (1990), practice defines what people actually do when they conduct their business. Practice is conceptualized in terms of how things unfold in action, where rules are situationally interpreted and where both discourse and actions are performative (Czarniawska, 2001, p. 256; Clegg et al., 2006). Rather than claiming normatively what should be done or, in empiricist terms, merely reporting what was done with no comment other than to present 'the facts', a practice approach puts emphasis on the recursive constitution of ethics through everyday actions and discursive sense-making processes.

In this chapter we build on a recently emerging body of literature that can be denoted by the term ethics as practice (Jackall, 1988; Andrews, 1989 Stark, 1993; Paine, 1994; Kjonstad and Willmott, 1995; Keleman and Peltonen, 2001; ten Bos and Willmott, 2001; Thorne and Saunders, 2002; Clegg et al., 2006). In contrast to normative or empirical approaches, as defined by Donaldson and Dunfee (1994), the ethics as practice approach puts emphasis on the embeddedness and the enactment of ethics in everyday organizational processes, routines and practices. Rather than locating ethics squarely in organizational codes of conduct ethics are enacted when organizational members work in teams, negotiate with customers, and strategize about the future. The seminal work of Jackall (1988) illustrates this point. He researched the 'moral rules-in-use that managers construct to guide their behavior at work' and found that 'actual organizational moralities are ... contextual, situational, highly specific, and, most often, unarticulated' (Jackall 1988, pp. 4, 6). Hence ethics does not equal what is formulated as rules of behaviour or codes of conduct. Compliance with rules is not necessarily ethical as Kjonstad and Willmott (1995, p. 446) have suggested. Such codes of conduct might ensure compliance but they do not produce ethically sound behavior (Munro, 1992; Barker, 1993). Again, as Kjonstad and Willmott (1995, p. 449) argue, 'instead of acting to encourage and facilitate the development of moral learning and the exercise of moral judgment, [such] codes operate to promote routinized compliance'. Thus, from an ethics as practice perspective organizational members might utilize written codes as resources to negotiate their positions and make sense of events depending on context and situation; but ethics will not be determined by these rules and codes. Moreover, ethics is a highly ambiguous and uncertain business. 'Bounded morality' (Donaldson and Dunfee, 1994) causes organizational members to make ethical decisions based on highly complex, situational and incomplete information. Hence, the ethicality of a particular situation is constructed retrospectively (Ibarra-Colado et al., 2006). As Donaldson and Dunfee, (1994, p. 257) argue, 'the correctness of each moral decision must be referenced to an infinite array of facts, or subject to theories that clash with key moral convictions'. Hence, the tension between organizational practices and ethical decisions is constitutive for business ethics (see Margolis and Walsh, 2003). Finally, ethics is socially and discursively constructed (Clegg et al., 2006). Rather than assuming a priori ethically right and wrong answers to a particular situation, ethics is subject to and constituted through sensemaking processes of organizational members (Weick, 1995). In fact, to frame a particular situation as ethically charged is already a constructive move that reflects how ethics are constituted within knowledge/power, become relations (Nietzsche, 1969; Foucault, 1997). For instance, Gordon et al. (2006) have shown how ethics in a police organization was constituted by the power relations between organizational members and how the dominant discourse legitimized certain decisions and actions as ethical. Building on this ethics as practice approach will allow us to understand how ethics was constituted at our research site, the health-care center.

THE METHODOLOGY

Context

The empirical part of this chapter is based on qualitative research that was conducted by one of the authors from April 2004 until March 2006. The privately owned organization (for reasons of confidentiality referred to as 'Med Center') employs around 80 staff and can be described as one of the industry leaders in the fast growing market of private health care providers in Europe. The organization was founded in the 1970s as a leisure and holiday destination for tourists. A few years later the decision was made to focus on health care. By then only three out of the total staff of 30 were working in the medical/therapeutical area. Today's managing director was brought on board to facilitate this transition. Currently 60 percent of the Med Center's staff work in the medical/therapeutical area catering for 80 guests in a high tech and high touch environment. As we will argue, the biography of the organization (see Mueller and Carter, 2005) and its changing identity is inextricably linked to its ethics.

The Med Center offers products and services including medical treatment, therapy, exclusive hospitality, and dermatherapy treatments. One employee describes the benefit of the Med Center as 'guidance and assistance on the way back to a healthy life'. The customers are called 'guests' and while some of them visit the Med Center to achieve better work-life balance others seek treatment for more serious illness including drug and alcohol addiction, obesity and other health-related problems. The exclusive offer attracts wealthy guests from Europe (mainly from Germany, and increasingly from Eastern European countries) that are willing to spend between €2,500 and €15,000 for a week for treatments. The facility is located in the tranquil and beautiful environment at the heart of the Austrian Alps. Recently the Med Center has been facing increased competition from alternative service providers. Therefore, the management of the Med Center has embraced a strategy of product innovation, excellent service quality and continuous organizational learning. This strategy should ensure that the Med Center can maintain its position as leading private health service provider in Europe and grow its customer base. The Med Center represents an interesting research site for several reasons: first, its products and services are developed and promoted around value-laden attributes such as 'good', 'healthy' and 'beautiful'. However, following the logic of market capitalism the Med Center is managed as a business and as such it has to provide adequate profits and growth. Second, when we started researching the organization there was no formal code of ethics in place. However, ethics are of key concern to any organization operating in the health care industry including medicine, pharmacy, and other health services. Hence ethics were enacted in situ which led to conflicts and ethical dilemmas that provided an interesting empirical starting point for our inquiry into ethics as practice.

Data Collection and Analysis

The project was designed and conducted as an action-research project (Kappler; 1980; Winter, 1987; Passfield, 1996; Zuber-Skeritt, 2002; Zuber-Skeritt and Perry, 2002). The involvement of the researcher within the organization can be seen as potentially distorting our observations. However, we would argue that especially an empirical inquiry into the nature of ethics depends on open communication between researcher and researched organization. Throughout the research phase a close relationship with many organizational members was established. Through this personal relationship the research team gained insights into everyday organizational life that would not have been possible otherwise. Also, it is important to mention that because of this action research process both parties had an interest in the research and its outcomes. The organization used the research team as consultants and advisors which allowed the research team to participate in important meetings and observe how the organization dealt with critical issues.

We started our data gathering process in April 2004 and ended in March 2006. We entered shortly after several key employees left the organization and part of the organization was restructured. During this redesign the Med Center was closed for two months. In order to collect data we spent a total of 16 days participating in different aspects of organizational life: for eight days we worked in the organization helping in the kitchen, at the reception desk, assisting the management team and performing other more mundane activities such as cleaning; the other eight days were spent as observing guests of the Med Center to develop an understanding of the extent to which image, reality and processes of organizing were congruent. Moreover, we conducted 16 semi-structured interviews that ranged from 45 minutes to 90 minutes. Interviewees were selected from different parts of the organization, including employees from different departments, members of the management team, as well as guests of the Med Center. All interviews were tape recorded and transcribed. Also, informal conversations provided a valuable source of information. In many settings the conversation between the researcher and staff members could not be taped. The atmosphere of these conversations was quite relaxed and staff members revealed many 'insider' stories. Additionally, we could gain access to internal meetings and workshops: in total we observed four internal workshops over eight days, 16 ad hoc trouble shooting meetings and more than 150 routine meetings. During these events we studied how organizational members made sense of potentially ethically charged situations, how they interacted with each other both verbally and non-verbally, and how they responded to problems, challenges and opportunities that emerged as potentially ethically charged. We focused on how ethics were articulated in these situations, how and why particular situations were perceived as ethically charged, and how far ethics were deployed as a solution. These observations were documented and made accessible for data analysis. The plurality of data collection techniques ensured that the researchers could gain different perspectives that contributed to a more holistic image of the organization (Flick, 2003).

After the data collection was conducted by the first author of this chapter the research team started analysing the data by categorizing it according to theoretically derived and emerging key themes. Rather than taking for granted the existence of ethics as an 'object' we assumed that ethics result from constructive social moves by individuals and organizations (Berger and Luckmann, 1967). Working through our empirical data we found that the themes of values, identity, closeness and distance occurred repeatedly and were reflected in the different data (Weick, 1989). We put special emphasis on tensions, conflicts and apparent paradoxes between these different themes and ethics in practice. We moved between our preliminary understanding and our findings from the research both informing each other and allowing us to translate the data into a narrative.

Translating Data Into a Narrative: Writing the Case

Kirk and Millard (1986, p. 42) suggest that the *reliability* of case-study-based data is problematic. Researchers need to articulate both sources of data and the data analysis in order to make a case study credible (Eisenhardt, 1989). A narrative can be very high in accuracy (Langley, 1999) and validity (Tsoukas, 1989), but only if the author can convince the reader by an account of the construction of the case study. Golden-Biddle and Locke (1993) argue that conviction requires authenticity, plausibility and criticality. Given the research team's experience (Schneider and Laske, 1985; Laske and Schneider, 1986), by addressing these three criteria we sought to ensure that our narrative would be convincing (see Mueller and Carter, 2005).

Given that the Med Center's senior management team was very interested in ethics as key to their organizational success they agreed to provide generous access to meetings, staff interviews, and participant observation (see above). In return the research team agreed to feedback key observation and make recommendations on the basis of the analysis of the findings. Since the organization was rather small a good relationship between the researchers and organizational members was established quickly. This good relationship ensured that the research team could conduct interviews very openly and could also talk about emerging key themes during informal encounters. Obviously, such open interaction generated rich data. Also, trust was built between the researchers and the organization which made much more intimate observations possible. Therefore, the case study is built upon data from different sources that ensures authenticity of the narrative.

Secondly, the research process was such that every attempt was made to ensure that the narrative presents itself as plausible. To achieve this, following the data collection, the case study was written into a narrative and then presented and discussed with members of the organization. Doing so it was ensured that they recognized the events that were recorded and various positions taken on such events. Furthermore, during the data collection and the writing of the narrative several academic colleagues provided valuable feedback. Discussing our own understanding of the data with organizational members and colleagues provided an opportunity to make sense of the data intersubjectively and hence establish plausibility. The main findings of the research were presented and discussed during a half-day workshop with the CEO and around 50 organizational members. This was an important forum in which contradictions and ambiguities became obvious. We used these meetings with organizational members as sense-making process. Organizational members used the feedback to discuss values that they understood as important for the future development of the organization. Most organizational members understood the research process as vehicle to speak about taboos openly and reduce internal tensions. The importance of the open discussions that were encouraged by the research team are reinforced by spontaneous behaviour and feedback from the staff.

The final dimension of Golden-Biddle and Locke's (1993) notion of 'convincing' is the notion of criticality. This addresses the extent to which we were reflexive about our own work and the degree to which texts succeed in prompting other writers and managers to re-examine their own assumptions. Self-reflexively the research team discussed its bounded 'ways of worldmaking' (Goodman, 1978), the specific research interest that guided their data collection and analysis (Habermas, 1973) and the effects that these biases had on our conclusions. Whereas the limitations of our study will be discussed in more detail in the last section of this chapter, it is important to note that our research provided the organization with an opportunity to narrate its own identity. Reflecting on these effects of our research on our own understanding of the observed events ensured the criticality of our case study. Doing so, data collection and interpretation become a fluid process resulting in a mutually deeper understanding between the researched organization and the research team.

FINDINGS

As mentioned above the Med Center changed in its history from a leisure and tourist facility to a modern establishment focusing on health, therapy, well-being and holistic treatment of its guests. This development was achieved through, and made necessary, fundamental changes in its management structure. As one member of the management team put it:

In the early days, the organization was like a small plane, but now we changed and we are flying a fast jet – I need to check all instruments, I need to check navigation, I need all relevant information about the next landing and the next take off.

The culture of the organization has changed from a family-like, informal climate to a more professional, structured organization where administrative processes and organizational practices are defined and standardized. Conflicts between the old and the new way of doing things were evident throughout the research process. For instance an organizational member stated:

If things could become again what they were in the past: when our director did not know what to do anymore we all went for a walk up a mountain, had lots of fun and talked about everything. Then we knew again what to do ... back then we were one team.

When we started our research process two of the doctors that had been responsible for the development of the health and therapy related services over the past 15 years left the organization, and the two key managers from the therapeutical department and several of their staff left the organization for different reasons. The complex synthesis of medical treatment and exclusive hospitality experience created high expectations from guests and required the organization to integrate its processes and management systems much more thoroughly. As one employee put it the high expectations of guests were reflected in the high bills they had to pay:

you could hear: 'oh, that's a small family car' – or 'I could have bought a car for that or gone on a three month holiday'. ... we improved the service quality over the past 3 years ... you hear less complaints about high bills. Of course people still say 'Au' and might catch their breath for a second .... But nowadays there are less 'stupid' remarks then before.

In the past, information about guests, their current state and their medical schedule was communicated informally and spontaneously. However, the 'professionalization' of the Med Center and the loss of key staff made a change in the communication structure necessary. Employees perceived this change in a negative way threatening the informal and open culture that provided them with a certain amount of autonomy and control over their work. Moreover, employees were increasingly expected to manage their and their guests' emotions at work. Mistakes and failures in the organizational services delivery process (such as having no capacity for a special treatment that a guest requires) had to be managed through personal and emotional engagement of staff. This put enormous pressure on staff as one employee said: 'This week almost killed me, mentally. ... I was afraid to go to work ... and then at the weekend I collapsed and just cried for three days. I said to myself 'I cannot stand this any longer' and took my resignation with me to work. 'Ironically, situations such as this one occurred in an organization that promotes values of health, mental balance and well-being. Surprisingly, employees perceived this gap between talk and actual practice as hypocrisy (see Brunsson, 1994). In fact, in analyzing the values put forward by the organization conflicts and contradictions become obvious. For instance the organizations promoted emotional engagement, intuition, innovation and individual development as core to its success; simultaneously as a business it needed to control processes, establish quality standards and ensure operating at (almost) full capacity. In summary, the organizational changes led to conflicts and tensions. In the following sections we will report areas in which these conflicts and their impact on ethics in practice became most obvious.

Identity

Employees described the benefits for the guests as follows: 'our guests are people that work hard and that find themselves alienated from their self. Now they arrive at the Med Center ... there are people [working here] that do not only give them the feeling that we are there for them but we are really there for them. I believe this is the secret of the Med Center'. Another employee described the Med Center as a 'big family' where 'guests feel comfortably looked after from the very first day to the last'. This quality is seen as being threatened by the changes of the organization: 'what I feel as big danger ... is that the Med Center turns into an economic machine or whether the human element remains'. However, this ethics of a humanistic environment is subverted by the unreconciled diversity of the employees of the Med Center. As mentioned above, at the end of our research project more than 80 percent of staff were working in the medical/therapeutical area and only 20 percent were working in the more traditional hospitality area. The self-perception of the organization did not reflect these changes. For instance, payment standards are derived from other comparable hospitality businesses; the software that the Med Center used is a hospitality package; and most importantly, leadership structures were modeled after hospitality structures: the managing director and the hotel manager acted as an executive team. Their decisions affected all medical staff, including the medical doctors. Pricing models for the different medical services were developed by the executive team not by the medical team. Medical decisions such as the rule that guests should not speak during meals were often overruled by the management team which held feedback interviews with guests over lunch. These examples demonstrate the dominant logic of the Med Center that is modeled after structures, systems and practices common in the hospitality industry. However, they do not reflect the change towards a more health care focused organization. Medical and non-medical staff members often had conflicting ideas about the identity and the culture of the Med Center. As one non-medical staff member put it: 'we from hospitality get together and have fun ... Then there is the other block ... the guys in white [meaning the medical staff]. They sit at another table, they talk about work and about what we could invent next. This cannot be very constructive.' Moreover, the medical staff were seen as 'theorists' not knowing how things work in practice. For instance, one employee saw the growth in the medical area as the reason for the current problems:

> I can tell you, if we were more lean in the therapeutical area, if we – and that's just a number – if we did not employ 35 but only 25 staff, and they would all work efficiently, then we would have the calmness of the old days. Work would be done more efficiently, it would be less hush-hush – he is doing a bit of this, and then we put his feet into water and a bit of floating and a bit of that – that's all bullshit, nobody needs that. It's all a waste of time.

The cracks in the collaboration between medical and non-medical staff became obvious when guests complained about lack of service quality. As one employee who manages guests' feedback put it, the 'biggest problems occur when communication and collaboration between hospitality and therapy do not function'. The differences between non-medical and medical staff were embedded in everyday practices, organizational processes as well as organizational discourses that the two groups use to make sense of their environments. Using the example of the 'guest' we will argue that these different discourses constitute the customer as different subject – either from a hospitality perspective as 'guest who is king' or, from a medical perspective, as 'guest as human being' who does not always know what is good for her or him. These different discourses and practices constitute a very different subject 'guest' and hence constitute different ethical relations between staff and guests.

'Kings' or 'Human Beings' – The Discursive Constitution of Customer Ethics

The different roles and responsibilities of medical and non-medical staff are reflected in different discourses that they employ to make sense of their environment. One member of the management team put it as follows:

> It needs to be made clear to some of our employees that we are not simply employees – hospitality needs to be lived 100 percent. The guest really needs to say 'I feel comfortable here' and he must mean this truly not simply 'hello' and 'good bye'. It must come from the heart. Hospitality must be lived 100 percent – you cannot learn that, you cannot study that, the service mentality simply needs to be there; you need to be open towards your guests, and satisfy almost each of their needs and wishes. In this respect we will have to work extremely hard on the attitude of some employees who do not agree with this approach.

In this quote the customer is literally conceptualized as king; each of his or her wishes needs to be addressed and if possible fulfilled. The discursive model for this attitude is taken from the hospitality industry in which the 'customer is king' attitude prevails. This attitude is reflected in the hospitality part as one employee says: repeat customers get 'their' preferred room, 'their' preferred staff and 'their' spot in the dining room:

> some of them have been coming for twenty years – twenty years! And he wants to have his staff, his room. The staff know exactly when Mr Mueller arrives which pillows, which bathrobe, the hard or the soft bed, a table and a chair although this is not part of the standard room equipment. Everything is done perfectly. Eighty percent of our guests are repeat guests.

This quote from an employee working in hospitality demonstrates their service attitude. Staff are committed to retaining customers and treating them accordingly. Obviously such an emphasis on 'mundane things' such as which pillow is preferred by different repeat customers makes the task of a lower ranking staff member more important. From the staff's perspective they are part of the institution just as much as the service offer itself. As the next quote demonstrates this service attitude 'bends' organizational processes as one employee from hospitality suggests:

> Here a typical case: a guest arrives, cannot occupy his preferred room although he booked it … Kurt [the receptionist] changes all the room bookings and makes sure that the guest gets his preferred room. Then the guest goes and sees the doctor who

is busy right now. Again we change all bookings to make sure the guest gets to see the doctor. It goes on like this from early morning until late night – everything is done for the guests. It's always the same. It's typical for our guests. He arrives and wants something although we are booked out he'll get it – he is bending and breaking [our rules]. We are bending and breaking. That's typical.

The quote shows that the organizational members working in hospitality are committed to 'bend' and 'break' normal practices to satisfy guests. However, from a medical perspective it might be advisable that a guest is prescribed a different treatment than she usually receives. In sharp contrast the medical-therapeutical staff assumes that the best treatment is the medically most appropriate one. Their ethics towards the guest is not to 'bend over backwards' but to treat the guest as a human being whose physical condition has the highest priority. These two different ethics towards the customer are constituted and reinforced through different discourses and practices that take their legitimacy from the two different worlds of medicine and hospitality. Inevitably, conflicts occur between these different discourses and practices. Also they establish different power relations: from the hospitality perspective, the customer dominates the relationship towards the employee; from a medical perspective, the customer is subordinate to the expertise of the medical-therapeutical staff. The latter have superior knowledge compared to the customer and are therefore in a more powerful position.

The Practice of Care – Closeness and Distance and the Constitution of Customer Subjectivity

As we have seen above, everyday work practices at the Med Center were demanding and stressed organizational members. As one employee put it, the contact with patients made him feel like 'mental garbage cans', open for guests to 'dump' their psychological problems. The stress levels varied throughout the organization. Medical-therapeutical staff were exposed to very intimate stories from guests' lives, as one employee who changed position from hospitality to the medical department explained:

even in the dining room you have a relationship with guests. It's not as intensive as in the therapy but even when they have afternoon tea some drop in only to see you and have a conversation. Although you are only service personnel … if you had a day off they asked you the next day where you've been, and they say they have missed you.

The employee also notes that this relationship is something special, and that it makes her feel special to have the attention of wealthy and sometimes well-known guests. As she tells, some guests bring presents from home. As she interpreted it the fact that they thought of her before coming to the Med Center means that they value their relationship with staff.

However, in the medical-therapeutical area there is a different, much more intense level of closeness. The fact that most guests are enjoying their treatments half-naked translates directly into their psychological openness. It also adds to the asymmetrical power relation between medical staff and guests that has been discussed above. As one staff member told:

> [during the different therapies] I spent easily one hour with the guest. And during this hour, well, you have intimate conversations. Actually you find out pretty much everything. You hear the worst stories. I have heard stories about abuse and so on, stuff that really affects you. They just tell you what comes to their mind. Now, with the new infusion treatment room, it is different, there are five people in at once, which was not the case before. Before, we had one room with one bed and one patient and one therapist. ... at the beginning I regretted this change but now I find it protects the employee, because these stories really get to you, if you listen to so intimate and horrible stories.

Another employee from the medical-therapeutical department told the following story:

> Eighty percent of our guests are mentally exhausted. I think what I have realized is that people build-up trust very quickly. ... people you've never seen before open up, talk about their lives, about their sorrows, about stuff I would hesitate to tell my best friend. ... people open up ... it is one thing to get a prescription and swallow a pill but it is a different story to open up emotionally. That's what they do. There are stories – I brought someone to lasering [a treatment] and she told me about her son who is a drug addict and about her marriage and whether she should continue it or not.

Another therapist told about a 65 year old guest who explained to her

> she was sexually abused as child and that she has never really overcome this experience. I was deeply moved by this story, because you would not guess that this lady made this experience. To the outside world she always pretended to be happy but she said 'well, at some point I have to tell somebody' and she asked whether there would be a way that she would get over it with 65 years.

DISCUSSION AND CONCLUSION

At the Med Center ethics are not articulated in a code of ethics but embedded in discourse and practice. As we have seen, ethics are not an 'object' but are performed through practices such as interacting with customers, performing routine work, cooperation between the different divisions etc. The routines that therapeutical staff perform constitute different ethics from the practices of hospitality. Similarly, the discourse of the therapeutical staff creates a different ethical relationship and responsibility towards guests: they are seen as 'human beings' that need treatment. The power imbalance between therapeutical staff and guests reinforce these ethics towards the guest. On the other hand, hospitality staff constitute their ethical relationships based on the discourse of 'the customer is king'. Emerging from this discourse, ethical relationships between staff and guest are very different, focusing on customer satisfaction and the economic imperative to create loyalty and repeat visits. Although there is no written code of conduct the practice of therapeutical staff (spending time with guests who physically and psychologically strip down, etc.) contributes to an ethics in sharp contrast to the ethics of the hospitality staff. The hospitality staff's practice (providing special amenities for repeat guests, etc.) is the basis of a different ethics towards the customer. In fact, ethics can be understood as a response to internal and external environmental challenges and a way of making sense of them. In this perspective ethics are socially and discursively constructed (Clegg et al., 2006).

Rather than being judgmental and arguing for one or the other side as being 'more ethical' we suggest to accepting the plurality of ethics that, each taken by itself, might be valid and reasonable. In accordance with Derrida we would argue that real ethical questions arise when such conflicting value systems collide (see Jones, 2003). As seen in our case, there is no simple logical calculation that we could resort to in order to make a decision in regards to which ethics is more appropriate. Rather, we could argue that true ethical decisions can occur only in these contested spaces. In these contested spaces power is exercised. Hence we would argue that power relations play an important role in the constitution of ethics. As our case study shows, ethics takes shape through power relations that are played out between different actors. In our case therapeutical staff had considerable power over their guests. This led to a different constitution of their subjectivity (Foucault, 1977) and contributed to the constitution of ethics in practice. In contrast the hospitality staff was in a far inferior power relation which influenced the way they framed their ethics. Hospitality staff understood themselves as serving their guests and got satisfaction out of positive feedback such as small presents given to them by their guests. The clear subordination of the hospitality staff constituted, and was constituted by, a different way of speaking about guests, different practices that were deemed appropriate and ultimately a different ethics towards them.

Although both hospitality and therapeutical staff work in the same organization their ethics are vastly different and provide reasons for conflicts. We would argue that ethics is an inherently conflict laden business (Nietzsche, 1969). Ethics is a negotiated order that emerges as organizational members argue for and over resources and responsibilities. As our account reveals, ethics changed with the organizational change of roles, structures and processes that were introduced. Hence ethics will be an especially highly contested and tension-laden business during organizational change. Also, the positive reception of the research project and the breaking of taboos that organizational members associated with it provide evidence that an open discourse about values and ethics is important during change.

Finally, and perhaps most importantly, ethics are characterized by a high degree of ambiguity and uncertainty. Organizational members of the Med Center experienced what Donaldson and Dunfee (1994) termed 'bounded morality': they had to make ethical decisions based on highly complex, situational and incomplete information. For instance organizational members from the hospitality division displayed a traditional and rather conservative attitude towards innovation. Whereas they 'broke and bent' the rules and achieved change incrementally, medical-therapeutical staff learning, professional development and innovation were central values. Organizational members in hospitality explained this passion for innovation with the fact that most of the medical-therapeutical staff did not have family and used seminars and training session as opportunities to socialize. This way of relating to and representing the Other (see Rhodes and Westwood in this volume) was obviously based on incomplete information and a selective perception. Also, often they were about to make ethical decisions not knowing that their decisions were touching on questions of ethicality. None of the organizational members interviewed reflected explicitly on ethical dilemmas when they talked about conflicts, patient rights, or, as in the case of one doctor, about the acceptance of money from a pharmaceutical company where he had placed a large order. Hence, we would argue that ethics is largely constructed in retrospect. Improvising on Karl Weick's dictum, the Med Center's organizational members acted according to the premise 'how can I know whether I have been acting ethically until I have seen what I have done'. Whereas this dictum provides arguably less direction than the Kantian ethical imperative it might be more helpful in understanding how organizational members make ethical decisions and 'muddle through' (Lindblom, 1979) their everyday organizational life.

REFERENCES

Andrews, K. (1989), 'Ethics in Practice', *Harvard Business Review,* September-October, 99-104.

Astley, G. (1985), 'Administrative science as socially constructed truth', *Administrative Science Quarterly*, **30** (1), 497-513.

Barker, J. R. (1993), 'Tightening the iron cage: Concertive control in self-managing teams', *Administrative Science Quarterly*, **38**, 408-437.

Berger, P. L. and T. Luckmann (1967), *The Social Construction of Reality: A Treatise in the Sociology of Knowledge*, New York, US: Anchor Books.

Bourdieu, P. (1990), *The Logic of Practice*, trans. R. Nice, Cambridge, UK: Polity Press.

Brass, D. J., K. D. Butterfield and B. C. Skaggs (1998), 'Relationships and unethical behaviour', *Academy of Management Review*, **23**, 14-32.

Brunsson, N. (1994), *The Organization of Hypocrisy: Talk, Decisions and Actions. Organization*, Chichester, UK: Wiley.

Clegg, S., M. Kornberger and C. Rhodes (2006), 'Ethics as practice', *British Journal of Management*, forthcoming.

Czarniawska, B. (2001), 'Is it possible to be a constructivist consultant?', *Management Learning*, **32**, 253-266.

Donaldson, T. (2003), 'Editor's comments: Taking ethics seriously – A mission now more possible', *Academy of Management Review*, **28**, 363-366.

Donaldson, T. and T. W. Dunfee (1994), 'Towards a unified conception of business ethics: Integrative social contracts theory', *Academy of Management Review*, **19**, 252-275.

Flick, U. (2003), 'Triangulation', in U. Flick, V. E. Kardorff and I. Steinke (eds), *Qualitative Forschung – Ein Handbuch*, 2nd Edition, Hamburg, pp. 309-311.

Flyvberg, B. (2003), 'Rationality and Power', in Scott Cambell and Susan S. Fainstein (eds), *Readings in Planning Theory,* second edition, Oxford, UK: Blackwell, pp. 318-329.

Foucault, M. (1977), *Discipline and Punish*, London, UK: Allen Lane.

Foucault, M. (1997), *Ethics, Subjectivity and Truth – Essential Works of Foucault 1954-1984*, P. Rabinow (ed.), New York, US: The New Press.

Francis, R. and A. Armstrong (2003), 'Ethics as a risk management strategy: The Australian experience', *Journal of Business Ethics*, **45**, 75-385.

Gatewood, R. D. and A. B. Carroll (1991), 'Assessment of ethical performance of organization member', *Academy of Management Review*, **16**, 667-691.

Golden-Biddle, K. and K. Locke (1993), 'Appealing work: An investigation of how ethnographic texts convince', *Organization Science*, **4**, 595-616.

Goodman, N. (1978), *Ways of World Making*, Indianapolis, US: Hackett Publishing.

Gordon, R., S. Clegg and M. Kornberger (2006), 'Ethics in the NSW Police Service', Working Paper.

Gouldner, A. (1954), *Patterns of Industrial Bureaucracy*, New York, US: Free Press.

Habermas, J. (1973), *Knowledge and Human Interests*, London, UK: Heinemann.

Ibarra-Colado, E., Clegg, S. R., Rhodes, C. and Kornberger, M. (2006), 'The Ethics of Managerial Subjectivity', *Journal of Business Ethics*, **64**, 45-55.

Jackall, R. (1988), *Moral Mazes: The World of Corporate Managers*, New York, US: Oxford University Press.

Jones, C. (2003), 'As if business ethics were possible, "within such limits"...', *Organization*, **10**, 223-248.

Joyner, B. and D. Payne (2002), 'Evolution and implementation: A study of values, business ethics and corporate social responsibility', *Journal of Business Ethics*, **41**, 297-311.

Kappler, E. (1980), 'Aktionsforschung', in E. Grochla (eds), *Handwörterbuch der Organisation*, second. edition, Stuttgart, pp. 52-64.

Keleman, M. and T. Peltonen (2001), 'Ethics, morality and the subject: The contribution of Zygmunt Bauman and Michel Foucault to "postmodern" business ethics', *Scandinavian Journal of Management*, **17**, 151-166.

Kirk, J. and M. Millard (1986), *Reliability and Validity in Qualitative Research*, London, UK: Sage.

Kjonstad, B. and H. Willmott (1995), 'Business ethics: Restrictive or empowering?', *Journal of Business Ethics*, **14**, 445-464.

Knights, D. (1992), 'Changing spaces: The disruptive impact of a new epistemological location for the study of management', *Academy of Management Review*, **17** (3), 530, 533.

Langley, A. (1999), 'Strategies for theorizing from process data', *Academy of Management Review*, **24**, (4), 691-710.

Laske, S. and U. Schneider (1986), '... Und es funktioniert doch! – Selbstverwaltung kann man lernen', second edition, Vienna: Bundesministerium für Soziale Verwaltung.

Leithäuser, T. and B. Volmerg (1988), *Psychoanalyse in der Sozialforschung – Eine Einführung*, Opladen.

Lindblom, C. (1979), 'Still muddling, not yet through', *Public Administration Review*, November/December, 517-526.

Margolis, Joshua D. and J. P. Walsh (2003), 'Misery loves company: Rethinking social initiatives by business', *Administrative Science Quarterly*, **48**, 268-305.

Meyer, J. W. and B. Rowan (1977), 'Institutionalized organizations: Formal structure as myth and ceremony', *American Journal of Sociology*, **83**, 340-363.

Mueller, F. and C. Carter (2005), 'Scripting TQM in its organizational biography', *Organization Studies*, **26** (6), 221-247.

Munro, I. (1992), 'Codes of Ethics: Some Uses and Abuses', in P. Davies (ed.), *Current Issues in Business Ethics*, London, UK: Routledge, pp. 97-106.

Nietzsche, F. (1969), *On the Genealogy of Morals*, New York, US: Vintage.

Paine, L. (1994), 'Managing for organizational integrity', *Harvard Business Review*, March-April, 106-117.

Passfield, R. (1996), 'Action learning for professional and organizational development: An action research case study in higher education', PhD Dissertation, Brisbane, Australia: Griffith University.

Raiborn, C. and D. Payne (1996), 'TQM: Just what the ethicist ordered', *Journal of Business Ethics*, **15**, 963-972.

Schneider, U. and S. Laske (1985), 'Produktivgenossenschaften. Gesellschaften mit beschränkter Hoffnung?', Vienna.

Soule, E. (2002), 'Managerial moral strategies – In search of a few good principals', *Academy of Management Review*, **27**, 114-124.

Stark, A. (1993), 'What's the matter with business ethics?, *Harvard Business Review*, May-June, 38-48.

ten Bos, R. And H. Willmott (2001), 'Towards a post-dualistic business ethics: Interweaving reason and emotion in working life', *Journal of Management Studies*, **38**, 769-794.

Thorne, L. and S. Saunders (2002), 'The socio-cultural embeddedness of individuals' ethical reasoning in organizations (cross-cultural ethics)', *Journal of Business Ethics*, **35**, 1-14.

Tsoukas, H. (1989), 'The validity of idiographic research explanations', *Academy of Management Review*, **14** (4), 551-561.

Weick, K. (1979), *The Social Psychology of Organizing*, New York, US: Random House.

Weick, K. (1989), 'Theory construction as disciplined imagination', *Academy of Management Review*, **14**, 516–531.

Weick, K. E. (1995), *Sensemaking in Organizations*, Thousand Oaks, CA, US: Sage.

Wicks, A. C. and R. E. Freeman (1998), 'Organization studies and the new pragmatism: Positivism, anti-positivism and the search for ethics', *Organization Science*, **9**, 123-141.

Winter, R. (1987), *Action-Research and the Nature of Social Inquiry*, Aldershot, UK: Avebury.

Wittgenstein, L. (1968), *Philosophical Investigations*, Oxford, UK: Blackwell.

Zuber-Skeritt, O. (2002), 'A model for designing action learning and action research programs', *The Learning Organization*, **9** (4), 143-149.

Zuber-Skeritt, O. and C. Perry (2002), 'Action research within organisations and university thesis writing', *The Learning Organization*, **9** (4), 171-179.

12. The Guest as a Friendly Foe? Hotel Service Encounters In-between the Face and the Gaze of the Guest

Dirk Bunzel[*]

AN ETHICS OF EXCELLENCE OR MORAL SLAVERY?

With Max Weber's treaty on the spirit of capitalism, we are acutely aware of the intimate link between moral convictions and the conduct of work and business. Yet, while in the early days of capitalism, *work ethics* developed in the light of religious principles, in today's secularized and post-industrial societies alternative resorts prevail. Now, such ethics 'is promoted primarily in terms of work being a responsibility, both to family and to the nation' (Beeder, 2000, p. 2). Consequently, contemporary organizations are keen to reinvent themselves as business families to bestow a new work ethics upon their employees (Casey, 1995; Parker, 1995); while the ensuing ethics delineates *passion for excellence* as being both a moral obligation and a condition of organizational and national citizenship (e.g. Peters and Waterman, 1982/1994). Notably, the term 'passion' indicates that such obligations are not purely performative but entail an almost spiritual element – one that concerns individuals' values, convictions and sentiments, and that is constituent of what commonly is dubbed 'emotional labour', (Hochschild, 1983). Thus, contemporary work ethics are part and parcel of a form of membership that is provisional and dependent upon both dedication to and mastery of excellence (Munro, 1999) – albeit there is still debate as to whether such membership amounts to 'citizenship' or 'vassalage' (Hancock, 1997; Parker, 1997).

[*]Thanks to Mihaela Kelemen and Martin Kornberger for their helpful comments

Apart from being secularized and post-industrial, contemporary work ethics and the obligations it stipulates commonly pay tribute to a third party: the customer. A whole body of literature has emerged that cherishes sensitivity for and responsiveness to customer wants and needs as road to economic prosperity and as a doctrine of business conduct. In the excellent organizations, we are told, the passion for excellence is that pervasive, the desire to excel in the provision of service is so strong, that organizational members eagerly subdue their will to the dictates of the customer (Peters and Waterman, 1982/1994). Evidently, where customers reign supreme, such passion is rendered into a normative demand that unanimously applies to management and employees, while failure to arouse the sentiments demanded equates to deviancy and moral failure. Hence, this heroic tale of service excellence and the romantic attachment to customers wants and needs that it portrays transpires as an ideology. In fact, there is an abundance of evidence that the cult of the customer gives rise to strategies, practices and identities that, ultimately, do not serve the well-being of customers but the expropriation of maximum profit for corporate shareholders (e.g. Willmott, 1993; du Gay, et al., 1996; Sewell, 1998). Under the spell of corporate culturism, the stimulation and management of feelings and sentiments perverts into 'emotional labour' – a form of work that thrives on the exploitation and instrumentalization of employees' feelings, sentiments and ingenuity to generate surplus value (Hochschild, 1983; see also Seemann, Laske and Kornberger in this volume).

Critical accounts of customer service, however, seem to concede a partial corporate victory in the 'battle for the hearts and minds of employees' (Knights and Willmott, 1989; Deetz, 1998; Jackson and Carter, 1998). Notwithstanding their post-Marxist, commonly Foucauldian vocabulary, much of this critique seems to imply that emotional labour, per se, is alienated and corrupted, and that a sincere concern with service excellence signifies no more than 'false consciousness' – with surface acting being the logical, almost heroic alternative to subservience (Hochschild, 1983). From that perspective, a work ethics that embraces a passion for (service) excellence relapses into 'moral slavery', (Willmott, 1993). If we assume, however, that for-profit service as such is corrupt or that it is fundamentally insincere, if provided by someone who primarily wants to earn a living, then most of us face an ambiguous and probably undesirable future. In times of dwindling welfare states, of aging societies and of eroding family and kinship structures, many of us will depend upon care provided by private organizations whose main responsibility lies with pleasing their owners or shareholders. Clearly, one may wish that this did not inevitably mean that staff working for those organizations would only act as diligently, empathically and authentically as we can financially afford. On the contrary, it seems that '[t]he more the heart is managed, the more we value the unmanaged heart', and not everyone may be willing to settle for authenticity as a surrogate for sincerity (Hochschild, 1983, p. 192).

Without a doubt, matters of morals are elusive when it comes to emotional labour and simple dichotomies may not serve well in this regard. At the time of writing this chapter, doctors in Germany's public hospitals are on strike for higher wages and restrictions to the common culture of excessive overtime working, with patients being subject to industrial action. Hence, while numerous medical operations have been cancelled or postponed, and as the waiting lists for treatment and admittance to hospital have extended exponentially, medical staff quite warrantedly claim that their resistance to a culture of long hours serves the interest and safety of patience. Nonetheless, albeit recent surveys show overwhelming public support for those on strike, and although they have made sure that emergency services are kept running, effectively patients have been taken hostage by both (!) employers and employees in the process of bargaining.

Incidents like this clearly concern matters of an ethical nature – not only when individuals are 'suffering'. Emotional labour indubitably thrives on the exploitation and manipulation of individuals' sentiments, of their need for help, for care, or for sympathy. Yet, manipulation pertains to both sides of this bargain – service providers and customers – as the subjects and objects of service encounters constantly swap places within a game that attains a seductive quality (Bunzel, 2001). Significantly, though, service also differs from manufacturing in that the object of manipulation is not a thing but a person.[1] Thus, when those providing a service refuse to meet customer expectations – as justified as their cause might be – this is of ethical concern too. After all, service providers directly affect the well-being of their guests, patients, or clients; hence, they cannot eschew a certain responsibility for their object: 'the other'. Given the seductive, interactive nature of service encounters, such responsibility applies, conversely, also to customers. Limits to that responsibility are not easily defined. A 'war of smiles'[2] constitutes a legitimate act of resistance to some, a form of 'Ludditism' to others. And, while some uphold the sovereignty of their majesty, the customer, others criticise any abuse of his/her power.

Accordingly, the question driving this chapter reads: What do we owe to the other of customer service? Needless to say, perhaps, that this other could be a client, a patient, or a guest or someone else; yet also a doctor, a waiter, or a cleaner. And, is whatever we owe to him or her confined to the stipulations of an (employment) contract? The issue raised here thus concerns the very nature of emotional labour and addresses, in a rather distinctive manner, the non-contractual element, to borrow Durkheim's vocabulary. Emotional labour – and it is from this perspective that we shall address the matter in this chapter – seems to seek for extending this non-contractual element to include both the object(s) of production, the other, as well as the sentiments of the producers.

To explore the moral foundations of emotional labour, we shall now turn to a thinker who – like few others – has placed responsibility and care for the other at the centre of his philosophy: Emmanuel Levinas. We shall illustrate the tenets of his ethics by drawing on sequences taken from an ethnographic study of a five-star luxury hotel located in a small town on the Australian East Coast.[3] At the time of the study, the Grand Seaside Hotel, as we shall call it, had just been taken over by an international hotel chain that sought a speedy and plentiful return on their investment.[4] Complementary to the streamlining of business operations, a customer service programme was introduced that propagated service excellence as a panacea for business success and profitability. The discussion to be presented presented below will highlight the ambiguities of both moral sentiments and emotional labour in the light of Levinas' reasoning.

LEVINAS: ETHICS AS FIRST PHILOSOPHY

Emmanuel Levinas was born into a traditional Jewish family in Kaunas in 1906. Having been exposed to the works of famous Russian writers – Puschkin, Lermontow and, most notably, Dostoyevsky – from an early age, the issue of transcendence, so eloquently raised by these masters, was to concern him ever after (Malka, 2003). After studying philosophy in Strasburg and Freiburg, attending the lectures of Edmund Husserl and the young Heidegger, Levinas went to Paris to teach philosophy and soon became one of the foremost interpreters of contemporary German philosophy in France.[5] Levinas, a French soldier by that time, survived the Second World War in a German camp for prisoners of war, while most members of his family in Lithuania – including his parents and his two brothers – were murdered by the German occupation troops.[6] After the war, Levinas took over the directorship of the Ecole Normale Israelite Orientale, which he headed in the thirty years to come while simultaneously holding a professorship at the Sorbonne. Until his death in 1995, Levinas continued to influence philosophic discourse well beyond the French academic community and has been a source of inspiration to many of his colleagues and friends, among them Jean Wahl, Paul Ricoer, and Jacques Derrida (Malka, 2003).

Absolute Otherness and Infinity

The fate of his loved ones and the sheer inconceivable horrors of the Holocaust provided the traumatic background for Levinas' reasoning and philosophizing. Engaging with phenomenology and existentialism – most notably Husserl and Heidegger – and drawing on the religious philosophy and theology of Buber and Rosenzweig, Levinas did not settle for creating a humanist philosophy; more radically, he was determined to ground all philosophy within a religiously inspired humanism. He did this by asserting a *universal and unconditional responsibility to care for the other*.[7] This responsibility, which to him was part and parcel of the human condition, calls for opening oneself up to the radical otherness of the other, while leaving his alterity intact. This led Levinas to ground his philosophy within a new concept of selfhood; one that surpasses the transcendental ego of Husserl's phenomenology. Departing from both traditional subject philosophy and dialectic reasoning, he not only refutes monadic conceptions of the self, which define the latter as existing prior to and independent of both the external world and other; he also criticizes interactionist understandings of identity that conceive of the other in purely negative terms. To him, it was not permissible to conceive of the other in analogy to the self, thereby reducing this otherness to yet another version of the same. Instead, he maintained that a gulf ultimately separates the I and the other, and that this gulf cannot easily be bridged. The other is absolutely the other: 'We' does not confine itself to a plurality of Is. Hence, the alterity of the other is transcendental and can only be approached as infinity (Levinas, 1961/2004)

The Other as Revealed

Significantly, Levinas argues that a sense of infinity cannot be gained with an intentional attitude, in the phenomenological sense of the term; one in which the noetic consciousness sets the noema, the object, as his teacher Husserl had it (Levinas, 1993):

> The idea of infinity ... does not proceed from the I ... here the movement proceeds from what is thought and not from the thinker (Levinas, 1961/2004, p. 61).

Nor is infinity 'the "object" of a cognition' (Levinas, 1961/2004, p. 62). Instead, transcendence is 'a presence in thought of an idea whose ideatum overflows the capacity of thought' (ibid., p. 49). It arises from the object as desire and as such is distinct from an object, which is apprehended by need (ibid., p. 62f.). This desire is metaphysical and 'at each instance thinks more than it thinks', which is why the absolute other cannot be an object proper of thought (ibid., p. 62; emphasis original). Absolute otherness, therefore, cannot be subsumed to abstract principles, nor can it be constituted as knowledge (of the other). Instead, absolute otherness is 'revealed, in the strong sense of the term' (ibid.; emphasis original). Hence, to Levinas the absolute otherness of the other therefore relates to a spiritual dimension (ibid., p. 64).

The distinction Levinas establishes between radical otherness as revealed, as arousing a metaphysical desire, amounts to the difference between ontology and ethics. In contrast to ontology – where the other is integrated and neutralized as 'a theme or an object' – Levinas emphasizes 'respect for exteriority', for that casts doubt upon my taken for granted assumptions and everyday routines and thus appears disturbing and divergent (ibid., p. 43). In so doing, he subordinates ontology to ethics and devalues attempts at knowing the other as acts of violence that integrate the alterity of the other to a total(itarian) order of the same. Against such violence, he wishes to welcome otherness, disturbance and divergence.

The Face of the Other

While referring to infinity, the absolute alterity of the other reveals itself in a rather concrete manner: through the face of the (concrete) Other: 'The other qua other is the Other', as Levinas puts it (ibid., p. 71, emphasis original; see also Rhodes and Westwood in this volume). Face to face with the Other, this is *the* ethical situation. Here one recognizes the very nakedness of his face; a nakedness that reveals the Other as being both defenceless and irresistible. The face of the Other speaks: 'Thou shall not kill' – and the relationship build upon this primordial obligation is both unconditional and limitless.[8] This primordial obligation is 'prior to all contract' and grounds a sociality as being for-the-other, one that ultimately demands sacrifice (Levinas, 1991/1998, p. 233). Encounters with the face of the Other thus arouse an insatiable desire to welcome the other, to protect him, to be at his service. Such desire is not only metaphysical; it is essentially gratuitous and non-reciprocal, while it leaves the other's alterity intact. There is, then, a fundamental asymmetry at the heart of Levinas' philosophy. This asymmetry is of a double nature though: ethically, it demands self-subordination to the dictate of the other; epistemologically, it ascertains the dominance of the other within the process of creating (self-) knowledge.[9] Levinas radically de-centres the subject, which is no longer creator and master of self and world, but which has been taken hostage by the other.

THE GUEST AS THE OTHER OF HOTEL SERVICE

Excellence as Transcendence?

In the face of the gulf that ultimately separates me from his alterity, how should I approach the other? Moreover, how can I ever come to get to know him adequately, given that his alterity is absolute and infinite? Within the cult of the customer, Levinas' claim that absolute otherness resides within infinity translates into a principal limitlessness of customer wants and needs. Excellent firms do not settle for pleasing wants and needs; in fact, they aspire to exceeding whatever is demanded. At the Grand Seaside Hotel, Tim Chang, the newly appointed General Manager, was convinced that:

> Nowadays, customer service is the key to survival in an ever more competitive market. I have to do more than the other competitors; I have to provide service-excellence, really outstanding service. I can only do that by listening to what the customer says and by listening to my staff. But, actually, it's about more. It's not just meeting customers' expectations; that's what all do. It means *exceeding* them, providing service *beyond the customer's expectation*, that's my philosophy. And you can only do that by training your people properly.

Accordingly, Tim was eager for staff to share his concern with customer service. Be it during the regular management meetings – the 'Morning Briefings', as they were referred to in the hotel jargon – or social events such as the annual All-Staff Meeting, Tim used every opportunity to instruct staff on how to develop a 'passion for service excellence'. He also spread this message using the monthly hotel newsletter, the notice board, or even the walls of the staff canteen.

Know Thy Guest

Staff thus instructed on the importance of service excellence, however, faced the problem of identifying what it actually was that they were supposed to exceed. For that matter, a comprehensive system of guest questionnaires and informal quality circles were set up, all aimed at defining those customer wants and needs that provided the threshold to be surpassed. Accordingly, questionnaires were provided to guests at their rooms, and Elsa, Tim's secretary, entered the information thus gathered into a database, with the latest findings being regularly announced at the Morning Briefings. Yet, Tim and his management team would not settle for meeting – respectively exceeding – demands raised by corporeal guests of the hotel. During the Morning Briefings, managers would commonly report on their own experience and fantasy, surrogating for potential guests' service evaluation. In the due course of such imaginary service encounters, Tim projected hypothetical needs or wants upon equally hypothetical guests, as the following sequence, taken from one of the Morning Briefings, illustrates:

Tim: Just a reminder to you that the front-desk is a public area for customer service and not for socializing of staff; even if they are not busy with a guest at that moment. Sometimes when you pass by there, the guys from concierge are chatting with each other or hanging around. This does not lead to a good impression, *if* guests are passing by. This morning I saw even Celine (an administrative assistant, DB) standing around there having a chat with some of the guys. I mean, she is not even from reservations; so what does she have to do there? So, please inform your staff: The front-desk is not a staff room! It's not a chatting area!

Often, Tim would also point at the aesthetic dimension of the service experience – occasionally, he would do so rather bluntly.

Tim: Where is Housekeeping? (He gazes around the table.)

Elsa: She's not in, today.

Tim: Okay! Then tell her that the area around the hotel looks
                  like (He hesitates for a moment.) . . . well, it really looks
                  like *shit*! So, they have to clean it regularly!

On another occasion, Tim criticized Amanda, a supervisor of cleaning staff:

Tim: I just wanted to remind you that you have put the slippery
                  sign away. It's such a nice gangway from The Garden
                  Terrace to the pool and then you have this ugly sign there.

Encouraged by Tim's example, other managers also called upon the
imaginary voice of this ghostly guest. Keenly, they shared their service
experiences and fantasies to satisfy the suspected wants and needs of the
elusive but omnipresent guest. In so doing, however, they reminded, more or
less explicitly, their colleagues of their failure to live up to the standards of
service excellence. One of the Security Managers, for instance, claimed 'on
behalf' of (imaginary) customers that the car park 'has become the most
messy place in the whole hotel – an insult to our guests'. On other occasions,
participants of the meeting reminded Bill, the Engineer responsible for the
maintenance of the building, that some light bulbs had to be changed or that
one of the toilet flushes was not working properly. Others informed the
meeting participants about dirty carpets, empty bottles around the pool area,
or the inappropriate dress code of staff members, putting those responsible
for the deficient service provision on public display. Although such
comments were usually expressed in a helpful and collegial tone – e.g. 'by
the way, I just wanted to let you know that' – the people addressed often
appeared embarrassed by these 'helpful reminders' and usually responded in
an apologetic manner.

Responding to Metaphysical Desire?

Having thus transcended organizational reality and having extended customer
wants and needs *ad infinitum*, staff were instructed on how to meet –
respectively exceed – these want and needs. To that end, training sessions for
staff were held that were designed and run by Di and Leo, two members of
the management team. Their training programme, significantly called 'Make
the Little Things Count', raised awareness for the mundane and frequently
overlooked 'little things' in the process of service delivery. Echoing Tim,
they told their audience that these days merely meeting customers' demands
is no longer good enough. 'Winning companies' have to deliver 'service that

exceeds customer expectations!' The key to such an excess, the trainers explained, lies precisely with those notorious little things. Again the little things could be associated with the spontaneous side of human interaction which cannot be managed on a grand scale. It is the anticipation of customers' needs and wants that determines the quality of service delivery and that, ultimately, define service excellence. Hence, the trainers concluded, staff have to 'expect the unexpected', if they want to deliver service that 'exceeds customer expectations'.

To render this philosophy more tangible, Di, Leo, and another member of staff performed a brief role-play during the training session. This scene was based on a service encounter that had taken place just a few days ago, when a room cleaner on duty discovered, through the open door of a hotel room, how a young mother tried to give her baby the bottle. As the baby was crying unremittingly and the mother obviously did not find a way to calm him down, the cleaner suspected that the milk in the bottle might be too cold. Obviously, the mother looked overwhelmed and in need of assistance, so the cleaner turned to her and offered to warm up the bottle. The mother agreed, and when the cleaner came back with the warm milk, the baby drank it and eventually calmed down.

At that point, the play stopped. The trainers turned to their audience and pointed out that the mother was 'over the moon' and that she went to the General Manager of the hotel to thank the cleaner for her effort. This, the trainers stressed, was precisely the sort of proactive approach that staff have to develop and that would be appreciated and rewarded by management. For that matter, the trainers elaborated, management had introduced the 'Make the Little Things Count reward programme'. According to the principles of this programme, each employee was held to identify exemplary incidents of service provision and to nominate the respective staff for a reward.[10] The trainers concluded their session pointing out that winners of the Make the Little Things Count Award would be announced on a monthly basis. Apart from a gift-voucher they would receive 100 Australian dollars and a T-shirt carrying the newly designed logo of the programme on the front and the sentence 'I Made a Little Thing Count' on the back.

SERVICE EXCELLENCE AS CARE FOR THE OTHER?

When considering the sequences of life at the Grand Seaside Hotel represented above, it appears that care for the other – here the guest – is pivotal to business operations and, arguably, a hallmark of organizational identity.[11] The ideological undertones of this discourse of customer service, as in the public declarations during training sessions, meetings and social gatherings, do not quite justify challenging the genuine concern of both management and staff for the well-being of their guests. Hence, when the cleaner offers to warm up the bottle for a baby; when a conference organizer lends one of her dresses to a lady whose dinner-dress got ruined when squeezed in a car door; or when a concierge drives to the next chemist to organize some headache-tablets for a guest, they are not just 'walking the extra-mile', as Tim would put it, but they sincerely seem to care for the other: the guest. In fact, such incidents show staff exhibiting indeed the universal and unconditional responsibility to care for the other that Levinas demands.

Similarly, the various strategies and practices that aim at developing a passion for excellence seem to echo at least some of Levinas' claims concerning absolute otherness. The guest, as the other in service encounters, is granted a reservoir of wants and needs that can be extended infinitely and that thus bestow a limitless responsibility upon staff. Staff are not only asked to heed customer wants and needs as their command; they are even expected to be subservient to hypothetical wishes of imaginary guest. The 'proactive attitude' advocated by management – an attitude that asks to 'expect the unexpected' and to 'provide service beyond expectation' – exponentially widens the scope of potential customer wants and needs to be met. Hence, this attitude is one that should allow for welcoming the other, for being disturbed by his otherness, for respecting his exteriority, his radical difference. Such an attitude thrives upon a metaphysical desire to care for the other – one that constantly requires 'thinking more than one thinks'. Somewhat paradoxically, the dictum of service excellence, which asks for exceeding customer expectations that are already principally limitless, evokes a double infinity. Hence, the doctrine of service excellence amounts to an overkill; yet one that truly reflects the metaphysical nature of such care.

Some doubt remains, though, as to whether care for the other as practiced at the Grand Seaside Hotel indeed matches Levinas' imaginary scenario. First, one may question whether the ways in which the infinity of guest wants and needs are ascertained reflect the absolute otherness of the guest. Often, customer expectations are read off the face of the Other – that is, from a concrete guest within a service encounter. On such occasions, the face of the Guest will reveal his nakedness, his need for help, support, or attention, and will arouse the metaphysical desire to care for her. As seen above, a cleaner, a conference organizer or a concierge may respond to that call and accept their moral responsibility. However, such genuine examples of caring for the other differ from the various strategies to know the other that turn her into an object of reasoning, objectification, and ultimately manipulation. Hence, when lessons are drawn from guest questionnaires to regulate future service encounters; when 'guest histories' stipulate the treatment of VIP guests; when categories of guests receive 'special attention' as identified 'trouble-makers', their otherness is integrated and neutralized qua objectification. Here, as in the case of hypothetical wishes of imaginary customers, expectations concerning a concrete Other (Guest) are extrapolated from their original context and are authoritatively ascribed to other guests in future encounters as representing their (suspected) wants and needs. In other words, within such strategies that seek to know, objectify and regulate the other, the Guest of a past/imaginary encounter defines the otherness ascribed to (whole groups of) future guests. With the alterity of the latter being modelled upon the former, absolute otherness is annihilated and reduced to a version of the same. Far from welcoming absolute otherness, the objectified guest – whether real or imaginary – is idealized and demotes into a mere mirror image of management and staff preferences.

On another account, there also remain doubts concerning the ethical status of customer service as practiced at the Grand Seaside Hotel. When incorporated into a system of rewards and sanctions, the dictum to 'exceed customer expectations' and 'expect the unexpected' acquires a disciplinary quality. The helpful reminders so routinely voiced at the Morning Briefings frequently point to failures to meet guest expectations, as are the readings from the guest questionnaires. And, while the staff is encouraged to look out for exemplary instances of service provision and to nominate those performing well for rewards within the 'Make the Little Things Count' programme, such an appeal simultaneously introduces principles of peer surveillance through the back-door (Bunzel, 2001). The routines and rituals can be manifold by which staff, management and customer alike are subjected to a discourse that – while being seemingly concerned with exceeding customer expectation – establishes a disciplinary regime of organizational rationality and management prerogative (Barker, 1993; Sewell, 1998). In fact, the obsessive concern with service excellence, as practiced at the Grand Seaside hotel, even extrapolates customer wants and needs into a virtual domain, with imaginary service encounters routinely informing, and thus shaping, the organizational life at the hotel. When staff are sanctioned on the basis of imaginary complaints by hypothetical guest, as common practice during the morning briefings, the (gaze of the) guest seems omnipresent and provokes a culture of self- and peer-surveillance with virtually Panoptic qualities (Bunzel, 2001).

In other words, to staff of the Grand Seaside Hotel, the dictum of service excellence – i.e. exceeding customer expectations – translates into 'it's never enough'. In the name of service excellence, it provokes a corporate colonization of fantasy that demands self-subordination to the guest and, most significantly, to those who speak on his behalf: Tim and his management team. Hence, in a perverse twist, the face of the Other appears as the gaze of the other, while responsibility for the guest serves to legitimize management's prerogative. In this constellation, staff is taken hostage by both the guest and the high priests of the cult of the customer.

TOWARDS AN ETHICS OF CUSTOMER SERVICE?

Ethics as Eschatology

The portrait of customer service at the Grand Seaside Hotel painted with Levinas' brush, so to speak, demonstrates that our attempts at knowing the other are at best futile, if not a violation of her otherness. Even our desire to serve the other can go astray and be rendered as (self-) exploitative. So, does our primordial responsibility to care for the other then suggest moral slavery? Or should our relationship with the other be that of equals and rest upon equality and commonality?

Clearly, Levinas does not offer straightforward advice on these matters – nor does he intend to do so. In fact, he deliberately constitutes his ethics as eschatology and turns to religion as a foundation for a bond that associates the same and the other 'without constituting a totality' (Levinas, 1961/2004, p. 40). Nor is his ethics egalitarian or communal in a traditional sense. In radically privileging the other, he advocates a social asymmetry of a special kind. Against the mechanic or organic solidarity that grounds Durkheimian sociality, Levinas is sceptical of similarity and complementarity as constituting a viable and durable 'social glue'. Instead, he envisages a society that cherishes difference and divergence as guiding presumptions to moral conduct and sociality. In line with Durkheim, though, he conceives of society as a profoundly religious order, and situates the non-contractual element within the elementary forms of a quasi-religious life. Literally, Levinas envisages a *pre*-contractual element, a fundamental liability of men 'who, before all loans, have debts, owe their fellowman, are responsible' (Levinas, 1991/1998, p. 231). This primordial liability requires a spirituality of 'responsibility for the other'; one 'to which the I is chosen – or condemned' (ibid., p. 202). To Levinas, this spirituality is essentially ethical and religious and opposes ontology and politics. Hence, against the spiritualities of consciousness, of knowledge, and of truth, as underlying the passion for excellence, Levinas sets a spirituality of love and charity. Most radically, this spirituality not only defies ontology, cognition, and knowledge; it also dispenses with utility, a pillar of Western reasoning.

The obsessive concern with service excellence that shapes the culture of the Grand Seaside Hotel leaves little room for respecting the alterity of the other. Nor does it create a spirituality of love and charity, as Levinas envisages it. On the contrary, the guest enters the discourse of customer service as a gaze – not as a face – and the ensuing attitude is one of a fearsome subordination. In fact, beneath the sur*face* of customer service, lie hostility and violence, considering that

> violence does not consists so much in injuring and annihilating persons as in interrupting their continuity, making them play roles in which they no longer recognize themselves, making them betray not only commitments but their own substance, making them carry out actions that will destroy every possibility for action (Levinas, 1961/2004, p. 21).

Consequently, life at the hotel is in a state of war, as Levinas calls it, as the discourse of customer service constitutes a total(itarian) 'order from which no one can keep his distance; nothing henceforth is exterior' (ibid.., p. 21). This is an inherently violent order that corrupts genuine concern for the other, devalues the moral potential of human encounters, and perverts sociality. Thus, while the face of the Guest makes her a friend; the gaze of the guest turns him into a foe.

Staff of the Grand Seaside Hotel responded to the war waged upon them in various ways, including subservience, cynicism, or exit, and frequently resorted to surface acting when the scenario became too stressful or oppressive (Bunzel, 2001). Yet simultaneously, they also displayed generosity and sincere concern for their guests in an attitude of peace and compassion in the midst of violence. Thus, they developed a *bounded emotionality* that defied the crude instrumentalization of emotional labour and infused a predominantly inauthentic culture with humanity (Mumby and Putnam, 1992; Martin, 1998).

Against the constitution of customer service as war, Levinas' ethical stance seeks diversion from the totality of business and economy by providing an eschatology of messianic peace that does not annihilate the otherness of the other and does not constitute the other as an object either. Our attempts at knowing the guest, at scripting service encounters, at managing customer service are firmly rooted within the realm of ontology and thus, to Levinas at least, they are bound to moral failure. Being true to absolute otherness entails an element of undecidability, as Derrida would have it, and is, as such, opposed to standards and practices of business management. Only in instances of genuine care, when a cleaner, a conference organizer, or a concierge respond to the 'face of the Guest', is the original humanity restored. At that time, a moral spontaneity surfaces that emanates from an I that is aware of its own unworthiness and that accepts his 'asymmetrical responsibility for the other', as Levinas would put it.

Evidently, Levinas' imaginary scenario is utopian and evokes a future social and ethical state of humanity. So perhaps, for the time being, we have to settle for bounded emotionality as a controlled but non-instrumental opening up to the other, particularly as the future Levinas refers to is not deferment: it is an absolute one, outside the temporal horizon of our personal existence, and may never become our present. In this, his eschatology seems to echo Camus' Sisyphus in calling for relentless struggle against the absurdity of life and Being – a struggle defying all concern for utility or reciprocity. To be precise, Levinas insisted upon the difference between philosophy and praxis, and he did not suggest an existence outside of society and economy. His ethics encourages us to welcome the other and to develop our hospitality as a concrete *Sittlichkeit*, while it denounces attempts to know, possess and effectively annihilate otherness. In his sense, it takes virtuous people to realize instances of true hospitality, and such people may be at work even in the most total(itarian) organizations. In effect then, Levinas calls for 'cultivating a moral sensibility of love and charity' to balance our inclination to objectify, to normalize, and to control the protagonists of service encounters. This sensibility, however, is less an antidote to excellence as it undermines management by suggesting other forms of organizing (Parker, 2002).

NOTES

1. I exclude here, for the sake of brevity, considerations concerning ecology and animal rights.
2. Ingvar Carlsson, CEO of Scandinavian Airlines in the 1980s, labelled 'war of smiles' the strategy of his employees to express their dissent with corporate policies. As part of this strategy, stewardesses, for example, deliberately behaved inauthentically polite, thus to 'alienate' customers as an act of resistance against management policies.

3. During the fourteen months of ethnographic research I interviewed all managers and about one in seven members of (regular) staff at the hotel as well as several industry representatives; I regularly attended the Morning Briefings as well as other meetings and social events; and I worked as a participant observer in virtually every unit of the hotel. The interviews were taped and subsequently transcribed before archived and coded with the help of NVivo, as were the observation notes made during meetings and work. For matters of securing anonymity, all members of staff and the management team at the Grand Seaside Hotel have been given code-names in this chapter.

4. During the restructuring, several parts of the hotel business were outsourced or subcontracted, among them the shopping outlets and cafés in the arcade surrounding the property, the hotel fitness club, and the provision of an audio-visual service to conference guests. Other departments, such as conferences and Food and Beverages were merged and the hotel restaurants were reorganized into profit centres. Most managers, if not made redundant, found themselves in unfamiliar situations, often having to cope with increased levels of responsibility and work intensity. The restructuring was also accompanied by the dismissal of numerous staff, which induced an atmosphere of underlying anxiety and distrust among employees.

5. Most notably, Levinas became the first to translate the works of Husserl into French.

6. It was only thanks to the help of a friend, the writer Maurice Blanchot, that Levinas' wife and daughter escaped deportation to Auschwitz.

7. In line with the English translation of Levinas' first major work 'Totality and Infinity', I shall use the term *other* to designate the generalized conception referring to alterity in general (third person), whereas Other refers to the concrete 'you' within encounters between human beings.

8. To be precise, Levinas does not envisage our encounter with the face of the Other as the sensing of any particular part of the human body: 'The face, then, is not the colour of the eyes, the shape of the nose, the ruddiness of the cheeks, etc.' (Levinas, 1991/1998, p. 232). The face could be anything that conveys the very proximity and nakedness of the other. It quite literally *speaks* to us, it is essentially expression; while at the same token it is impossible to approach the other without speaking in return. Thus the ultimate situation and the dialogue with the other it initiates eschew their articulation in terms of common knowledge; rather they institute sociality 'through a relationship that is ... irreducible to understanding' (ibid.: p. 7).

9. Albeit Levinas confines the privileged status of the other to the social domain and relationships among human beings; in principle, one could extend this privilege to matters of ecology or animal rights, for example. A discussion of these aspects, however, is beyond the scope of this chapter.

10. Of course, such nominations are a double-edge sword. Perhaps, more often staff 'nominated' peers that had performed rather ill, when pointing out deficiencies or failures of service provision during the Morning Briefings, for example. For a more elaborate discussion on peer-surveillance and Panopticism at the Grand Seaside Hotel see Bunzel et al. (2002).

11. The role of the guest as hallmark of organizational identity is discussed in Bunzel (2001).

REFERENCES

Barker, J. R. (1993), 'Tightening the iron cage: Concertive control in self-managing teams', *Administrative Science Quarterly*, **38** (8), 408-437.

Beeder, S. (2000), *Selling the Work Ethic – From Puritan Pulpit to Corporate PR*, London, UK and New York, US: Zed Books.

Bunzel, D. (2001), 'Towards a virtualization of social control? Simulation and seductive domination in an Australian coastal hotel', *Administrative Theory and Praxis*, **23** (3), 363-82.

Bunzel, D., S. Clegg and G. Teal (2002), 'Disciplining customers at the Grand Seaside Hotel', *Journal of the Australian and New Zealand Academy of Management*, **8** (2), 1-13.

Casey, C. (1995), *Work, Self, and Society – After Industrialism*, London, UK: Routledge.

Deetz, S. A. (1998), 'Discursive Formations, Strategized Subordination and Self-Surveillance', in A. McKinaly and K. Starkey (eds), *Foucault, Management, and Organization Theory*, London, UK: Sage, pp. 151-172.

Hancock, P. (1997), 'Citizenship or vassalage? Organizational membership in an age of unreason', *Organization*, **4** (1), 93-111.

Hochschild, A. (1983), *The Managed Heart – Commercialization of Human Feeling*, Berkeley, US: University of California Press.

Jackson, N. and P. Carter (1998), 'Labour as Dressage', in A. McKinlay and K. Starkey (eds), *Foucault, Management and Organization Theory*, London, UK: Sage, pp. 49-64.

Knights, D. and H. Willmott (1989), 'Power and subjectivity at work – From degradation to subjugation in social relations', *Sociology*, **23** (4), 535-558.

Levinas, E. (1961/2004), *Totality and Infinity – An Essay on Exteriority*, Pittsburgh, US: Duquesne University Press.

Levinas, E. (1991/1998), *Entre Nous – Thinking-of-the-Other*, New York, US: Columbia University Press.

Levinas, E. (1993), *Outside the Subject*, Stanford: Stanford University Press.

Malka, S. (2003), *Emmanuel Levinas – Eine Biographie*, München: C. H. Beck.

Martin, J., K. Knopoff and C. Beckman (1998), 'An alternative to bureaucratic impersonality and emotional labour – bounded emotionality at The Body Shop', *Administrative Science Quarterly*, **43** (June), 429-469.

Mumby, D. K. and L. L. Putnam (1992), 'The politics of emotion – A feminist reading of bounded rationality', *Academy of Management Review*, **17** (3), 465-486.

Munro, R. (1999), 'Membership work in the team of technology', *Organization*, **6**, 429-450.

Parker, M. (1995), 'Critique in the name of what? Postmodernism and critical approaches to organization', *Organization Studies*, **16** (4), 553-577.

Parker, M. (1997), 'Organizations and citizenship', *Organization*, **4** (1), 75-92.

Parker, M. (2002), *Against Management*, Cambridge, UK: Polity Press.

Peters, T. J. and R. H. Waterman (1982/1994), *In Search of Excellence – Lessons from America's Best Run Organizations*, Sydney, Australia: Harper Collins.

Sewell, G. (1998), 'The discipline of teams: The control of team-based industrial work through electronic and peer surveillance', *Administrative Science Quarterly*, **43**, 397-428.

Willmott, H. (1993), 'Strength is ignorance; slavery is freedom: Managing culture in modern organizations', *Journal of Management Studies*, **30** (4), 515-552.

Index